B62022

SOLDIERS OF LIGHT AND LOVE

THE FRED W. MORRISON
SERIES IN SOUTHERN STUDIES

JACQUELINE JONES

Soldiers of Light and Love
Northern Teachers and Georgia Blacks, 1865–1873

The University of North Carolina Press Chapel Hill

© 1980 The University of North Carolina Press

All rights reserved

Manufactured in the United States of America

ISBN 0-8078-1435-0

Library of Congress Catalog Card Number 79-27129

Library of Congress Cataloging in Publication Data

Jones, Jacqueline, 1948–
    Soldiers of light and love.

    (The Fred W. Morrison series in Southern studies)
    Bibliography: p.
    Includes index.
    1. Freedmen in Georgia—Education. 2. Teachers—Georgia—
History. 3. Reconstruction—Georgia.
I. Title. II. Series: Fred W. Morrison series in Southern studies.
F291.J67   975.8'041   79-27129
ISBN 0-8078-1435-0

To My Parents, Albert and Sylvia Jones,
and My Brothers, Kent and Randy

Contents

Acknowledgments

A work of historical scholarship is often "autobiographical" in the sense that it reflects the author's own personal and political concerns. My study of the northern teachers of the Georgia freed people is a good case in point. Dealing with a "timely" subject, the history of women and race relations in the United States, it has possessed an immediacy for me that inspired and sustained the research process over the last few years. But more importantly, the several stages of this project represent my growing understanding of ideas and problems that transcend the specific story of the teachers. To the many persons and groups who have assisted me I owe therefore a personal as well as intellectual debt, for I learned that the lessons of history go beyond relevance to modern-day issues of personal interest and suggest a realm of human experience that is significant just because it is so far from and alien to our own.

In the formative stages of this study John Munroe served as an eminently knowledgeable counselor and introduced me to the rigors of scholarly research. James M. McPherson early encouraged me to conduct an in-depth study of the northern teachers and offered many helpful suggestions. His own work provided me not only with an understanding of the freedmen's aid societies but also with a model of lucid scholarship.

Paul K. Conkin and Daniel T. Rodgers commented on the study at length and suggested new directions for research. Carl F. Kaestle patiently listened to my latest theory on this or that and read numerous drafts of the manuscript with painstaking care. His criticism was at once demanding, fair, thorough, and encouraging.

Several scholars urged me to sort out the threads of class, sex, and race that made the teachers' story so fascinating. Claudia Foster, Steven Schlossman, and Martha Coons each read individual chapters. The comments of my colleagues in Wellesley's Department of History led me to refine my generalizations about the relationship between Afro-American culture and black education after the

Civil War. Clarence Mohr shared his own work on Georgia with me, and Raymond Wolters offered several valuable suggestions. James L. Roark asked all the right questions and in large measure the shape and scope of this study can be credited to his interest and perceptiveness.

I would like to acknowledge additional forms of assistance from individuals, institutions, and foundations. The staffs of several research libraries went out of their way to help me locate relevant materials. Lee Alexander, reference librarian at the Atlanta University Center Trevor Arnett Library; Clifton H. Johnson, executive director of the Amistad Research Center, New Orleans, and his efficient staff; Wilson Flemister, librarian at Gammon Theological Center in Atlanta; and Elaine Everly, researcher in the Military Archives Division of the National Archives all gave of their time and expertise. Three other staffs merit special thanks for their aid and forbearance over extended periods of time: the circulation, reference, microfilm, and interlibrary loan departments of the State Historical Society of Wisconsin; pages and reference librarians at the American Antiquarian Society in Worcester, Massachusetts; and the interlibrary loan, circulation, and reference librarians at Wellesley College.

Aid in the form of fellowships and grants allowed me to devote several uninterrupted years to research and writing. The Ford Foundation, Woodrow Wilson National Fellowship Foundation, American Antiquarian Society, American Association of University Women, State Historical Society of Wisconsin, Graduate School of the University of Wisconsin, and American Council of Learned Societies provided generous financial support.

The Amistad Research Center of New Orleans (American Missionary Association Archives and John A. Rockwell and Martha D. Ayres Scrapbook) and the Trevor Arnett Library of Atlanta University (Edmund Asa Ware Papers and Frederick Ayer Papers) kindly granted permission to cite from correspondence in their respective collections. Portions of chapters II, IV, and VII appeared in slightly altered form in volume 19 (Spring 1979) of the *History of Education Quarterly* and are herein used with permission.

Finally, the contributions of a special group of friends/colleagues were crucial. Robert Halstead and Patricia Kelleher, in their work on the Americans in Tampico and the Irish in Chicago, respectively, taught me what a commitment to the study of history means in both intellectual and emotional terms. Karin and Jon Knudsen more than once rescued me from self-imposed isolation, and in their home

I found laughter, warmth, and cheerful commiseration. And last but far from least, Jeffrey Abramson provided much-needed support via long distance while the manuscript was in the last stages of revision; during that busy year he had the good sense to be three thousand miles away.

SOLDIERS OF LIGHT AND LOVE

"The war with bullet and bayonet
is over at the South; the
invasion of light and love is not."

American Missionary,
May 1869

CHAPTER I

Introduction

This book tells the story of the northern women and men who went south to Georgia after the Civil War amid the ruins of the Confederacy to teach the freed people—why they volunteered, how they lived and labored, what they accomplished, and what they learned about themselves. Sponsored by various freedmen's aid societies, they conducted classes, organized religious programs, and established self-improvement groups to help the blacks achieve what the northerners hoped would be an "orderly" transition from slavery to freedom. In the process, however, the teachers faced innumerable challenges both from within and without their small and isolated circles that crucially tested their sense of missionary self-sacrifice. Their activities and problems reveal not only the strength of the neo-abolitionist impulse as well as the limits of liberal reform, but they also incorporate the "three Rs" of mid-nineteenth century American history: race, reform, and Reconstruction.

The teachers responded to—though they sometimes believed they inspired—a great eagerness for schooling among the freed people. Denied the opportunity to learn to read and write by law, slaves had nevertheless recognized the symbolic and practical significance of literacy. After emancipation, going to school became a political act as well as a means of personal edification. Black people joined together to establish schools and hire teachers for old and young alike, and their collective effort represented both defiance to white authority and an expression of community self-interest. Consequently, this strong commitment to formal schooling was not, as some historians have suggested, either mysterious on the one hand or "pathetic" on the other.[1] Yet there were limits to what black people could accomplish on their own, and there were limits to what education could help them to achieve as members of a caste group within southern society. In Reconstruction Georgia, only 5 percent of the state's nearly half-million freed people attended school in any one year, and very few were able to do so with any regularity. For blacks, the war had left a bittersweet legacy of both emancipation and protracted bondage in the form of poverty and racial prejudice. Schooling was a luxury for people of all ages and both sexes; those who had the opportunity to learn, or provided that opportunity for other family members, soon discovered that education was an expensive proposition.

And so when northern benevolent societies, in cooperation with the United States government (through the agency of the Bureau of Refugees, Freedmen, and Abandoned Lands) offered assistance, blacks accepted it enthusiastically. Just released from slavery and having little in the way of personal possessions, community-owned buildings, or cash, the freed people appreciated northern largesse, including construction materials, textbooks, money for salaries, and the services of Yankee teachers. But this relationship between New England freedmen's aid societies and the "objects" of their benevolence was often fraught with tension. The problem went far beyond the attempt of northern whites to help blacks acquire literacy skills. Simply stated, the aid came with strings attached. According to many Georgia blacks, relinquishing any control over neighborhood institutions was a high price to pay for northern philanthropy.

The direct link between the antebellum abolitionist impulse and freedmen's work has been well established by historians in recent years. As Ronald G. Walters notes, abolitionism "began with a call for individual outrage and repentance and ended with the Yankee schoolmarm in the South." James M. McPherson has shown convincingly that abolitionism survived the war intact and provided both the ideology and fervor that sparked the northern-sponsored education effort during and after Reconstruction.[2] The missionary teachers sought to "uplift" the blacks by purging them of the baneful effects of slavery and preparing them for the duties of responsible American citizenship. The goals of the teachers were political and religious as well as educational; they believed that individual regeneration would eventually culminate in a more stable, "godly" society. In practical terms, freedmen's "education" encompassed a number of specific antebellum reform programs, including physical relief, temperance work, and religious instruction, but schooling constituted the focus of the effort. For most of these northerners, their incursion into the "enemies' land" was brief but intense, as they did battle with hostile southern whites and sometimes with black people who seemed unappreciative of Victorian "moral instruction." Often crowded together in tiny mission homes, the teachers even experienced difficulty getting along with one another. But, if they encountered disappointment and frustration in their attempts to "Yankeeize" the freed people, they often derived a good deal of personal satisfaction from missionary work in the South. Most of the teachers assigned to Georgia were young, well-educated, unmarried women from middle-class northern homes. Intensely idealistic, they embraced the rugged life and a chance to perform hard, "useful" labor on behalf of those whom they believed were "degraded," but more sinned against than sinning.

Within the context of the federal program of Reconstruction, the teachers served as uneasy allies of the Republican party. Overall, freedmen's work, emphasizing as it did physical relief, schooling, and social welfare, complemented the federal effort to restore some measure of social stability to the postwar South. As conservative reformers, the teachers shared with Republicans the vision of a truly unified American society in which competing interests would be cemented together in national purpose by the tenets of Protestantism and capitalism. The missionaries served as the fervent agents of this bourgeois faith by combining evangelical zeal with cultural self-righteousness to lift high a banner of Republican individualism strongly tinged with the notion of Christian responsibility.

But, as neoabolitionists, freedmen's workers often expressed impatience with politicians regardless of party affiliation. The national aid societies dissented sharply from prevailing northern ideas on race, even in some cases arguing for "social equality" between blacks and whites. Few serious office-seekers during this period ever went so far, though a handful of Radical Republicans boldly advocated civil rights for the freedmen. Most northerners had considered it a war for the Union, rather than for the liberation of the slaves. In Georgia, teachers demonstrated their ambivalence toward federal policies by supporting prolonged military occupation and the Freedmen's Bureau while criticizing soldiers, congressmen, and President Andrew Johnson for their callousness toward black people. The mistrust was mutual and natural, for the politicians sought to obey the will of the people, but the missionary teachers were more interested in divining the will of God.[3]

Until a few years ago, historians paid slight attention to the teachers of the freedmen. (An exception was Henry L. Swint, who in 1941 published an impressionistic, rather unsympathetic overview of their effort in the South.) Still, those scholars who only mentioned the teachers in general works on the Civil War era wrote with more passion than the length of their discussions would seem to warrant. The teachers have inspired strong feelings. Indeed, the women in particular came to symbolize a "New England" spirit that historians might praise or condemn, but could rarely ignore. In his almost mystical evocation of black culture, *The Souls of Black Folk* (1903), W. E. B. Du Bois paid homage to the calico-garbed "saintly souls" who presented their black students with "the gift of New England": "not cash, but character." According to this black scholar, the northern education effort represented the "finest thing in American history."[4]

Almost four decades later, Wilbur J. Cash, chronicler of white southern mythology, agreed with Du Bois that the teacher was "a living epitome of the Yankee mind" but then proceeded to condemn her for her "meddlesome stupidity"; "she was, of course, no proper intellectual, but at best a comic character, at worst a dangerous fool, playing with explosive forces which she did not understand." (Cash's attack conjured up an image of the teacher as "horsefaced, bespectacled and spare of frame"—an image associated with the rather derogatory label "Yankee schoolmarm.") Although obviously writing from quite different perspectives, both Du Bois and Cash agreed that the teachers had exerted a considerable impact on southern society. The black writer cited the teachers' attempts to raise the freed people "out of the defilement of the places where slavery had wallowed them"—an effort that Cash charged brought "southern fear and hate to explicit focus." In any case, the teachers embodied New England character, for good or evil.[5]

Not until the 1960s and 1970s did the subject of freedmen's work begin to receive the extensive treatment it deserved. Writing from the perspective of the Civil Rights Revolution, James M. McPherson has drawn a compelling portrait of those northern men and women whose dream of a casteless society set them apart from the vast majority of Americans in their day, and a considerable number in our own. In two separate full-length works, McPherson concentrates on persons active in the antebellum abolitionist movement who later devoted much of their lives to the cause of black education. He is not insensitive to the issue of Yankee indoctrination of black students; he readily admits that the teachers were paternalistic (or maternalistic) "culturalists," but refrains from indicting them for their narrow-mindedness. He argues that the reformers were not racists— they believed that blacks had the same intellectual capabilities as whites—and that many Afro-American leaders supported their efforts to instill Puritan values in black students.[6]

In her study of twelve teachers whose memoirs or correspondence have been published, Sandra E. Small delves deeper into the ambiguities and contradictions in freedmen's work. She explores the teachers' attitudes toward race, white southerners, charity, and the Freedmen's Bureau. Because the teachers faced a number of moral dilemmas, they cannot be labeled "cocksure invaders," according to Small. However, she refrains from offering a thorough assessment of the teachers and their mission. She concludes that the women were "unsure of their way in frequent conflicts between prevailing customs and their own perceptions of human values."[7]

Like McPherson, other scholars who have recently studied the issues of race and reform during Reconstruction distinguish the abolitionist sensibility from majority public opinion at the time; the teachers' idealism presents a striking contrast to the intransigence of most Americans on the race question in general, and southerners on the issue of black education in particular. Today, the teachers no longer symbolize "New England," and they have been redeemed from Cash's spiteful diatribe.[8]

McPherson deals primarily with persons who made a lifelong commitment to black higher education during the period 1861 to 1910. He suggests that "married couples and unmarried women over 30 . . . were generally better teachers than the younger single women, among whom the 'missionary spirit' was often frail," and adds that "unsuccessful teachers were usually weeded out after a year or two." This volume complements and expands on McPherson's. The group he studied represented a hard core of long-term reformers, but the focus here is on elementary-school teachers, who were more typical of freedmen's workers in general.[9] The case-study method has been employed to examine the 368 northern teachers who served in Georgia at some time between 1865 and 1873, years of feverish excitement and grand hopes for the future. Most of these women and men taught in the South for only a few years; they worked hard, but felt that they could not "afford" to spend their whole lives there. Unlike the works of McPherson, this one refrains from making the judgment that these persons were less "successful" or competent than others who were older or stayed longer. Although temporary in a literal sense, their devotion to missionary work was nonetheless heartfelt. Moreover, though McPherson finds ample reason to laud the northerners' achievements in the field of higher education for southern blacks, this book remains ambivalent in its assessment of the Yankee common-school program in the South.

The drama of Reconstruction features familiar characters: self-sacrificing northern teachers and unrepentant rebels, freed people struggling to keep body and soul together, opportunistic scalawags and power-hungry carpetbaggers. But these players wrote their own lines, and they refused to conform to the traditional roles of hero or villain. For example, northern whites at times subverted black attempts at self-help, and some native white Georgians defied their neighbors and joined in the effort to aid black education. White Republicans collaborated with Democrats to depoliticize the race issue as both parties succumbed to racist political opportunism. The teachers on occasion found themselves preoccupied with in-group scandals and controversies that were the inevitable result of close quarters and clashing personalities. Thus there were many scenes at the state level within a larger nationwide performance. And, throughout the drama, the teachers were often tragic figures.

In discussing the teachers' motivation, this study examines their group ideology—that of evangelical abolitionism—and the personal circumstances that made the prospect of southern missionary work so attractive. The burgeoning literature on the images and roles of women in mid-nineteenth-century northern society has made it possible to examine the Georgia freedmen's teachers in their capacity as women. Like many reformers, they joined the cause in order to liberate themselves from the comfort and complacency of a middle-class existence. This is not to belittle or detract from their commitment to the freedmen, only to suggest that the work fulfilled some of their needs and enabled them to understand their own situation more clearly.

In terms of modern notions of "feminism," the teachers defy categorization. Granted, they wanted to escape from the cult of domesticity and embrace the physical, mental, and emotional challenges of missionary work far away from their parents' homes. These were not "ladies" of the Lydia Huntley Sigourney variety; by April most of them had rolled up their shirtwaist sleeves and, hot and sweaty, had begun drilling their students for the upcoming final "exhibition." During the year, they taught Sunday school classes, distributed food and clothing, tended the ill, and fired off eloquent letters to northern churches begging for cash and supplies. Some even managed to challenge some of the male bureaucrats whom they considered inadequately trained as educators or incompetent as moral leaders. In a couple of dramatic cases, young women argued persistently on behalf of "equal pay for equal work" (male teachers received higher salaries). But these were exceptions. On the whole, the teachers' struggle to assert themselves within the female-missionary-teacher sphere of moral reform reveals the strength, as well as the flexibility, of role designations based on sex in early Victorian America.

Within the context of Reconstruction social history, freedmen's work is an intricate web spun with the threads of race, class, sex, and culture. At the most basic level, the encounter between the teachers and freed people represented a meeting between white and black. The teachers professed a belief in the "equality" of the races, at least theoretically. But some demonstrated overt prejudice in the South by refusing to board or sit down at the same dinner table with blacks. Others admitted to overcoming initial feelings of dislike for black people. These examples suggest that the problem was more widespread than the *American Missionary* and other freedmen's aid society journals might indicate.

If the evidence pointing to racial prejudice among the teachers is sporadic and indirect, the problem of cultural conflict between the two groups stands out in stark relief. The teachers' values of evangelical piety, self-control, and hard, steady work formed the trinity of northern-sponsored freedmen's education. (In the industrializing North, these values were functional, if not universally shared by all classes and ethnic groups.) The teachers understandably congratulated themselves, and cited the similarity between the curriculum of New England common schools and their black institutions in the South as proof of their own racial egalitarianism. In the long run, they perceived the goal of public schooling to be the same in both sections of the country: to effect moral character reform and thereby guarantee social stability in the face of increasing fragmentation based on class, political, religious, and racial tensions. This nationalistic individualism clashed with the freed people's "ethos of mutuality," which arose during slavery as a protective reaction against white oppression.[10]

Eugene Genovese has suggested that Afro-Americans "developed their own values as a force for community cohesion and survival, but in so doing they widened the cultural gap and exposed themselves to even harder blows from a white nation that could neither understand their behavior nor respect its moral foundations." It is certainly true that blacks in Georgia soon discovered that their own way of life was neither understood nor respected by the northern whites. Yankee teachers rarely saw them as equals in any meaningful sense of the word; freed people were malleable beings to be "elevated," to be shaped and molded in the image of Protestant evangelicals. In no area of their work did the teachers encounter more overt hostility from blacks than in their denominational proselytizing. Congregationalists, in particular, harvested few Georgia converts, despite their desperate efforts to till the soil of black religiosity.[11]

And, finally, personal relationships between the northern teachers and black adults are revealing. Some freed people continued to act out the "deference ritual" in their encounter with these women, just as they had affected fawning, servile behavior with their masters under slavery. The teachers were also white authority figures, and, if their attempt to shape black behavior represented a form of social control much less insidious than that of slavery, it too was based on a notion of white cultural superiority. In any case, several black communities in Georgia made it clear they preferred schoolteachers of their own race. Such expressions of group solidarity left the northerners puzzled and resentful.

Thus the story of freedmen's work highlights the white teacher-black pupil conflict, which was based on race, culture, and class. But it also suggests a parallel between sexism and racism as sources of ascribed status in nineteenth-century American society; similar patterns of socialization and legal discrimination severely limited the opportunities of both blacks and white women for independent action and personal achievement. During the Civil War era, middle-class northern reformers, male and female, made explicit the female-Negro analogy on two levels. Women's-rights activists like the Grimké sisters charged that the chains of prejudice and deceit that bound the slave also confined the white "lady" to her sphere of genteel domesticity. Some abolitionists concurred; wrote one: "Anti-slavery is peculiarly woman's work—slavery man's. Man is a tyrant. He has enslaved woman along with his other slaves." This radical critique centered on power relationships between black and white, male and female.[12]

"Racialist" reformers and sentimental writers of the period agreed that the analogy was apt, but they offered a quite different interpretation. They believed that both women and slaves were inherently passive, religiously inclined, and "child-like" in their emotional configurations. Even racial "egalitarians" adhered to this view. For example, in 1863 Theodore Tilton wrote, "Is not the religious nature the highest part of human nature? . . . In all those intellectual activities which take their strange quickening from the moral faculties— processes which we call instincts, or intuitions—the negro is superior to the white man—equal to the white woman. The negro is the feminine race of the world." He intended this as a compliment to both groups, of course.[13]

For their part, the freedmen's aid societies institutionalized a separate, inferior position for women within their educational bureaucracies by maintaining they were by nature incapable of exercising administrative authority. The most active society in Georgia discriminated on the bases of race and sex in its salaries for clergymen and teachers. This is not to suggest that nineteenth-century middle-class northern women in any way experienced emotional or physical oppression remotely akin to that endured by black people under slavery. But both groups suffered from a prejudice deeply ingrained in American society. This fact points up several significant themes: the similarities and differences between the two groups in their struggles to free themselves in this period of social dislocation, their roles within the northern-sponsored educational bureaucracy, and their rather ironic confrontation with each other.

For a number of reasons, the state of Georgia is an especially appropriate focus for this study. In 1860 Georgia was the largest of the Lower South states in terms of total population, voters, slaves, slaveholders, and nonslaveholders.[14] Its leaders played an active, if not always constructive, role in the fight for the Confederacy. (For example, Governor Joseph E. Brown spent almost as much time and energy doing battle with the centralizing policies of Confederate President Jefferson Davis as with the Yankees.) Members of northern freedmen's aid societies considered Georgia a particularly attractive "field of labor" in symbolic and practical terms as a result of its economic and political prominence within the Confederacy.

Moreover, the state early acquired among many freedmen's workers a reputation for being rather dangerous in two respects: the climate was hot and exceedingly "unhealthful," especially during the summer; and the "rebs" seemed exceptionally bitter and prone to violence. The teachers had a heightened sense of missionary self-sacrifice, and some found a Georgia assignment appealing for just these reasons. But other candidates made it clear in their letters of application to a sponsoring society that they would prefer to work closer to home in a tried and proven field—Virginia, for example—rather than venture so far into the steamy heart of the Confederacy.

William Lee Rose, Louis Gerteis, and others have examined in detail the evolution of the federal government's and northern societies' policies toward blacks during the war. By the time General William Tecumseh Sherman swept through Georgia in late 1864, "experiments" on the South Carolina Sea Islands, the coast of Virginia, and throughout the Mississippi Valley had hardened into public and private programs of limited physical relief, religious and educational instruction, and a concern for economic and social stability (manifested later in the labor-contract system of the Freedmen's Bureau). Northern aid societies had played an active role in this "rehearsal for Reconstruction," and had taken heart from early evidence that the former slaves would be willing to work, learn, and pray as free men and women.[15]

The American Missionary Association (AMA), the largest evangelical freedmen's aid organization, entered the Reconstruction era with a long history of radical abolitionism and an impressive record of black education work during the war. Shrewd to the point of ruthlessness in its ability to stake out southern territory for its own missionaries, the association followed closely on Sherman's heels when he entered Georgia, determined to plant itself firmly in this new field and dominate the state's education effort at all costs. This the AMA managed to do by the spring of 1865. It was soon rewarded for its persistence with close cooperation from Freedmen's Bureau officials, a bond strengthened by hard cash and personal friendships. Thus the Georgia freedmen's school system rose phoenix-like from the ashes of wartime devastation; the time for experimentation had passed, and the impressive bureaucracy engineered by association and bureau officials indicates that few of these men doubted the best way to proceed from this point forward.

The convergence of several major events within a five-month period from December 1864 to May 1865—the fall of Savannah, passage of the Freedmen's Bureau bill in Congress, and Appomattox— inspired the first northern workers in Georgia with a sense of excitement and optimism for the future. As McPherson has shown, the freedmen's education program continued long after Reconstruction. This volume concentrates on the eight years immediately after the war because of the scope and intensity of the effort within that limited time span. The war had inspired an evangelical missionary crusade that rivaled the military conflict in the fervor and determination of its combatants.

By 1870 the national aid societies had raised millions of dollars, and more than five thousand women and men had gone south to teach in black schools. The late 1860s and early 1870s marked a period of retrenchment, if not retreat, in the voluntary and government effort. Contributions dropped off, the number of missionary teachers declined, the Freedmen's Bureau withered away. A number of dedicated souls persisted in the fight for freedmen's education, but the battleground had changed somewhat. In 1870 Georgia re-entered the Union. Soon AMA officials found themselves in the uncomfortable position of negotiating with local school boards who offered to rent association buildings for black pupils within the new "public" system. Old animosities lingered, and the continuing violence in race relations revealed that the wounds of war were still open and festering. Yet freedmen's work had lost its aura of immediacy for young New England women. In the cycle of American reform, their daughters would choose settlement work later in the century, just as their mothers had formed branches of antislavery societies before the war.

Historians have debated the implications of educational segregation for Afro-American community development. Should the freedmen's aid societies and late nineteenth-century philanthropists have pushed vigorously for the integration of southern public school systems? What type of black leaders were trained in the white-sponsored institutions: men and women estranged from their own people and culture or persons well-prepared to lead the struggle for civil rights and integration? The short time period spanned by this work precludes the presentation of any fresh insights on this subject, which covers a one-hundred-year period in American history. But this book does explore the significance of schooling as a force for social change during Reconstruction. The northern teachers assumed that education would serve as a means of personal and group advancement, though they were uncertain how much time this process would take. The longer they stayed in the South, the further into the future they pushed their projections for "success." Eventually they hoped to see some signs of "moral improvement" and a higher standard of living among southern blacks.[16]

But the overall freedmen's education effort in Georgia was so limited, and the effects of racial discrimination so pervasive, that the teachers could derive hope only from increments—day-to-day triumphs in the classroom, or the impressive achievements of the few students who attended colleges and normal schools, for example. The intensive higher education program yielded more in the way of visible "results." By the mid-1870s the AMA had focused its energies on Atlanta University and a handful of other prized institutions and had yielded up its elementary schools to public authorities. A shortage of funds demanded cutbacks of some sort; for better or worse, they were made at the expense of common-school education.

The pages that follow describe the aspirations, struggles, achievements, and missed opportunities of those gentle "soldiers" who went south as teachers armed only with the weapons of romantic reform. They were "ordinary" women and men destined for extraordinary experiences. As individuals, they never gained national prominence for their work in the South, but their story illuminates some of the major themes of early Victorian America.

CHAPTER II
Teachers and Sponsors

The antebellum reform impulse emerged bright and burnished from the Civil War crucible. Indeed, freedmen's work represented an extension of prewar movements for moral and institutional reform; northern aid societies incorporated the ideology of abolitionists, common-school reformers, temperance workers, Sunday school organizers, and distributors of tracts and Bibles in their educational and social welfare programs for southern black people. The machinery, tactics, and goals of freedmen's work mirrored the antebellum effort in large part because the agents of reform in both periods included many of the same people, especially those active in the antislavery cause. But, although the Reconstruction campaign rested on antebellum philosophical foundations, its field of action expanded out of New England and the Midwest and into the southern arena. When the American Missionary Association (AMA) called for a "national system" of public education in 1865, it echoed the call of early common-school reformers. Yet the association perceived real possibilities for national integration—a social and political union between North and South that schoolmen and other northerners before the war had only dreamed about. The elimination of slavery and the subjugation of the rebels provided reformers with a grand new opportunity to influence the destiny of the entire country.[1]

The freedmen's teachers derived justification for their work from the ideology of evangelical abolitionism. Slavery was a sin against God and man; it denied the black person the ability to function as an independent moral being. Deprived of responsibility for his own spiritual and physical welfare, the slave had descended to a state of moral degradation in which he had no ability or incentive to take care of himself. Slavery represented a form of personal anarchy, for the limits to personal growth were shaped by the whim of the slaveholder, and his power depended on physical violence and not moral authority. Freedmen's workers believed that, in order to be truly "free," blacks needed to be liberated from the chains that bound them body and soul. Each freed person possessed an intuitive moral sense, and it was the teachers' duty to help pupils sharpen their capacity to distinguish right from wrong. "Education" involved moral as well as intellectual growth. Men and women who were really "free" were naturally pious, thrifty, and chaste because they were able to obey their own moral inclinations. The conscience liberated the soul.[2]

The freedmen's teachers and sponsoring societies viewed their work as a natural, benevolent continuation of the war. They agreed wholeheartedly with politicians and government policymakers who thought a transition period was necessary to deal with the "Negro problem" on the one hand and the defiant rebels on the other. (Somewhat inconsistently, in the field these associations did their best to avoid all contact with southern whites and concentrated their efforts on the former slaves.) But the overtly moralistic rhetoric of the freedmen's aid groups presented a striking contrast to the attitude of federal officials responsible for carrying out the laws and programs of Reconstruction. Although most northerners, regardless of their feelings on the race issue, hoped to see "order" reestablished in the South as quickly as possible, freedmen's workers maintained that black character reform was imperative before the war effort could be judged completely successful. The clash between reformers and government officials over this point revealed deeply conflicting perceptions of the war between two different segments of the northern population.

As private benevolent organizations, the freedmen's aid societies depended on northern volunteers for funds and service to promote the cause. The institutional selection process, plus the existence of a relatively large pool of eager and willing young women in New England and the Midwest, helped to shape the profile of the wartime reformer. She was the well-educated daughter of a farmer or professional and was highly conscious of her duty to God and country. In the South, the teacher faced the difficult task of demonstrating her society's high ideals. But she rejoiced in the opportunity to be "useful" and hailed self-sacrifice as a privilege. Truly she went south to save and be saved, for she sought a personal salvation both earthly and spiritual.

Organized efforts to send northern teachers south began just five months after the first roar of cannon shook Fort Sumter. The AMA, a group established fifteen years before the war, commissioned a Congregational clergyman to instruct the "contraband of war" at Fortress Monroe, Virginia, in September 1861. From 1862 until 1868, several regional and denominational associations were formed exclusively for the education of black people in Union-occupied areas, and, after 1865, in all parts of the South. These newly formed groups included one large national organization unaffiliated with any sectarian group, eventually called the American Freedmen's Union Commission (AFUC), and several freedmen's aid societies sponsored by major northern churches, including the Methodists, Baptists, and Presbyterians. All groups coordinated the efforts of local chapters to raise funds, solicit donations of food and clothing, and recruit teachers. The AMA and the denominational societies also sent ministers to proselytize in the South, and considered all their workers religious "missionaries." In scope and funds expended, the overall effort peaked in 1866–67, and then began to fall off at the end of the decade. But, at its height, the freedmen's aid program involved thousands of persons—some of whom were paid minimal salaries as national and regional administrators, southern teachers, ministers, and missionaries, and others who were members of local groups and contributed their own time and money.[3]

In Georgia, the AMA established an early lead in freedmen's work. Agreeing with rival groups that each society should have exclusive "fields" in the South (ostensibly to "harmonize" the effort), the association took forceful steps in the spring of 1865 to insure its "control" of the entire state. In large part, this was accomplished through a series of skillful political maneuvers in the key city of Savannah, where a native black organization as well as two branches of the AFUC began operations soon after Sherman occupied the city. By 1873 the AMA had sponsored 290, or almost 80 percent, of all the state's northern teachers (Appendix A).

The Methodist Freedmen's Aid Society (MFAS), which assigned thirty-one workers to the state over the eight-year period, represented the next most active group. The society cooperated closely with official missionaries of the Methodist Episcopal Church (North), who had begun their southern activities in 1864. Methodist teachers remained concentrated in the northern and western sections of Georgia, an area included in the Tennessee Conference, which had been established a year and a half after the war's end. By 1867 the state contained two administrative, or presiding-elder, districts centered in Oxford and Atlanta. Although the abolitionist founders of the MFAS doubted the regular missionaries' commitment to evangelizing among the freedmen, the strong antislavery sentiments of the most prominent men in the field gave all of Methodist work in Georgia a distinct profreedmen bias. And yet protracted disputes between the white missionaries and members of black churches (especially the African Methodists) over buildings, potential converts, and doctrine made the society's educational work frustrating and difficult. The Methodists considered the religious effort to be primary, and they used their schools to lure black adults and children away from rival denominations. The AMA was not above using the same tactics, but so few freed people responded to the Congregationalist style of worship that association teachers never enjoyed the chance to share the Methodists' grandiose dreams of expanded church membership.

Teachers representing the New England branch of the AFUC were equal in number to the Methodists. They concentrated their efforts in the city of Columbus, on the state's western border. Self-consciously "secular," this group remained much more active in the Upper South, especially in Maryland, Virginia, and North Carolina. Instructors and ministers connected with the American Baptist Home Missionary Society (ABHMS) and another Baptist group, the National Theological Institute, together made up only 3 percent of the total Georgia teachers. They also stayed in one town, which they eventually came to dominate: Augusta, on the Savannah River. The New York Yearly Meeting of Friends (one teacher) and New York branch of the AFUC (four) both abandoned activities in the state soon after their brief and rather unpleasant initial encounters with the AMA in Savannah. The Freedmen's Aid Committee of the Old School Presbyterian church, a conservative wing of the northern denomination, did establish a few schools in the state during this period, but it apparently sponsored no northern teachers. It preferred to commission native whites and blacks as its freedmen's workers.

To understand why the teachers volunteered and what they did and hoped to accomplish in the South, it is necessary to examine the ideology of their sponsoring societies. A coherent world view based on certain assumptions about human nature and the will of God undergirded freedmen's work, defined its purpose, shaped its goals, and fired its proponents with religious zeal. Like abolitionism, freedmen's work became a "religion," interdenominational in character and guided by a set of compelling beliefs that called the faithful to action.

The AMA provides a suitable focus for a discussion of this religious impulse and how it affected the Georgia education effort in terms of objectives and personnel. Not only did the organization sponsor a large majority of all the northern teachers assigned to that state between 1865 and 1873, but it articulated a philosophy of reform also shared by most women and men commissioned by other groups. Although unofficially affiliated with the Congregational church, the association made explicit its commitment to interdenominational evangelicalism by excluding only Unitarians and Universalists from the fold of Protestant true believers. A stretching of the definition of nonevangelical church members and elimination of all Episcopalians and Quakers reveals that fully 98 percent—or all but five—of the Georgia teachers (whose membership has been determined) could be considered evangelical Protestants. It is true that the AFUC and the sectarian groups (including the AMA) engaged in a spirited debate at the national level over the appropriateness of proselytizing among the freedmen. Moreover, all the groups made strenuous efforts to appeal to potential supporters, at home and in the South, at the expense of their rivals.[4]

Yet the two types of groups did not differ sharply in either ideology or the practical application of those ideas. A comparison of the correspondence and publications of the freedmen's aid societies in Georgia reveals that most workers, regardless of denomination or sponsorship, shared similar beliefs on the general purposes and nature of the work. Although some teachers held opposing views on certain issues, these disagreements usually cut across society lines and did not necessarily represent philosophical differences among the sponsoring organizations. Almost all the Georgia freedmen's teachers assisted in revival meetings, Sunday school classes, and church services as part of their regular duties; the handful of AFUC teachers did not, though several participated in religious activities in an unofficial capacity. But that is the extent of a meaningful distinction between the groups at work in the state, and should not imply that AFUC workers were any less concerned about the spiritual well-being of their pupils.

During the Civil War era, the AMA functioned like a combination tract, temperance, Sunday school, mission, charity, and common-school reform association. But the guiding principle behind these various impulses was abolitionism. Founded in 1846, the association originally brought together a number of small missionary groups committed to the immediate abolition of slavery and the conversion of black people to Christianity. In the process, it allied itself with the evangelical wing of American Protestantism.[5]

This religious orientation posited a belief in the inherent sinfulness of each person and the need for spiritual regeneration through repentance and faith. Antebellum evangelicalism contained within it a strong tendency toward mission work stemming from a combination of doctrinal and social factors. These included a millenarian faith that all Christians must assume responsibility for the conversion of the heathen in order to prepare for the day when Jesus would return to earth and reign for a thousand years; an increasing emphasis on the importance of "good works"; and the growing fear among many American Protestants that the moral fiber of society was crumbling under the weight of economic change and the emergence of "dangerous classes"—the poor, Roman Catholics, immigrants, and free thinkers. As a means of converting those from without, and inspiring those already within their ranks, the evangelicals relied heavily on the religious revival, a worship service during which participants experienced first an emotional awareness of their own unworthiness and then the tender forgiveness of God.[6]

The relationship between revivalism and reform, both of which flourished between 1815 and 1860, remains murky, at best. Historians have cited the exhortations of the Reverend Charles G. Finney, one of the most famous of antebellum revivalists, as proof of some connection between the two phenomena. Finney called for "disinterested benevolence" among the faithful—charity work that would provide evidence of spiritual redemption and help the sinner to glorify God. Still, revivalism actually encouraged, indeed depended upon, extreme introspection, and the record of Finney and others of his calling in major reform movements was not at all impressive. But perhaps, as Ronald Walters has suggested, the impulse for reform came after the fires of revivalism had inspired a personal awakening and then died out, or at least diminished to a point where the convert could begin to direct attention toward sinfulness outside, as well as within, himself.[7]

In any case, evangelical Protestantism did turn outward during the early years of the nineteenth century and seek to purify the entire nation. Americans who (in the words of Aileen Kraditor) "took literally the teachings of their religion" provided much of the support for the multitude of voluntary moral-reform associations that sprang up in New England. Many of these groups represented extensions of individual Protestant denominations. Yet, if their ultimate objective was religious conversion, they nonetheless demonstrated great concern for personal behavior. They hoped to make Americans more moderate in their drinking, more pious in their reading habits, more faithful in their church attendance, and more responsible in work and family relations. (Whether the person whose personal and public behavior conformed to the highest standards of Puritan virtue was actually regenerate or not still remained something of a mystery to the evangelicals; in the South, freedmen's teachers would often have to content themselves with evidence of good manners in their pupils, and pray that these signs indicated a deeper spiritual awakening.)[8]

The AMA soon assumed a prominent position within the "Evangelical United Front" of tract and missionary societies. Forming a network based on overlapping personnel and financial contributors, these organizations were characterized by interdenominational cooperation, lay control, and a complex hierarchical structure that coordinated local branches in a national effort. Their emphasis was on moral suasion as a means of social change; abolitionists, for example, called for the religious conversion of individual slaveholders who would then feel morally obligated to liberate their own bondsmen. Although the AMA conformed to the general patterns of ideology and administration typical of reform societies within this "Benevolent Empire," it soon gained a well-deserved reputation for radicalism on the race issue. The mission work of the association in Africa, the West Indies, Canada, and the northern United States, plus its public pronouncements on civil rights, all revealed a firm commitment to political equality and economic independence among black people at home and abroad. During the antebellum period, association officials often chided other evangelical reform groups for their silence on the question of slavery.[9]

In Georgia, freedmen's work derived its impetus from, first, the association's analysis of the institution of slavery, and, second, its aggressive missionary impulse created by evangelical fervor. Within the context of antebellum reform, the AMA and the teachers it sponsored were evangelical abolitionists (or, after the passage of the Thirteenth Amendment, neoabolitionists.) Although the AMA's clearly articulated stand against racial prejudice placed it "in the vanguard of racial liberalism," the group formally allied itself with mainstream American Protestantism. This accommodation to denominationalism can be contrasted with the radical "come-outerism," or antiinstitutionalism, of William Lloyd Garrison and his followers. They refused to support religious and secular governments, and charged that the major denominations as well as the United States government were corrupt by virtue of their inaction on the slavery issue. This wing of the antislavery movement also repudiated the evangelicals' emphasis on original sin in favor of a more hopeful view of human nature. Still, Garrison and AMA leaders agreed on the basic outlines of a radical critique of slavery, which included explicit condemnation of the system itself and a call for immediate emancipation.[10]

Slavery was a sin, a crime against God, primarily because "the slaveholder interfered between God and another moral agent, the

slave, and thereby placed himself in the sinful position of contend-
ing against divine sovereignty." Thus, as Lewis Perry argues, the
key issue for abolitionists was moral authority, specifically the master's denial of the slave's accountability to God. This idea was closely
related to the Puritan belief that each person must stand alone
before God, without the intercession of priests or other mortal inter-
mediaries. The abolitionists also believed that everyone, whether
black or white, had an innate moral sense. Although slaves possessed the potential to act as moral human beings, they were stunted
spiritually, for they had never received instruction or encouragement to help them strengthen this capacity. The system also denied
the human instinct and need for close family ties.[11]

According to abolitionists, slavery left an indelible imprint on the
character of its victims; slaves behaved like willful, irresponsible
children acting out of fear of physical punishment rather than any
comprehension of right or wrong. Human vices attributed directly
to the effects of bondage included ignorance, laziness, lying, and
stealing. The prime fault was "intemperance" in personal habits
(especially sexual activity, language, drinking, and tobacco use) that
left slaves "degraded" and lacking a conception of their own worth
as moral human beings. Abolitionists thus adhered to a belief in
environmentalism, but only within certain bounds.

The AMA, for example, argued that although slaves were "ignorant, superstitious and demoralized," they were not fully to blame:
"the circumstances of heathenism, in which they have always lived
. . . have made them such, and not anything that inherently pertains
to them as a race." Yet few abolitionists could ever bring themselves
to exculpate the slaves entirely from their sins; that would come
dangerously close to the moral relativists' heresy that human beings
could not be held responsible for their own behavior. In any case,
freedmen's workers believed they could help the black person to
achieve his or her own character reformation, which was defined as
the development of a "conscience," or inner moral sense, as evidenced by a change in behavior. However, as McPherson points out,
many of the teachers were also "romantic racialists," for they thought
that blacks—in their love of music and childlike faith in God—
would always be "different" from whites (though not inferior) despite radical changes in their personal conduct.[12]

These reformers also held that they, as individuals, and the northern population in general, shared guilt for slavery equally with the
most sadistic overseer. The AMA admitted, "As a nation we have
sinned and provoked the God of heaven and earth. . . . Slavery has
been THE COUNTRY'S SIN. It is true that the seat of slavery has been

chiefly at the South, but the people of the North have consented to the deed; and therefore the sin is national." Passivity amounted to moral complicity. This view provided abolitionists with a powerful incentive to act, for they were both the victims and accomplices of southern slaveholders, and emancipation would guarantee "their own liberation" from sin as well as the slave's release from his chains.[13]

The AMA derived from this critique a compelling argument on behalf of racial egalitarianism: "Let all be treated according to their merits, their capabilities, and their character." Slavery would not be crushed until whites searched their own hearts and destroyed the "spirit of caste" that permeated American life. In practical terms, this meant the association supported full civil and political rights for blacks; integration of schools, churches, and public facilities; and equal economic opportunities for all regardless of race. The AMA strongly condemned the pervasiveness of racial prejudice in the North; even self-proclaimed evangelical Christians harbored deep in their hearts a "mean prejudice" against blacks who lived or worked near them, according to society spokesmen. In their view that black and white Americans should be "one people," all equal before the law (as they were before God), the AMA and other abolitionists offered an explicit challenge to prevailing northern opinion on the race issue.[14]

The ideology of freedmen's work was identical to the beliefs of Garrison on slavery in several significant respects. He and his supporters also asserted that slavery was foremost a moral issue, that compromise was impossible (it must be ripped out of American society "root and branch"), and that the elimination of racial prejudice should constitute an important goal of the antislavery movement. But the AMA and the Garrisonians diverged sharply on their overall assessment of American life. Specifically, they differed on the role of religious institutions as agents of moral reformation and on the significance of patriotism to the abolitionist cause. Garrison argued that slavery was sustained by established political and religious institutions in the United States, that it was part of the national fiber, woven into the Constitution by Founding Fathers who knew very well what they were doing. The evangelicals on the other hand maintained that, despite the sin of slavery, the American political and economic system was basically good. AMA literature, for example, was rife with an intense and strident nationalism. Slavery went against the principles of republican government, and emancipation would result in purification, rather than repudiation, of the Constitution, according to the AMA. The quest was "to realize utopia under the American form of government," and to infuse the state, church, school, and family with a new awareness of God's will. The Reverend Henry Ward Beecher served as the chief spokesman of this evangelical patriotism. Although many abolitionists deplored his laxness on the slavery issue before the war, the association shared his belief in a divinely appointed national order.[15]

Within this evangelical world view, the Civil War assumed the proportions of a great conflagration between the forces of righteousness and evil. The AMA welcomed physical combat as a means to suppress the "wicked conspiracy against law, republican government, and the rights of man." The war for the Union would also be a war for the liberation of the slaves, according to the abolitionists, and in the heat of the times they abandoned the idea that the spiritual conversion of slaveholders afforded the quickest route to emancipation. This "accommodation to violence" among abolitionists amounted to wholehearted support of the conflict "as a purifying act of God," a means of both retribution and collective salvation. The association followed wartime military and political activities closely, and even reminded its members to vote for the "party of the Union."[16]

This raises the question of the relationship between the AMA and the Republican party. McPherson has shown quite clearly that the abolitionists in general and freedmen's workers in particular remained justifiably skeptical of the party's commitment to the black man's cause during the war. And yet the association shared with Republicans a northern middle-class view of sectional differences and the need for national economic and social unification. For example, the AMA dealt easily and often in stereotypes; the land of vicious slave-owning "aristocrats," semicivilized poor whites, and "degraded" blacks offered a striking contrast to its image of New England populated with rugged, thrifty, pious men and women. Most importantly, according to the association, southern whites had no real comprehension of the value of hard, honest labor; they were "utterly indolent and shiftless." It is clear that the North had its own fire-eaters among the evangelical segment of the population.[17]

Implicit in freedmen's aid society ideology was an impulse to act swiftly and decisively on behalf of the blacks once the way south was cleared by northern troops. Like other mid-nineteenth century reformers, proponents of freedmen's work believed they should not only come to understand God's moral law, but work to establish it here on earth: everyone "must be prepared to stand in his lot, holding himself, and all he has, consecrated unreservedly to the master's service, to be used, as he sees fit, for the establishment of his Kingdom of peace and righteousness in our land and throughout the earth." Military victories alone could not redeem sin-ridden New England. The incursion of Union soldiers into Confederate territory represented only the first step on the path to salvation, and the end of the war signaled opportunity, not respite. "Opportunity is always a duty," intoned the New England branch of the AFUC. "A great opportunity," exclaimed the New York chapter, and the AMA echoed that the freedmen's pitiful condition amounted to a "rich and grand opportunity in a new field of usefulness." One Baptist clergyman tried mightily to convey in writing his excitement over the prospect of educating the newly freed slaves: "*I know,* I KNOW *there never was such an opportunity,* THERE HAS BEEN NO SUCH DAY."[18]

Northern societies often used military images and metaphors to delineate the challenges of the wartime era. In introducing its missionary "muster roll" one year, an editor of the *American Missionary* wrote, "The war with bullet and bayonet is over at the South; the invasion of light and love is not." Another writer for the journal questioned whether northerners were "taking as much pains to enlist . . . under the banner of the great Captain of Salvation as under the flag of their country, whether they are contributing their means to the support of the holy army of warriors with as much liberality as they are for the support of the army of their government." In effect, the Protestant voluntary societies' traditional rhetorical emphasis on Christian "soldiers," reinforced by a military-like chain of command from the national level into the field, took on a literal meaning during and after the war. And the AMA, which boasted a fifteen-year history of agitation on the race issue and well-oiled institutional machinery, considered itself sufficiently armed with expertise and support among northern evangelicals to do battle with the infidels of both races in the South.[19]

From 1861 on, the association cut back its foreign missions and concentrated on work among the freed people. Although its philosophy of freedmen's work derived from the abolitionist critique of slavery that evolved in the antebellum period, wartime exigencies led the AMA to expand and make more specific its views on race and reform in American society. In light of the enormous northern sacrifice in terms of blood and physical resources, the call for missionaries took on an added note of urgency. Specific goals continued to include character reform among the former slaves and the eventual incorporation of southern blacks and whites into a more godly, "orderly" America united in morality as well as political purpose. During the war, however, the association introduced a new theme: the threat that, if ignored by northern evangelicals, the freedmen would become a permanently dangerous segment of the population, a potential source of violence and social disruption. The AMA outlined the problem in graphic terms: "leave the field for a few years to Romanism, to plant and sow;— to intemperance, superstition, and infidelity, to poison and corrupt;— to Southern teaching, and preaching; and the case is hopeless. The time for us to work is now." Emancipation must not become a "curse" to blacks and to "our common country." Thus freedmen's workers waged both a defensive and offensive battle against the forces of sin and dissolution.[20]

In practical terms, the association translated its fears and hopes into a number of specific programs designed to meet the special needs of the former slaves. On the most basic level, efforts to distribute food and clothing among the destitute refugees constituted an important part of mission work, both as an expression of humanitarianism and as "an admirable means of opening the hearts of the people, securing their confidence in their friends at the North, and preparing the way for [AMA] educational and spiritual labors." From the beginning of the war until 1869 or so, benevolent groups sent shoes, coats, blankets, medicine, and grocery staples to the freedmen via government transportation. The teachers, in their capacity as Reconstruction social workers, delivered these supplies to individuals and families deemed worthy of aid.[21]

Of course, the AMA and denominational societies engaged in aggressive proselytizing among the freed people by sponsoring revivals and Sunday school and Bible-study classes, and by establishing new churches. Religious work, supplemented by temperance meetings and a variety of other measures aimed at personal "uplift," were intended to instill in blacks a code of middle-class Protestant morality. This emphasis on self-improvement (i.e., the development of one's conscience to regulate behavior and thought) combined the evangelical quest for piety with the Victorian obsession with self-control. Freedmen's workers looked forward to the day when black people could become truly independent of their white benefactors, when they had internalized the values of steady work, thrift, honesty, and chastity and no longer needed the supporting props of moral-reform societies.[22]

In their fears that Romanism, rum, and ignorance posed serious threats to the stability of American society, and in their concern for personal morality, the freedmen's aid societies closely resembled New England school reformers of the antebellum period. Recent scholarship on the origins and purposes of common-school reform offers a convincing argument that Horace Mann and others saw the public school as a force for social cohesion. Groups that deviated from the mainstream of northern middle-class life—the poor, immigrants, Roman Catholics, and wage workers—represented divisive factors in American society and threatened to fragment national culture into a myriad of competing interests. The common school would supposedly absorb the children of all classes and ethnic groups, instruct them in certain "universal" values they might or might not also be taught at home, and release them fully prepared to function as responsible American citizens. In the words of Carl F. Kaestle, the common school represented a general Yankee "ethos of efficiency, manipulation, and mastery." The freedmen's school, which received financial support from both the private sector and the federal government, was a unique experiment in national institution building during this period in American history.[23]

The northern societies thus defined "education" in its broadest sense. Schooling for the freed people included training in literacy skills, moral instruction, and, for a very few, higher education. In Georgia, these three different components met with varying degrees of success. The intention was to create a comprehensive system of black education that would enable the mass of freed people to read newspapers and labor contracts and write letters; provide them with rudimentary lessons in moral behavior; and insure a steady, reliable supply of teachers of their own race in the years to come. The societies hoped that their work would eventually be incorporated into the political structure of each southern state. Systems of tax-supported, free public education would remain a permanent legacy of freedmen's work, the first in a series of great northern institutions transplanted to southern soil. Such an achievement would "enable the inhabitants of the South, without distinction of color [to] vie in morality and intelligence with the hearty sons of the North."[24]

In addition to these general concerns, the American Missionary Association in particular devoted special attention to the specific issues of civil rights and property ownership among blacks. The association strongly supported black suffrage and all other political rights that the freed people had been denied under slavery. For example, Lewis Tappan, one of the group's founders, had maintained that freedom and property ownership were inseparable, and the AMA sponsored several land-distribution programs for West Indian blacks in its antebellum missionary work. During the war, abolitionists took heart from initial, tentative efforts on the part of the federal government to settle black people on land that had been confiscated from Confederates. Later, the AMA specifically proposed that Congress or northern businessmen invest in southern lands and create a homestead project for the freedmen. The long-range goal was the incorporation of blacks into a casteless American society.[25]

Throughout the Civil War and Reconstruction, the abolitionists remained ambivalent toward the federal government and its specific policies on blacks—policies that were shaped more by military necessity and political considerations than humanitarian concerns. Northerners sympathetic to the plight of the slaves reacted angrily when President Abraham Lincoln revoked General John C. Frémont's order freeing the Missouri slaves in 1861, but they praised the chief executive for his courage and foresight when he released the Emancipation Proclamation. Most abolitionists mourned Lincoln's death in April 1865, but they quickly came to view his successor as a traitor to the cause of freedmen's rights. The reformers' racial egalitarianism prompted them to lash out continuously at military officials who regarded the former slaves as nuisances at best, cannon fodder at worst. Thus the reformers placed principle over politics, justice over expediency. Indeed, their well-founded doubts concerning the moral commitment of the federal government during Reconstruction represented a continuation and intensification of abolitionist mistrust of the Republican party before the war.[26]

Freedmen's aid societies hailed the passage of the Freedmen's Bureau Bill in March 1865. In the beginning, this new agency seemed to answer the reformers' calls for comprehensive government programs to provide blacks with parcels of confiscated and deserted lands, to establish common schools, and to aid loyal whites. But the bureau never lived up to its promise. Chronically understaffed and underfinanced, it received no support from President Johnson and very little from members of Congress. Its efforts to distribute what little land the government did own failed miserably; in the Sea Islands off the coasts of Georgia and South Carolina the bureau even forced blacks off territory that General Sherman had proclaimed should be theirs in his Special Field Order #15. During most of its existence, the agency concentrated on enforcing a labor-contract system intended to effect an orderly transition from war to peacetime by insuring that blacks would continue to toil as agricultural workers for (white) landowners.[27]

Given the reality of the situation, the AMA position on land distribution for blacks seemed hopelessly out of step with federal intentions. An editorial in an 1865 issue of the *American Missionary* presented a perceptive view of the black man's rights and needs that garnered little government support after the war: "when the freedman is established upon a farm of his own he succeeds, . . . he is happier and more ambitious when permitted to be independent than when retained as a mere laborer for the white man and subject to his will." In other areas also, such as the protection of the freed people's political rights, the bureau's weakness was disappointing to northerners who perceived the postwar period as a "great opportunity" to effect major social and economic changes in the South.[28]

And yet the moral reformers' work complemented and reinforced government policy in a manner that even they did not always recognize. The major emphasis on education and moral suasion—rather than vigorous agitation for civil rights, for example—fit in well with congressional programs to relieve the most obvious instances of physical suffering and prevent further economic dislocation. The AMA might have favored the creation of a black yeomanry, but it was immediately concerned with the importance of productive labor and urged the freed people to go back to work until they could purchase land on their own; in the meantime, blacks would study "the industrial and business habits" of the northern whites who settled among them. Predictably, the Freedmen's Bureau's efforts to encourage the former slaves to eschew idleness and revelry in the months after emancipation received the enthusiastic support of northern aid societies. On the issue of black welfare, the government and the reformers differed radically in their rhetoric and goals, but the general overall program of Radical Reconstruction, sponsored by both public and private funds, was consistent in its conservative purposes.[29]

Moral education, inculcation of the Protestant work ethic, and charitable relief programs represented a neat package of self-help and short-term benevolence. When confronted with the hostility of most southern whites toward any aid at all for the blacks, the northern teachers and bureau agents in the field found themselves ideological allies. Many years after the war, a black man in Augusta, Georgia, recalled the first days of freedom when he and others were addressed by "all the Yankees" who had just arrived in town. He remembered that they had "told the negroes: 'You are free. Don't steal! Now work and make an honest living. Do honest work, make an honest living and support yourself and children. There are no masters. You are free!'" He did not bother to identify the "Yankees," but they could just as well have been teachers sponsored by the AMA as bureau agents.[30]

It would be misleading to suggest that the freedmen's aid societies and government military and bureau agents differed only in style, though it is true that confrontations over rhetoric and symbols could escalate tensions between the two parties in ways that formal policy disputes never did. Two incidents in Augusta soon after the war suggest the intensity of conflict between teachers and federal officials at the local level.

In 1866 a spirited young AMA instructor assigned to Augusta, where the teachers were noted for their zeal and evangelical commitment to black education, made no secret of the fact that she considered General Davis Tillson, assistant commissioner of the Freedmen's Bureau in Georgia, a less than enthusiastic advocate of the freed people. (Historians have since confirmed her charge that Tillson often allied himself with former slaveholders in opposition to the blacks.) According to one bureau official, in his counterattack the general charged that all the AMA teachers in Augusta were "damned whores." The entire incident caused a great deal of embarrassment among AMA officials in New York and a great deal of indignation in the Augusta mission home where the teachers stayed.[31]

About the same time, the association gave widespread coverage to an attempt by its teachers and a group of black children to place flowers on the graves of Union soldiers in a local cemetery. Augusta's mayor and an armed police force forcibly prevented them from entering the graveyard, and the federal troops stationed nearby feared that intervention on their part would precipitate a race riot. Fumed one northerner living in Augusta at the time: "has it *already* come to this; that the graves of men, who fought to overthrow our Government can be covered with flowers, . . . but that the colored friends of our brave Union boys, who have died to serve their country, can not honor their memory by strewing flowers upon their graves!" For AMA teachers in Georgia the event signified both the strength of southern resentment toward the Yankees and the complicity of northern troops in postwar "outrages" perpetrated by the unrepentant rebels.[32]

The actual short-term success of the freedmen's aid societies depended on several factors, including their ability to arouse and sustain the enthusiasm of New England contributors; their effectiveness in efficiently operating large-scale independent, yet cooperating, educational systems; and the receptivity of the freed people to schooling and to northern-sponsored benevolence in general. Ultimately, however, responsibility lay with the teachers who volunteered to go south. These women and men faced the difficult task of applying high-minded evangelical beliefs to situations they encountered daily. Although their northern superiors told of glorious plans and outlined far-reaching goals in the *American Missionary*, the teachers adhered to a list of unofficial priorities and ran into problems not easily solved by ideology or policy. For example, AMA workers in Georgia usually ignored the issue of land distribution and focused their energies on religious work and common-school education. The *American Missionary* could rejoice in a whole new "field of missionary labor in the South," and point to "millions of non-slaveholding whites" to be "raised to the level of manhood," but the Georgia teachers had little contact with the native white population, whether out of choice or necessity. And always the idealistic rhetoric of racial egalitarianism proved difficult to match with deeds. One Georgia superintendent confessed to his superior that he preferred not to board black people in the association's Savannah mission home. He wrote, "I know it is hard to satisfy colored people. I am of the old abolition stamp. I stand by the principle of equal justice to all men. The A.M.A. is right. But if I have my choice I prefer white boarders, they are less trouble and then it does not bring down the wrath of the whites of the South." He was exceptional in his confession, and perhaps in his ambivalence toward blacks, but his words reveal that local conditions and personal prejudices could often dilute AMA ideology, if not abolitionist fervor.[33]

For those who remained faithful to the guiding principles of their sponsoring societies, freedmen's teaching amounted to grueling work often marked by frustration and disappointment. McPherson suggests that initial faith in the automatic healing powers of education became modified over time to the point where freedmen's workers believed the whole process of personal and social regeneration would take much longer than they had originally anticipated. Yet, if the teachers bore the brunt of the clash between evangelical idealism and southern realities, they also enjoyed a sense of personal fulfillment experienced by few administrators or financial contributors who remained at home in the North.[34]

In their personal characteristics—especially their race, age, denominational affiliation, education, socioeconomic status and place of birth—the teachers assigned to Georgia reflected the constituencies and needs of their sponsoring societies. For the most part, these were young women and men drawn from the ranks of the farmer and professional classes in New England and the Midwest. Few Georgia freedmen's teachers ever became famous for their contributions to the reform cause, and so biographical information on most of the 368 persons is incomplete. Still, the federal manuscript census for the years 1860 and 1870, family genealogies, obituaries published in society journals, and teachers' letters of application yield enough data to provide a starting point for answering the questions: Who went south, and why?

Several group patterns provide a clear picture of the "typical" teacher in Georgia. She was white, in her late twenties when she first applied for a commission, a member of a Congregational church, well educated, single, and experienced as a common-school teacher. She came from a relatively comfortable small-town or rural "Yankee" home. Her father, a native New Englander, was likely to be a clergyman, farmer, or skilled tradesman. About three-fifths of all the teachers lived in New England, and almost a third of the total came from the state of Massachusetts alone. More than 80 percent of all parents had been born in New England, though half of that number resided in the Midwest or Middle Atlantic states when their daughters went south. Most volunteers began their freedmen's teaching between 1865 and 1868.

Spouse, parent-child, and sibling relationships among the teachers indicate that one out of every four served in Georgia with at least one close family member. Sketchy data concerning family status suggest that as few as one-third of the teachers possessed two living parents when they left for Georgia. The remaining number were divided equally between those who were parentless and those who had either a mother or father still living. Of the 35 percent who fell in the latter category, teachers whose mother was alive outnumbered those with only a father by more than three to one. The "average" teacher came from a family with from three to six children. Less than 2 percent of the teachers were only children, and their sibling rank indicates a marked tendency toward first children, or at least toward children who were older than one-half of their brothers and sisters. Almost a third ranked first among their siblings (Appendixes B, C, and D).

The teachers represented a select group within the northern population. Their similarities were striking in terms of their sex (four-fifths were women), age (more than half were in their twenties), and level of education (nearly all for whom this information is available had attended normal school, a female seminary or academy, or college). The large percentage of Congregationalists, of course, revealed the AMA preference. Most of the teachers came from a segment of the New England and Midwest population best described as the literate (and literary) self-conscious Protestant middle class, the group primarily responsible for the creation and support of evangelical reform movements in the antebellum period.

Descriptions of three representative young women provide a closer look at the collective portrait of Georgia teachers. Jennie F. Stowell and Sarah and Fanny Hunt were living with their parents in rural Massachusetts when they applied to the AMA for teaching commissions. The two Hunts were sisters; they had no other siblings. Jennie was the third in a family of five children and the older daughter. These three young women had much in common. They were all about the same age when they first went south; Sarah and Jennie were twenty-seven, and Fanny was twenty-six. They had received formal preparation as public school teachers, the Hunts by completing the full course of study at Mount Holyoke Seminary and Jennie by graduating from the Massachusetts state normal school at Westfield. All three had practical teaching experience. Fanny had taught at the grammar and high school levels and the other two in their neighborhood common schools. All were confirmed members of the Congregational church. Their fathers owned and operated family farms. The 1860s brought a modest increase to Zebina Hunt's holdings near Sunderland; his real and personal property values increased from $3,400 and $734, respectively, in 1860, to $5,500 and $1,250 in 1870. He employed two young farmhands who lived in the Hunt household. Cyrus Stowell reported real estate and personal property worth $5,000 and $200 when the federal census taker visited his South Deerfield farm in 1870. He had the help of a seventeen-year-old Irish laborer.[35]

In their decision to go south, the three women encountered some initial difficulties in obtaining their parents' blessing. (When their daughter left for Georgia, the Stowells were each about sixty years old; Fanny and Sarah Hunt left at home their father of about the same age and stepmother—their mother had died in 1853.) Jennie first contacted the AMA in May 1864, when she reported that all three of her brothers had enlisted in the Union army. The youngest had been killed by a rebel sharpshooter at Port Hudson, and the other two still had time to serve; in fact, the middle brother had just signed up for three more years of duty under General Ambrose E. Burnside. Jennie abruptly discontinued her correspondence with the association until December 1867, when she renewed her request for a teaching position. Shortly thereafter her father, a graduate of Williams College and former state representative, wrote an anxious note to the society. Only one of his sons had returned home from the war alive, and he and his wife had serious misgivings about Jennie's headstrong determination to engage in such dangerous work as freedmen's teaching. In fact, Stowell managed to delay his daughter's latest effort to receive a commission, but in September 1868 she accepted an assignment in Macon.[36]

The Hunts also faced some resistance from their parents, who insisted their daughters go no farther from home than Georgia; they vetoed an Alabama assignment for Sarah. She taught in Savannah from 1865 until 1867, and then in Macon from 1869 until 1871. Fanny joined her sister in Savannah for the 1866–67 school year. The two, who showed that freedmen's teaching was often a family affair, served in Savannah under the supervision of their uncle and aunt, the Reverend and Mrs. E. A. Cooley, also natives of Sunderland. The three young teachers considered freedmen's work a temporary endeavor; Jennie and Fanny married upon returning home to the North, and Sarah wed nine years after she left Macon.[37]

Those workers who do not fit this general pattern merit special mention. A fifth of all persons sponsored by northern freedmen's aid societies were men. Most of them served as superintendents or principals; few of them taught elementary classes regularly or fulltime. They tended to be slightly older than the women (in their thirties). Most were married clergymen and had probably attended a college or seminary (Yale, Dartmouth, Amherst, and Oberlin were favorites). Apparently few had seen active duty in the army, though one minister served as a chaplain in Union hospitals in the North, and another man held the rank of captain (at the age of twenty-five) in the Twenty-third Regiment. The military status of a third, a Dartmouth graduate, is unknown, but he managed a dramatic escape from a Columbia, South Carolina, prison camp in November 1864. Many of the ministers demonstrated a long-term commitment to missionary service of some type on behalf of their own church or interdenominational evangelizing society. Their service in the South was relatively brief (most stayed only a year).[38]

Edmund Asa Ware, an AMA superintendent in Atlanta who became the first president of Atlanta University, was exceptional in a number of ways. A layman and professional educator, he devoted his life to freedmen's education and achieved some prominence for his work. Of all the Georgia workers during the eight years after the war, only Ware and five others, including two ministers, command McPherson's attention in his discussion of prominent neoabolitionists active in the freedmen's cause.[39]

In spite of incomplete evidence on these men, a few tentative suggestions may be offered about the nature of their participation in freedmen's work. Most had not served as soldiers during the war, perhaps obtaining exemptions by virtue of their profession (clergymen), youth, or status as college students. However, a commission from the AMA or some other sponsoring agency enabled these men to play an active role in the postwar effort. The small pool of northern ministers supplied most of the men who took part in freedmen's education. Because of the stability of their professional status during the war, their experience in living on a meager income, and their personal missionary commitment, some clergymen found the southern alternative appealing, if only for a year or two.

Freedmen's work, noted for its hardships and frustrations, held little attraction for men who had just survived physical combat. Several *American Missionary* articles, all entitled "Men Wanted," revealed the difficulty in obtaining male volunteers. Each of the groups needed men to serve as superintendents in the South, yet there were barely enough applicants to meet even this minimal need. While letters of inquiry from women wishing to join the cause piled higher and higher, the societies' calls for "young, healthy, brave men, with good education, high moral purpose, and some experience in teaching" went unheeded. The AMA constantly lamented the shortage of applications from men like Congregationalists Edmund Asa Ware, Thomas Chase, Frank Haley, John Rockwell, and Egbert B. Bingham—young Ivy League graduates who possessed administrative abilities and were already in the organization.[40]

Only eighteen (seven women and eleven men), or 5 percent, of the Georgia teachers were black. Again, most of the men were ministers. The Reverend Hardy Mobley affords an interesting example. Born a slave in Augusta, Georgia, he had eventually saved enough money to free himself and his wife and children from bondage (at a total cost of $3,000) and move to Brooklyn, New York. At the war's end, he received a commission from the Union Congregational Church in that city to serve as a missionary to the freed people. Before embarking on the journey to his native state, he declared that he wanted to return to "labor for the improvement of his old neighbors who [had] been less fortunate than himself." He received support from both the Brooklyn Freedmen's Friend Society and the AMA in his work in Georgia and later in Louisiana.[41]

Little is known about the black women who volunteered as teachers with the exception of Harriet Brent Jacobs. Aided by the prominent abolitionist Lydia Maria Child, in 1861 she had published her autobiography, entitled *Incidents in the Life of a Slave Girl, Written by Herself.* It recounted the story of her life as a slave in Georgia and her extraordinary escape north. Mrs. Jacobs, who wrote under the pseudonym Linda Brent, received a commission from the New York Society of Friends, an affiliate of the AFUC. She and her daughter taught in Savannah for one year.[42]

Standards set by the sponsoring societies themselves obviously played a large part in shaping the group profile of the teachers who went to Georgia. Sharing a similar philosophy, the northern groups agreed on the basic qualifications a candidate needed in order to receive a position as a freedmen's worker. For the most part, the personal characteristics of the teachers—patterns in sex, age, education, religious affiliation, and economic status—reflected the formal and informal criteria established by the two groups most active in the work, the AMA and the AFUC. In general, the commissioning of teachers represented a self-selection process, for both of these societies derived their financial support and leadership from the native, Protestant, propertied middle class in the North (i.e., from the teachers and their families, friends, and fellow church members).

By the time Georgia became "available" as a field of missionary labor, the AMA and the New England branch of the AFUC had firmly established application procedures for women and men who desired to teach the freed people. The New York headquarters of the AMA, which handled inquiries on a state-by-state basis, sent all candidates a printed application form and referred them to their state agent. The New England branch (NEB), based in Massachusetts, sorted through initial inquiries from all over the state and then encouraged promising candidates to arrange an interview with its teachers' committee at the main Boston office. Letters of recommendation, preferably from ministers and public school officials, completed the formal application requirements.

Because each society had more applicants than it could afford to commission, it was in a position to insist that its teachers meet certain standards, and went to great lengths to publicize the personal qualities deemed necessary for freedmen's work. For example, in its June 1864 issue, the *American Missionary* even published an "ideal" letter submitted by an "ideal" candidate. Both the AMA and the NEB provided standardized application forms, with questions concerning the person's teaching experience, health, reasons for wanting to go south and, in the case of the AMA, denominational affiliation.

General requirements differed little between the two organizations. The AMA called for experienced teachers with missionary spirit, a lack of "romantic or mercenary motives," physical health, "culture and common sense," and "benevolence, gravity and earnestness." The NEB matched its competitor virtue for virtue, with a similar plea for applicants possessed of "Health, courage, energy, high moral character, experience, good judgment, temper, good education, power of discipline, deep interest in the cause of the Negro, and earnest religious faith." (It is uncertain how many prospective candidates were dissuaded from applying by these rather formidable criteria.) Many persons found it difficult to demonstrate their own initial "earnestness of purpose" other than by writing of their concern for the freed people or by submitting testimonials to that effect from clergymen, friends, relatives, and school administrators. For example, the acquaintance of one hopeful candidate assured the AMA: "I learned that Miss Andrews is well-ballasted and free from all girlish nonsense, so that you may rely on her for good honest every day work." However, in such matters as sex, age, education, teaching experience, religious affiliation, and financial well-being, the selection committees had concrete information on which to base their decisions. And the two societies showed decided preferences in each of these six categories.[43]

The combination of several ideological and practical reasons, plus the fact that men were much more likely to serve as superintendents rather than regular elementary-school instructors, meant that freedmen's teaching soon became identified as "women's work." Closely linked to common-school reform, the feminization of the northern teaching force had gained momentum during the late antebellum period. Proponents cited both women's peculiar fitness for teaching and their "efficiency"—a euphemism for the fact that females could be paid lower wages than males. In ways that will be more fully explored in the following pages, the societies adopted and then slightly modified these arguments so that they became relevant to freedmen's work. In addition, middle-class women as a group represented a labor source largely untapped outside the home during the war. Women from financially secure families could afford to accept the low pay offered by the societies and move south for at least one year. As noted above, male volunteers were always in short supply.[44]

Although neither society specified an age beyond which it would not accept an applicant, the nature of the work tended to discourage older persons from applying. In addition, the requirement that all teachers possess the necessary physical fitness to endure the southern climate as well as the exhausting daily schedule served as an informal bar to committed, but older, women and men. For example, the AMA warned: "The toil, the frequent hardships, the tax of brain and nerve that may be encountered in the full and faithful prosecution of the work, will justify us in giving an appointment to no one, not enjoying good health. This is not a *hygenic* [sic] association, to help invalids try a change of air, or travel at others' expense." Moreover, unspecified but implicit criteria, such as flexibility and ability to fit easily into a mission home living situation, all worked against elderly men and women.[45]

The relatively high percentage of college and normal school graduates reflected the societies' formal requirements that all teachers possess an educational and professional background appropriate to freedmen's work. An examination of several hundred letters in the AMA screening files (applications, testimonials, acceptances, rejections) revealed that association officials adhered to this stipulation fairly consistently. However, they sometimes considered an applicant's outstanding educational background (without experience) or exceptional teaching record (minus formal training) sufficient qualification. Ironically, male superintendents, as clergymen, were likely to lack any common-school teaching or administrative experience. This sometimes provoked resentment on the part of female teachers in Georgia.

In addition to proof of teacher certification and experience, applicants to the denominational societies included letters concerning their church membership. The AMA ostensibly accepted affiliates of all evangelical denominations, though its reliance on Congregational churches as a source of funds and recruits resulted in the commissioning of an overwhelming majority from that group. The MFAS and the ABHMS, of course, selected teachers only from members of their respective churches. This requirement meant that successful applicants had undergone a personal religious conversion experience as evidenced by church membership; in few cases were baptism, parental affiliation, or experience in Sunday school teaching satisfactory substitutes. The AMA and the ABHMS had long traditions of sectarian mission work, and denominational societies formed during or after the war also made clear their intention to offer religious instruction to the freed people. The AFUC, while eschewing all connection with sectarianism, also required some evidence of "moral character," most easily filled by church membership in an evangelical, Unitarian, or Quaker group.

The teachers' ability to meet their own travel and living expenses in the South often directly influenced their chances for receiving a commission. As benevolent enterprises that depended wholly upon contributions to sustain their efforts, the freedmen's aid societies often found themselves "embarrassed" financially. Consequently, they strongly encouraged applicants to obtain patrons—church congregations, Sunday schools, private businesses, or individuals—that would pay all costs incurred in southern teaching, a figure usually set at three hundred to five hundred dollars annually per teacher. Indeed, both the AMA and the AFUC reached a point at the beginning of the 1868–69 school year where they were forced to announce that persons interested in going south need not apply if they could not find an outside sponsor who would pay at least some of their expenses.

Moreover, teacher selection committees at times went further and favored candidates with some measure of personal economic independence. Teachers who could afford to forgo a salary and rely on their own resources had a distinct advantage over others who needed some compensation from either the sponsoring society or a patron.

The AMA, for example, looked kindly on persons who offered to loan the association their salaries for the duration of their stay in the South even if they could not "donate" the whole amount outright. More directly, sponsoring societies soon recognized the benefits of employing teachers who could actually use their own funds in supplying instructional materials, superintendents who could dig into their own pockets and meet local financial obligations of the AMA in the South just in the nick of time, and matrons and missionaries who could buy food and clothing for the freed people with their own money. The AMA had its Frederick Ayers and Mary Conklings; subsisting on five dollars a month in Atlanta, he returned almost all of his salary to the association, and she bore the entire expense of operating an Augusta school in 1867. The Chase sisters, daughters of a prominent Worcester insurance agent, proved to be valuable assets for the AFUC because they channeled funds from home into social welfare projects in Columbus. Some teachers could even afford to lend their sponsoring societies large amounts of cash for an unspecified period of time and request only interest payments in return. Before she went south in 1864, one young Massachusetts woman deposited more than a thousand dollars with the AMA.[46]

The sponsorship system in general and salary levels in particular tended to make financial well-being an informal requirement for freedmen's work. The venture was certainly unattractive to fortune seekers, and few persons with dependents at home could afford to go south for fifteen dollars a month, the standard rate of compensation. Experienced teachers from large New England towns like Boston and Worcester necessarily suffered a salary cut. Even superintendents who made considerably more, from five hundred to eight hundred dollars for nine months, had trouble supporting a wife and children on that amount. One minister assigned to Georgia by the AMA reported that the work crippled him financially. Indeed, persons who lacked a secure source of income found themselves at a distinct disadvantage in the field. All the freedmen's groups exhibited the lamentable, if understandable, habit of letting months go by without paying teachers' salaries. One twenty-seven-year-old woman, the daughter of a Massachusetts clergyman, felt the AMA made life unnecessarily difficult for its teachers who were not independently wealthy. Noting that she had no money to make the trip home in June 1868, she remarked bitterly, "It might be better for the A.M.A. just now, if it had fewer 'poor country ministers' daughters.' . . . These classes are not supplied with bank stock, U.S. Bonds and independent friends who have a store of cash constantly on hand, from which supplies can be drawn in cases of emergency."

Money worries tended to distract those teachers from modest backgrounds and lead to awkward situations when they had to borrow money from their more privileged coworkers. In the end, this problem drove some persons out of freedmen's work altogether. A Savannah superintendent explained his resignation from the AMA this way: "My chief reason for not returning to the work was I could not afford it."[47]

As in most selection procedures where the number of candidates outnumbered the available positions, extraneous factors, as opposed to the candidate's personal qualifications, sometimes affected the committees' decisions. The need to keep a church or town in the society's fold or to lure it away from another group prompted a favorable decision in the case of certain applicants; AMA-AFUC rivalry was particularly intense in Massachusetts. And finally, of course, financial considerations always loomed large. Anne W. Phillips, thirty-three years old and a Boston resident, seemed to lack the AMA's most basic qualifications. She was an Episcopalian (often considered nonevangelical), lacked teaching experience, and had even "sympathized" with the South during the war (all the while professing concern for the blacks). Yet C. L. Woodworth, an AMA executive officer, wrote letters on her behalf to the teacher selection committee in 1867. He mentioned that she was "connected with some of the most aristocratic families of the city," and added that she had "property" and could go to Georgia "at her own expense." She received a commission.[48]

In their recruiting literature, freedmen's aid societies made little effort to conceal the fact that southern teaching was physically and emotionally demanding, if not exhausting. In loud and ringing terms, they sent out the call for dedicated young women to relinquish the material comforts of home and the companionship of family and friends to accept the challenge. Sponsors sought candidates who demonstrated a heightened sense of personal sacrifice—women who would make the long journey south and endure cramped living conditions, mosquitoes, and leaky classrooms for only nominal pay. Ultimately, this type of plea sustained and reinforced prevailing notions of women and their roles in mid-nineteenth century America.

Self-sacrifice was an important component of the early Victorian "cult of true womanhood." A rhetorical ideal popularized by Protestant clergymen and sentimental writers, it gained a certain amount of credence among the native northern middle class. Privileged women, stripped of their productive function in the industrializing economy, found themselves isolated in the home and responsible exclusively for domestic affairs. Within this framework of limited political and economic power, they were urged to exert "moral influence" over their families, to exude a pious refinement that would guarantee a nation of stable, happy households. Implicit in this idea of women's roles was the belief that wives, mothers, daughters, and maiden aunts owed a duty first to the people around them, and that personal "selfishness" had no place in a nation already divided on the basis of competing political and cultural interests. The "true woman" thought not of herself—her own desires or long-term interests in artistic or professional achievement—but of the comfort and welfare of her family. Carried to an extreme, the tenet of self-sacrifice became positively masochistic. Indeed, Catharine Beecher, high priestess of this female ethic and an early proponent of the feminization of common-school teaching, suggested that American women could find true happiness only through suffering for others.[49]

The Georgia teachers responded enthusiastically to their societies' call for self-abnegation, but some of the consequences were unexpected. A piecing together of their stories reveals that the teachers managed to break loose from home and family responsibilities and find a great deal of personal satisfaction for themselves, all in the name of "self-sacrifice." They took to heart the summons for women to extend their "moral influence" to others less fortunate than themselves—in this case, southern blacks. As white "mothers" who went south to "elevate" members of this "child-like" race, the teachers conformed to a Victorian ideal of "social guardianship" among middle-class women. But in their decision to leave their father's house and in their determination to exercise independent judgment in their teaching, they revealed the paradox of female missionary work. Like twenty-nine-year-old Jane Hardy of Shelburne, Massachusetts, who had been "cooped up all her life in such a still old town," these women knew that leaving home was a "great thing." They believed that the journey south, sweetened with self-sacrifice, would be the greatest adventure of their lives. Few were disappointed on that score.[50]

The teachers received appointments from their sponsors because they expressed a selfless devotion to the freedmen's cause and a willingness to forgo material comforts in the interest of the work. As young, idealistic Yankee girls, they had burned with shame as they heard for the first time of the horrors of slavery. Sympathy for the freed people "was planted in my heart in early childhood by a father of strong anti-slavery sentiments," explained one young woman from Clinton, Massachusetts, in 1864. Another came from a household of such radical abolitionist feeling that her brother had served with John Brown during the ill-fated raid on Harper's Ferry in 1859. Yet for these young girls, no compelling avenues of action were available; in large part, antebellum antislavery agitation was limited to raising funds, petitioning officeholders, and attending meetings. But at last the Union occupation of southern territory "opened" the South to northern missionaries and signaled the long-awaited call to moral arms among young women who longed to atone for the nation's collective sin against God.[51]

In their letters of application, the women told how they envied their brothers, fiancés, or husbands who had performed such heroic deeds in the war. They regretted that their own sacrifices at home seemed so insignificant in comparison and wanted the opportunity to serve as "soldiers" in the northern societies' "peace-making regiments." Throughout their letters runs a sense of relief from finally discovering a means to aid this holy cause: "I thought that I *must* do something, not having money at my command, what could I do but give *myself* to the work . . . ?" wrote one successful applicant, adding "I would go to them, and give them my life if necessary." Another expressed her thankfulness this way: "The voice we hear today is Go! work. This people must be educated, and may we rejoice that God permits us to aid in such a work."[52]

An evangelical Protestant world view provided the philosophical basis for the teachers' belief that they, as individuals, had both the duty and the ability to rectify certain moral and institutional evils. In the South, they served as informed representatives of their sponsoring societies. Their idealism was borne of religious fervor intensified by a bloody and horrible—but, in their eyes, righteous—conflict. This ideological impulse toward freedmen's work amounted to a form of group motivation in the sense that the teachers shared a common value system and out of it they perceived a certain course of action. Yet various factors in their personal lives made the decision to go south attractive—even imperative—to each of them. The dangers and excitement of Reconstruction Georgia beckoned them from their comfortable homes with promises of hard work that had some larger spiritual significance.

In September 1864 an Uxbridge, Massachusetts, father wrote to an AMA official concerning his daughter's request for a teaching commission. The family was well-to-do and had provided her with the finest cultural and educational opportunities. She had graduated from high school and devoted three years to study at Mount Holyoke Seminary. In 1863 she spent two months touring the European continent. Now, twenty-seven years old, she was unmarried and living at home. She had no teaching experience because it had never been necessary for her to work. Her father ended this letter of introduction by saying that his daughter was "anxious to place herself in some situation where she can do more good than she thinks she is doing at home." Later that year, she received an assignment and headed south as one of the first Georgia teachers.[53]

Her story was not unusual. Young, unmarried women, well educated and financially secure, revealed their restlessness and a wish to "do good." In many cases, parents and relatives were puzzled by their willingness to embrace the missionary life. A thirty-year-old widow who had no compelling economic need to return to teaching after her husband's death wrote, "I have a good home and all the comforts of life and my friends are surprised, that I can not be happy. But I feel that I must go among the Freedmen if possible. I will pay my own expenses." A friend testified of another applicant, "She belongs to a New London family, in such circumstances as to make it entirely convenient to live *at home* and *at ease*, so that *love of the work* it is clear moves her to seek the place." (She later received an assignment over the strenuous objections of her parents.) For middle-class women who possessed youthful spirit and energy, the rigors of freedmen's work presented an appealing alternative to a life of social pleasantries and "trifles," as one woman put it. A female seminary graduate, aged thirty-five and an experienced teacher, confessed, "My life . . . has been a life of ease, and I have felt for a long time that it was a useless one, and have been wishing for a more active life." A twenty-nine-year-old woman who had been teaching for ten years wrote, "I am a soldier's widow—left alone. I desire to be busy—useful." The need to be "useful" hardly lacked intensity because it was a moral, rather than economic, imperative: "When I wrote to you that I could not afford to be idle I did not mean in a pecuniary sense," declared a thirty-three-year-old teacher to an AMA official.[54]

A few years before she went south, one woman had experienced a spiritual awakening somewhat akin to religious conversion while attending an aunt dying of tuberculosis. It was then that she had decided there was "something better to live for" than the routine of household chores in her father's home and teaching in the neighborhood school. She hoped that a commission would satisfy her need for meaningful work, and apparently it did, for she remained in the South for nine years and taught in three different states, including Georgia. Indeed, many teachers chafed under the restrictions and responsibilities of home life in the North. As well-educated women in their twenties and thirties still living with their parents, brothers, sisters, and relatives, their own lack of self-sufficiency must have seemed like a painful extension of childhood's financial and emotional dependence. On returning home from boarding at normal school or a female seminary, they had begun a "domestic apprenticeship" under their mothers—helping with household chores, looking after the younger children, and learning social amenities such as the middle-class custom of afternoon visiting. Information concerning the teachers' family status suggests that many had assumed the duty of caring for aged parents and younger siblings, responsibilities that, in the rural tradition, devolved primarily upon the older daughter. For these women, going south offered an escape from family tasks they would never really "outgrow."[55]

Still, most teachers could never break totally from family influence, even temporarily. Obviously many depended upon their parents' approval in deciding whether to apply for a commission at all, and then when and where to go and how long to stay. Parents who maintained they needed their daughters at home took a dim view of this foray into freedmen's work. Older women who had spent a large part of their lives caring for fathers and mothers realized that home ties—which in some cases bordered on tyranny—remained strong. Wrote one applicant, who was at least fifty years old: "I have but little fear of the Rebs, but my Father is old [eighty-seven] and feeble and feels as though he could not have me go so far and where there is so much danger" (in 1868). Younger daughters also dutifully observed the wishes of their parents, at least to a point. One teacher in her early twenties sent a short note to the AMA, stating merely, "Mother says I need not stay at home next winter. I want to go south. May I?" Another teacher, about the same age, finally managed to escape from her parents in New Hampshire; they considered her undertaking "quite Quixotic" and she sought refuge with friends in Massachusetts until receiving final confirmation of her commission from the AMA. Little evidence exists that might explain how these women made provisions for younger or older relatives once they went south. Apparently some elderly parents agreed to fend for themselves; in other cases, sisters or female kinfolk agreed to take over various household chores. The prospective freedmen's teacher could argue that her mission was a temporary one, and that, by enabling her to fulfill this commitment, others who remained at home could indirectly participate with her in the work. Finally, a large number of women sent home all or part of their monthly sala-

ries to mothers, fathers, sisters, and brothers. This small amount—
fifteen dollars—might have symbolized their continued dependence
on and responsibility for home affairs.[56]

Those teaching candidates whose parents had died shared special
problems. Most resided with either friends or relatives or boarded
temporarily with other families. For these women, freedmen's teaching seemed a preferable alternative to their lives as permanent
"guests." For example, Jane McNeil of Charlotte, Vermont, included
a detailed personal history with her letter of application to the AMA
in 1869. In a family of fifteen children, she had been her parents'
"favor'd one." Consequently, until 1864 her "province" had involved
exclusively the duties of home, caring first for her father until his
death in 1860 and then for her mother until she died four years
later. Since that time she had lived with, or as she put it, "hung
upon" her relatives, a routine she found "not pleasant." Used to
strenuous activity and impatient with her "life of idleness," she
impressed upon the selection committee that she was "not permanently settled in any place [and] that . . . it would be in unison with
my mind to be in some way profitably employed." However, she felt
no need to work for financial reasons. Mature and accustomed to
responsibility, Jane McNeil found herself bored and uncomfortable
in the homes of her affluent relatives. As a freedmen's teacher she
could once more accept responsibility for other people, but this time
on her own terms. She served in Georgia from 1869 to 1870.[57]

Friends could play just as decisive a role as family members in a
teacher's decision to go south. The intensity and determination with
which female teachers maintained emotional relationships with
other women both before and during their work in the South illustrates a nineteenth-century phenomenon of mutual love and dependency among women friends; complex networks of friends, including
sisters, daughters, mothers, and cousins, as well as nonkinship relationships, played a large part in the lives of many women. Although
no examples of the teachers' correspondence with one another are
extant, their letters to freedmen's aid society officials suggest the
extent of their personal loyalties. At times a friend could be a negative influence and dissuade a woman from going south once she had
received a commission, or lead her to appeal for a different assignment because of fears for her physical safety or health. Apparently,
most teachers who served in Georgia eventually overruled these two
specific and often-mentioned objections. One teacher assured the
AMA's district secretary in October 1867, that "My friends have
been strongly opposed to my returning but I have finally overcome
their prejudices."[58]

Those women who served in the South with their friends avoided the problem. Letters of application to the AMA reveal that the decision to enter freedmen's work was often a collective, rather than individual, one. Sisters, cousins, and friends from school included in their applications the stipulation that, unless they could go south together, they preferred not to go at all. Others stated they had no preference of location as long as they were assigned together. Whenever pairs of teachers possessed satisfactory credentials and could raise some of the money for their own salaries, society officials tried to accommodate these requests. Teachers in Georgia also served as informal recruiters for freedmen's work when they persuaded friends at home to apply for teaching commissions and join them in the South. Those already in the field wrote to New York, supplied testimonials of "Christian character" for their friends, and requested that they, too, be sent to Georgia. From Augusta in 1867, one teacher wrote of a woman in New York City: "Miss H. is a person of more than ordinary talent and education, a sincere, earnest working Christian, has the interest of the freedmen very much at heart, and I feel would prove a valuable acquisition in your corps of teachers." Behind these stiff, formal letters of recommendation lay months of personal correspondence between the two women in which the teacher assured her friend that the work was safe and worthwhile.[59]

For each freedmen's worker, the rigors of southern teaching offered a sharp contrast to the genteel sphere of domesticity and dependence that middle-class northern society encouraged and expected her to occupy. How did she respond to these new challenges hundreds of miles away from home? Did she find some sort of personal satisfaction in her new life, or seek out the security of her New England home as soon as possible? One measure of the teachers' attitude toward their work is their length of stay in the South. Given the limited tenure for most schoolteachers in New England at this time (an average of two years), those in Georgia demonstrated a relatively strong commitment to the freedmen in terms of number of years devoted to their mission. One-third of them remained in the South for two or three years, and an equal number stayed for four years or longer. As a group they spent an average of four years in the South (range: one to forty-six; median, two). About half taught in other states in addition to Georgia, and one-sixth taught in three or more states. Some women left their homes early in the war and never returned to the North, except as visitors; these teachers made a lifelong commitment to black education.[60]

The state of their health in the South provides another indication of the women's ability to cope with the hardships and frustrations associated with freedmen's teaching. Contemporaries bemoaned the miserable condition of middle-class women's health and noted the susceptibility of wives and mothers to nervous exhaustion, depression, as well as a host of other maladies. Yet letters from Georgia reveal that, though the teachers were often plagued by ill health, it stemmed from physical causes—malaria, "chills and fever," and respiratory ailments—and not emotional ones. Most women exhibited the physical energy characteristic of persons employed in occupations requiring intellectual activity, physical stamina, and personal commitment. Soon after her return to Augusta in the fall, an older woman observed that the hard work enabled her to sleep better and that she had not "felt so contented" for three months (i.e., since she had left the work last spring). Declaring that she enjoyed the exercise of doing her own housework as well as teaching, a rural "pioneer" teacher explained, "I am very happy in my work and have no time to be lonely." Another confessed that, as the hectic end of the school year brought more responsibilities and excitement, "every day grows pleasanter."[61]

For many the demands of southern teaching represented a welcome change in their lives. "Oh! . . . My life here is so very *very* full," testified an Atlanta teacher. A coworker in Augusta declared, "The past winter has truly been the happiest one of my life." A Madison teacher told her superior, "My heart is filled with love for this work—Oh! I am so glad I could come." And some women actually embraced the dangers inherent in journeying to and teaching in the postwar South—the very hazards their friends had warned them about. A letter written by Fidelia Morgan, an experienced teacher from Bernardston, Massachusetts, provides a glimpse into her sense of daring and fascination with the unknown. Traveling alone from New York to Augusta aboard a steamship, she endured a terrible night in the midst of a hurricane. The storm had a dramatic effect on her and as she sat alone in her tiny room she mused, "And after all, I love this deep eternal sea—treacherous, soft, dreadful, inexplicable sea—I am fascinated by it perhaps *because it is dangerous* [with] its deep breathings, the mournfulest, most mysterious of all sounds." Two years later, Fidelia feared that the end of her freedmen's teaching would mean a "narrower life" for herself and fewer of those "precious opportunities."[62]

Teachers who spent summers in the North at home found themselves anticipating the time when they could return to Georgia. In anxious letters to society headquarters, they told of their restlessness and spoke of "longings" and "yearnings" for the work. A Massachusetts teacher expressed this happy conjunction of idealism and productive labor: "the time spent in teaching in Savannah has been by far the happiest period of my life, because I felt I was accomplishing more good in that length of time than I ever had the opportunity of doing before."[63]

Extensive follow-up information on the teachers is lacking. For most, of course, their experience in freedmen's work was only temporary. In 1869 one woman notified AMA headquarters, "You know this is my third year South, and I now think it my last; not because I do not love my work as well as ever, or feel as much interest in it as formerly, but because I cannot afford to spend more of my life here." Teachers left the field for a variety of well-defined reasons: illness and overwork, financial constraints, personality disagreements with coworkers and superiors, and requests of parents and friends to return home. Some, like one lonely teacher on an isolated Georgia plantation, found the work unbearably difficult; she wrote in March 1873, "I thought when I first came here [Walburg Plantation in Lowndes County] it was going to be a pleasant and comparatively easy situation; but I have found it anything but that. Nothing but the most decided convictions of duty could induce me to spend another such winter." She left at the end of the spring.[64]

Others resigned to embark on new careers and new lives, including marriage (some teachers wed immediately upon their return home, which indicated they had left fiancés behind to go south); traveling; teaching in the North; and missionary work among the Chinese in California, the Africans at the AMA Mendi Mission, the Turks in Constantinople, the Indians, and errant New Englanders in the old Northwest. But the continuation of strong friendships formed in Georgia, contributions to their sponsoring societies, reunions, and fund-raising efforts reveal a long-term commitment in many after they left the South.

With the exception of the progress of individual students and the limited effects of the distribution of relief supplies, signs of success within the overall context of freedmen's education were few and far between. But, like all faithful missionaries and reformers, the teachers derived a good deal of personal satisfaction from their efforts. Not unexpectedly, some even felt a bit guilty over the possibility that they were doing more good for themselves than for the freed people; this would hardly befit the role of a self-sacrificing missionary. One joyful twenty-eight-year-old in her first year of southern teaching confessed, "I am so happy that I sometimes wonder where are the self-denials of our work." Her words indicate that "self-denials" did not necessarily preclude personal emotional fulfillment. The teachers' experiences reveal the variety and complexity of ways in which they subverted the potentially destructive call for "self-sacrifice" and used it as a means of escape from the narrow confines of middle-class conventionality.[65]

CHAPTER III

"As a Thirsty Man Would Beg for Water"

The history of Georgia from 1860 to 1870 is fraught with irony. During this decade, the state underwent significant changes in its society, politics, and economy. Yet the tenet of white supremacy remained intact. Class tensions surfaced and became explicit in political rhetoric, but the weak postwar Republican party never confronted the race issue directly. The institution of slavery cracked and then crumbled under the weight of wartime exigencies, and blacks embarked on a quest for "soul liberty." Although the plantation system began to disintegrate in the latter part of the decade, the freed people continued to be economically dependent on white merchants and landowners. The cumulative effect of these trends was a climate of racial fear from which few Georgians, regardless of race, class, or political party, were insulated. And underneath the turmoil ran a river of continuity, deep and swift, polluted with violence and prejudice. These were the waters that would nourish the "New South."[1]

Formal education involves much more than learning how to read and write; it reflects society and economy, time and place. In Reconstruction Georgia, freedmen's education symbolized the new order in different ways to different groups. For black people, schooling represented individual and collective defiance to white authority and a means of expanding their horizons beyond the limits of the cotton plantation. Slavery had been a form of intellectual as well as physical bondage. Still, the efforts of blacks to establish their own schools after the war revealed that they had maintained an independence of spirit throughout their long ordeal.

For northern teachers and administrators, the school presented an opportunity to inculcate in the black population certain middle-class values that the whites assumed were universal among all "moral" men and women. They condemned rival black-operated schools as evidence of the race's ignorance and ingratitude toward its white benefactors. Indeed, no matter how radical their political beliefs, northerners in Georgia failed to appreciate the blacks' desire to control their own lives as much as possible, including what and by whom their children were taught. It is true that black communities would not have been able to achieve educational self-sufficiency soon after the war simply because they lacked the resources to establish and staff their own schools. The federal government and northern freedmen's aid societies supplied the cash and experienced teachers that many areas desperately needed. But those three groups most able and likely to aid the cause of black education—the Georgia Republican party, the Freedmen's Bureau, and northern societies—sometimes worked at cross-purposes with blacks who wanted to achieve some measure of freedom from all whites—paternalistic educators as well as tyrannical slaveholders.

Finally, to most white Georgians the school symbolized the breakdown of a social system that had formed the cornerstone of the southern "way of life." They quickly set about reconstructing that system after the war's end, and relied on legal discrimination, economic oppression, and terrorism to intimidate the former slaves. Black teachers and schoolhouses were logical targets for whites who were suspicious of all attempts at self-assertion on the part of their former bondsmen. Poor whites resented the fact that northern money went to aid black education while their own children were deprived of common schools, and for the first time they had to recognize black people as potential competitors in economic and political terms. Skin color bound whites fiercely together; except for a handful of Union sympathizers and Radical Republicans, white Georgians throughout the state shared, as one American Missionary Association (AMA) teacher put it, "a *perfect hatred*" for the Yankees who brought with them the subversive doctrines of antebellum abolitionism. Nevertheless, the freed people persisted in their determination to learn, and the school served as a rallying point for men and women, young and old, as they stepped out of the darkness of slavery and into the light of freedom.[2]

In 1860 Georgia was an integral part of the southern economy. Dominated by a rich and powerful planter elite, it was firmly committed to the slave system. This "peculiar institution" served as both the backbone of the state's economy and the chief determinant of social relations among whites and between blacks and whites. The population of 1,057,286 included almost half a million slaves. A tenth of all residents were registered to vote, and almost 40 percent of that number were slaveholders. Located in the center of the wide Black Belt, which girded the Piedmont area of the South, Georgia was a willing and obedient servant of King Cotton; it produced 701,840 bales of the staple crop in the year before the war. North of the central cotton belt lay the hill country and to the south of it was the less fertile wire-grass area, both regions populated by non-slaveholding farmers. The cotton Gold Coast, which included the rich Savannah River delta and subtropical Sea Islands, boasted large, prosperous plantations.[3]

Michael P. Johnson has examined in detail the events surrounding the state's secession from the Union in March 1861. Fearful that the contagion of northern Republican "free labor, free soil" ideology might infect poor whites in their state, wealthy Georgia planters waged an intensive and eventually successful campaign in favor of secession by arguing that all white men had a vested interest in the preservation of slavery. Their goal was to preserve their own hegemony against threats from their less prosperous white neighbors as well as New England abolitionists. Results of the election of delegates to the secession convention in January 1861 indicated that the voting public was evenly divided on the issue, split between men who owned slaves and those who did not. According to Johnson, slaveholders were determined to extend their own "patriarchal" influence over other whites (as they had over their slaves), and had little interest in promoting any vague notion of "democracy" within the context of the state's political system. After giving a secession ordinance their overwhelming approval, planter delegates to the convention consolidated their power by writing a new constitution that was "more responsive than its predecessor to the social, economic, and political leaders in Georgia and more insulated from any effects of electoral politics that might seriously threaten their interests in the status quo." The elite had in effect initiated a "double revolution," against native yeomen farmers and the federal government.[4]

But slaveholders did not need to create fears of race war and Yankee madness in the minds of their neighbors who were inclined to remain within the Union. John Brown's raid on Harper's Ferry in 1859, plus rumors of imminent slave insurrections and invasions by Garrison's disciples, led to a near-hysteria among all segments of the Georgia white population, urban and rural, rich and poor. As the state armed for war, and as slaveowners slowly lost control over their bondsmen in the haste to defend themselves and their new nation, racial fears intensified, and brutal suppression of the black population resulted. The old order was rapidly disappearing, and most whites and blacks realized it.[5]

Confederate Governor Joseph E. Brown fought the Civil War on several fronts during his tenure in office, which spanned the war years. The Yankee presence in coastal areas off South Carolina from late 1861 onward necessitated a vigilant military force in the southeastern part of Georgia for the duration of the conflict. Pro-Union sentiment, born of both philosophical commitment and extreme physical hardship among hill people who bore the brunt of this "rich man's war," produced pockets of resistance to the Confederate war effort. Yeomen farmers deserted from the army and banded together to skirmish with southern soldiers on Georgia soil. The state's antebellum economy collapsed as cotton production plummeted and farmers made a weak attempt to diversify their crops to keep the population alive.

As if he did not have his hands full with Yankees who threatened the coast and fellow Georgians who fought him in the mountains, Brown persisted in a principled but ultimately suicidal battle against the Confederacy itself by stubbornly opposing President Jefferson Davis's centralizing policies. Meanwhile, some slaves escaped to Union lines and others took advantage of wartime dislocation to loosen their fetters. By the time Sherman began his March to the Sea in late 1864, Georgia had already felt the ravages of war. The Union capture of Savannah in December was almost anticlimactic.[6]

Appomattox signaled humiliation for white Georgians, but few were prepared to capitulate completely to the victorious North. Delegates to the state's constitutional convention in October 1865 did their best to reestablish the slave system in the form of oppressive Black Codes. In January of the next year the former vice-president of the Confederacy, a Georgia resident, prepared to take his seat in the United States Senate, to which he had been duly elected by the defiant General Assembly. A few months later, that body refused to ratify the Fourteenth Amendment, which conferred citizenship rights on black people. Finally, Republicans in Washington could stand no more, and a coalition of radical and moderate congressmen established a military government over Georgia (and other recalcitrant states) in the spring of 1867. The state was readmitted to the union—for the first time—in June 1868.

Yet former Confederates still would not submit. White Democrats began a sustained campaign of terrorism against freedmen who tried to vote, and only 10 percent of eligible black voters cast ballots in the November presidential election, though the Republicans managed to elect key state officials, including Governor Rufus B. Bullock. Blacks chosen to serve in the state assembly that year were unceremoniously ejected by white legislators, Republicans and Democrats, who declared that the new constitution did not give blacks the right to hold office. The new body's rejection of the Fifteenth Amendment (granting black men the right to vote) provoked Congress to reinstitute military Reconstruction in December 1869. Governor Bullock resigned under a cloud of scandal in October 1871 to avoid impeachment, and his opponents capitalized on his hasty exit from the state. By late 1871, Georgia had finally achieved both readmission to the Union and political redemption; the Democratic party was firmly established in power at the state level.[7]

Throughout this period, the Republicans offered only a weak challenge to the state's traditional political system. Dominated by native white Georgians, the party began a statewide campaign in 1867 to attract black and poor white voters. Its platform included measures aimed at the state's small farmers—debt relief, homesteads, and public schools—and it had the potential to create an alliance between those two groups most feared by the antebellum planter elite. However, most Republicans were interested primarily in gaining political power, not in social change, and little came of their populist denunciations of "the ruling class at the South." Only a very few state party leaders shared the visions of congressional Radical Republicans like Charles Sumner and Thaddeus Stevens.[8]

In fact, black people in Georgia soon learned that they hardly needed Democratic enemies if they had Republican "friends." As Alan Conway has noted of Georgia Reconstruction politics in general, "Caucasian blood was thicker than party water." Black voters were courted vigorously by Republican politicians, but offered little in return for their support. Although "radicals" expressed a rhetorical commitment to interracial brotherhood when they were out on the campaign trail, they showed no interest in seeing freedmen achieve leadership positions within party ranks or jobs from the patronage system once elections were won. The moderates, who rarely made any secret of their personal dislike for blacks, "found the freedmen embarrassing" in their appeal for white votes. This segment of the party, which held the balance of power between black Republicans and white Democrats in the state legislature during the fall of 1868, was primarily responsible for the expulsion of thirty-two black legislators during that session. It was no wonder that black voters soon became disillusioned with the Republicans, and that their leaders began to stress racial solidarity above party interests. In his study of Georgia politics after the war, John M.

Matthews concludes that white Republican scalawags demonstrated a concern for the freed people that "was at best halfhearted and nearly always opportunistic."[9]

Amid the sound and the fury of Reconstruction politics—infighting among Republicans and Democrats alike, heightened racial animosities, a seemingly endless procession of different elected officials—nothing of substance materialized in the way of state aid to public education. Both the 1865 and 1868 (Republican) constitutions included vague provisions for tax-supported schools, and the expenditure of a great deal of Republican energy issuing promises in that direction indicated it was a relatively popular issue among whites and blacks alike. But, given the degree of overt racial prejudice within the Republican party, there was virtually no chance that the state would ever establish a comprehensive school system (let alone an integrated one) during Reconstruction. Indeed, the bloody game of racial politics dissuaded Republican legislators from even broaching the subject in any concrete way. A state system of public instruction would be the product of more stable, if not less heated, political climes during the post-Redemption period of the early 1870s.

The Republican party did offer some informal support to black schooling as part of its statewide campaign strategy. White members of the radical "Augusta wing" of the party, including future Governor Bullock, cooperated with blacks to form the Georgia Equal Rights Association in that city in January 1866. Ten months later, the group changed its name to the less offensive Georgia Education Association (GEA), and, supported by black leaders throughout the state, helped to organize schools. John H. Caldwell, an agent of the Freedmen's Aid Society of the Methodist Episcopal Church (MFAS), and John E. Bryant, carpetbagger from Maine and publisher of the *Loyal Georgian*, played prominent roles in the organization. Several black leaders, including James Porter, William Jefferson White, and Tunis G. Campbell (all of whom had ties at one time or another to the AMA), used the GEA as a base from which to launch their own political careers. By the fall of 1867, 120 black schools in 53 (out of a total of 131) counties claimed affiliation with the GEA, but the group was the short-lived victim of Republican opportunism. Still, it did serve as an impetus for grass-roots educational activity in black communities throughout the state.[10]

Northern Republicans in the United States Congress sought to influence southern society and politics indirectly through the Freedmen's Bureau. But the bureau, like the state party, could or would not deliver on its promises to protect the black man's civil rights. It was empowered to oversee the contract system between white landowners and black workers, administer relief to poor people of both races, and aid the cause of black education. The record of bureau officials in Georgia was mixed. In 1867 and 1868 they helped to register large numbers of newly enfranchised blacks, and many of the two hundred local agents cooperated with northern freedmen's aid societies in a number of ways, both official and unofficial, to establish a statewide system of black education that lasted from 1865 to 1870. The first and last assistant commissioners in charge of the district that included Georgia—Rufus Saxton (1865) and John R. Lewis (1868–70)—publicly and aggressively supported blacks in their struggle to gain land and the right to vote. But Saxton's successor, General Davis Tillson, was a staunch ally of Andrew Johnson, and in Georgia he quickly won favor with the conservative element of the population. Tillson played a pivotal role in divesting blacks of the lands granted to them in the coastal region under Sherman's Special Field Order # 15, and he came under fire from northern teachers for his contract-labor policies. In March 1866 a northern freedmen's teacher stationed in Columbus charged, "The Bureau we *found* made cruel contracts, and was *only* useful to the whites—no redress could the blacks find." Underpaid and overworked, most local agents probably did the best they could under the circumstances; surely they were unprepared to fight a major battle in the war against southern white racism. But the teacher's comments raise larger questions concerning the relationship between the state's agricultural system and public schooling. Patterns of land use and labor in postwar Georgia contributed to tensions between poor whites and the former slaves—tensions that were in turn exacerbated by the presence of northern teachers.[11]

The bureau sponsored a system of negotiated two-party labor contracts in an attempt to restore "order" in the southern countryside as soon after the war as possible. Its intentions were both reactionary and progressive: to preserve (at least temporarily) the basic economic relationship that had existed between the races under slavery, and to insure that blacks would receive some compensation for their labors at the end of the year (it was not uncommon for white employers to turn them off the land without any payment after the harvest was in). The terms of these contracts varied throughout the state from 1865 to 1869. The recommended agreements called for blacks to work for twelve dollars in cash per month and to receive food and medical care from their employers. The bureau also set up special appeals courts to deal with the strong resistance to the new program from planters, who charged that such terms would bankrupt them.[12]

In practice, however, the system was often quite harsh. Freed people who refused for whatever reasons to make contracts or who fled from physical punishment (contracts sometimes provided for the use of the lash) were liable to arrest for vagrancy under state law. One observer in Georgia remarked, "The excuse of the framers of this infamous law is, that without it, their Negroes will leave on every slight whipping, and all wholesome discipline is at an end." One Savannah agent threatened to put two freedmen in chains if they did not work under terms they considered unfair. Thus he and others who followed contract guidelines closely actually enforced a system of involuntary labor. Wage rates were very low to begin with (as little as two dollars per month in some areas of Georgia in 1865), and workers often had to provide their own tools. At the end of the year, few people had much to show for their hard work. An AMA teacher in Darien noted that the blacks there saw "but very little— if *any*—money; many think themselves fortunate if they do not come out in debt to the establishment which is oftentimes the case."[13]

In an agricultural society, land is the primary source of wealth and social status. A man measures his own self-worth by the amount and quality of land he owns; it is his major legacy to his heirs. After emancipation, the freed people correctly perceived that the ownership of land was the key to their collective and individual strength, that economic independence would help free them from the poverty and oppression they had endured under slavery. But they emerged from bondage with no cash and few material possessions. The Freedmen's Bureau actually distributed very little of the land the government had confiscated from Confederates during the war; much was returned to "repentant" rebels. Whites made agreements among themselves to refuse to sell land to blacks, and white merchants denied them the financial credit they needed in order to buy. For these reasons, Georgia blacks owned only one percent of the state's total acreage a decade after the war's end. The goal of economic self-sufficiency eluded them as a group.[14]

Nevertheless, the Georgia agricultural system underwent a major upheaval during this period. At first, the Freedmen's Bureau contract system reestablished a form of gang labor similar to that used by slaveholders, and almost all agricultural laborers continued to devote most of their energies to growing cotton as they had before the war. In 1866 many freed people lived in old slave quarters, suffered whippings by overseers when they slacked off, and received little pay for their year's labor. One Sea Island plantation mistress indicated her determination to grow cotton the same way despite emancipation when she admitted that her "old negro drivers" were "now called captains, out of complement to the changed times," but that their work routine had not changed at all. However, it was not long before the blacks themselves engaged in collective resistance to this way of life, which bore more than "an uneasy resemblance to slavery." They withheld their labor, broke contracts, and made clear their lack of faith in the bureau's promise to advance their interests. Although caught in a snare of Black Codes and bureau regulations designed to restrict their geographical and social mobility, Georgia blacks managed to express their strong dislike for wage labor. In the process, they forced whites to react and abandon the plantation system of cotton production.[15]

Black labor was a highly valued commodity. In the late 1860s, white landowners in Georgia and other Black Belt states began to respond in their own way to an increasingly frightening situation; the freed people's "unreliability," together with unfavorable weather conditions, had led to a decline in cotton production immediately after the war. To placate the blacks' desire for land, planters began to divide up their holdings and install individual families on small parcels. As payment for use of the land a family gave the owner cash or some fraction of the crop (by the end of the decade a "fifty-fifty" split was the most common form of sharecropping in the southern states). Between 1866 and 1869 the total number of "hands employed" declined by as many as 50 percent in the southwest area of Georgia, and other cotton-growing regions of the South also made the transition from wage labor to sharecropping.[16]

Blacks preferred the new system for good reasons. As tenants, they could move out of the old slave cabins clustered around an owner's house and into small homes scattered on his land. They could work alone, away from the overseer, with the understanding that they would be able to keep at least part of what they grew. This was an especially attractive prospect to young men with families, for they could make more money sharecropping. Paid a set amount each month according to their age and sex, plantation laborers had little incentive to work hard. Still, the freed people would rather have owned the land outright. Under the crop-lien system they had to pay exorbitantly high interest rates to local merchants for food and supplies and had no opportunity to save enough money to purchase land, assuming of course that they were able to find a willing seller. Economic institutions of credit and merchandising were warped by racial discrimination, and black people remained outside the "free" market economy.[17]

In their study of the postwar southern economy, *One Kind of Freedom*, Roger L. Ransom and Richard Sutch argue that the transformation of southern agriculture from the plantation wage system to sharecropping affected large numbers of poor whites as well as blacks. They further suggest that "the emergence of a white tenant class and the acquisition of independent family farms by many blacks brought the blacks and the middle- and lower-class whites into a more parallel situation than most of these whites would have preferred." This was one reason why Georgia Republicans failed so miserably in their attempts to appeal to small farmers of both races, especially blacks in the cotton belt and whites in the northern and wire-grass regions of the state. Not only did party members lack a commitment to interracial politics, but the historical antagonism between blacks and poor whites also intensified once the institutional barrier that had separated them under slavery was removed. Few white men liked the idea of competing with blacks for farmland or bank loans, even if that "competition" existed only in a theoretical sense. These whites also faced another new source of resentment: Yankee teachers, who entered the state with great fanfare and promised to "elevate" black people and teach them how to read and write. Yet education remained out of the reach of white children whose parents could not afford to send them to private schools.[18]

Freedom came in increments to black people in Georgia. During the Civil War, the chains of bondage loosened as slavery was disrupted by a variety of forces related to military preparedness. A few slaves gained their freedom by escaping from their masters; others won their liberation from the conquering Union army; still others had to wait months after the war before their owners finally released them. As soon as possible, most seized the opportunity to leave the plantation; many headed for nearby towns and some went to search for loved ones from whom they had been separated. As freed men and women, they shed the outer trappings of slavery and donned brightly colored garments. Their refusal to defer to whites on city sidewalks gave rise to reports of black "insolence" and "sassiness" throughout the state. Men left the fields early in the day, and insisted that their wives no longer work. Significantly, the response to emancipation quickly crystallized in the form of separate black political and cultural institutions created out of racial consciousness and an impulse for collective self-help. Many whites reacted fearfully to these acts of self-assertion and tried to reestablish the antebellum equilibrium between the races through violence. Indeed, the bloody history of Georgia race relations during Reconstruction reveals the freed people's struggle to resist an oppression that proved to be more durable than the institution of slavery.[19]

In this "quest for collective autonomy," schooling was of great symbolic and practical importance to blacks. It represented one form of independence from the class that had claimed literacy as its exclusive privilege: white landowners. A freed person who could read and write would be able to understand a labor contract, correspond with friends and relatives, keep informed of political affairs in the state, and study the Bible. Education was a means of breaking out of the confines of ignorance that had served the masters' interests so well, a means of thinking and acting on one's own. For a people just released from slavery, blacks in Georgia demonstrated an extraordinary commitment to formal education in terms of financial support and political self-awareness. In the words of one native black teacher, they begged for learning "as a thirsty man would beg his neighbor or a friend for a drink of water."[20]

Georgia slaves had had a keen sense of the limits of their own "education." Recalled an elderly man interviewed by the Federal Writers Project in the 1930s: "The only things that were taught the slaves were the use of their hands," and another echoed, "dey [owners] didn't teach 'em nothin' but wuk." One woman testified the whites had told her that "learning would git us so they couldn't do nothin' wid us." For this reason, Georgia's original slave code of 1755 had prohibited the teaching of slaves to read or write. A state law in 1829 included the same restrictions for free people of color. Whites reasoned that literate slaves would be able to read newspaper accounts of abolitionist rantings and communicate with one another to plot mass uprisings or other forms of collective resistance. All a slave needed to "learn" was how to work hard and respect white authority. Any wider awareness or learning was dangerous to a social system that relied on the ignorance of one group and the physical force wielded by the other.[21]

Ironically, through their own fears of the power of literacy, whites impressed on the black population the significance of education. In Georgia, the slaves' commitment to learning how to read and write had transcended the legal prohibitions of the caste system. Free blacks and urban slaves took advantage of clandestine schools taught by members of their own race; Savannah and Augusta both had long histories of secret schooling dating back to the mid-eighteenth century. On plantations, slaves showed great ingenuity in learning from "double-headed niggers" (other blacks who "could read and write and . . . knowed so much"). Some were taught their ABC's by the master's wife or children, who considered such instruction little more than a playful diversion for themselves.[22]

One black woman hid a schoolbook in her dress everyday and,

according to her son, "when de white chillun got home from school she would ax 'em lots of questions all 'bout what dey had done larned dat day. . . . She was so proud of every little scrap of book larnin' she could pick up." (After the war she became a schoolteacher.) The slaves who accompanied white children to school and waited outside the schoolroom door sometimes learned in bits and pieces. A few owners instructed favorite or highly skilled slaves, though they always ran the risk that these men and women would teach others. In Georgia, whites customarily punished slaves caught in the act of reading or writing by cutting off their thumbs or by amputating part of a finger to the first joint. In 1860 about 4 or 5 percent of Georgia blacks were literate.[23]

During the war, the set work routine associated with plantation slavery collapsed, and, as Clarence Mohr has argued persuasively, the whole system of slavery was shaken to its very foundations. Wild rumors of slave revolts shattered the image of a stable, harmonious antebellum society. Whites early initiated a reign of terror against free blacks, and owners attempted to control the slave plantation even more tightly by prohibiting worship services and limiting slave mobility. But these measures were only temporarily and partially successful. The slaves who were "refugeed" away from the coast, hired out for money, or impressed into construction work for the Confederacy encountered new situations that alerted them to the significance of the war and its potentially liberating effects. They took advantage of opportunities to assert themselves on plantations bereft of owners and overseers. In the cities they also "felt the easing of institutional restraints" as whites became increasingly distracted by the imminence of a Yankee victory. Although the war meant tremendous physical hardship for many blacks—white paranoia was translated into arbitrary acts of terrorism and food supplies dwindled—institutional changes "slowly, but inexorably broadened the perspective of many slaves and expanded their opportunities for freedom and personal autonomy."[24]

Slave literacy assumed heightened importance in the eyes of whites and blacks alike during this period of upheaval. As early as 1860, frightened Georgians had visions of northern teachers and clergymen invading the South to instruct their bondsmen in the gospel of social equality. Slaves who could read and write were regarded with more fear than ever before, and with good reason. Blacks behind federal lines on the Sea Islands received their first reading lessons from literate blacks and white naval personnel, and individual slave communities followed war events as best they could. One little girl in Georgia grew up remembering her slave mother's determination to gain an education; taking lessons from her master's children, the woman "was quick to learn and she never gave up." Recalled her daughter, "She would steal the newspapers and read up about the war, and she kept the other slaves posted as to how the war was progressing. She knew the war was over almost as soon as Marse John did." "Marse John," unlike some of the other slaveowners in the state, would have no chance to keep the fact of freedom a secret from his slaves for long.[25]

Like freed people all over the South, blacks in Georgia joined together to advance their own interests shortly after the war's end. In so doing, they manifested patterns of collective support that had been established under slavery. Demonstrating an "ethos of mutuality" that had permeated Afro-American culture for some time, communities formed black churches; Republican party clubs and Union Leagues; fire companies; mutual aid, protective, and fraternal associations; and schools. Recently, scholars have detailed the variety of other ways in which Georgia blacks asserted themselves as both a race and a class in southern society. For example, in late 1865 and early 1866, Sea Islanders staged a massive protest against a federal decision to restore to their former masters the land they had been working. Savannah dock workers protested low wages through a resolution of a newly formed Union League: they determined "to organize ourselves into associations whereby we may in the best manner avail ourselves of the means of enlightenment, of industry, of mutual help and protection within our reach." Blacks outraged over the ejection of their elected representatives from the General Assembly in October 1868 met in Macon to condemn the opportunism of all white politicians. In resolving to establish their own civil-rights associations, they declared to their brothers throughout the state, "We still have that potent weapon the ballot, and, if allowed to wield it without molestation, which seems very doubtful, we can remedy all evils. We do not recommend you to be satisfied with being a mere pack-horse to ride white men into office."[26]

It was against this backdrop of intense social and political activity on their own behalf that Georgia freed people formed local committees to establish neighborhood schools. In some cases, they elected trustees and set up a system of patrons to provide for the operation and financing of educational activities. When they could find no acceptable teachers in their area, they petitioned the Freedmen's Bureau or wrote directly to northern freedmen's aid societies for instructors. Samson Gardner, "presdent of the assozation [sic]," sent a letter to the state bureau superintendent in 1867, explaining, "We have nor Shool in Warrenton for Want of a techer the people say

Send them a teacher they can Depend on and they support him the best we can." Local auxiliaries of the GEA conducted meetings and raised funds for necessities—from pencils and fuel to the teachers' board and salary. People debated among themselves whether to hire a white or a black, southern or northern teacher. They made decisions about the length of the school term, charges for tuition, and the location of the schoolhouse.[27]

Of course, most communities required extensive outside aid for education. From Heard County in 1867 came a typical assessment of the situation: "Has nothing. Needs everything." Yet the amount of money some groups managed to raise was truly amazing. Small towns like Cuthbert, Albany, Cave Spring, and Thomasville, each having a black population no greater than seven hundred, raised up to $70 per month and contributed as much as $350 each for the construction of school buildings in the early years of Reconstruction. Outlays of cash came from the proceeds of fairs, bazaars, or bake sales; subscriptions raised by local associations; and tuition fees. Because most blacks received payment for their labor in crops, supplies, or promises, these amounts represented a substantial personal and group sacrifice to the cause of education. It is difficult to estimate the total amount raised by Georgia blacks for their own schooling from 1865 to 1873, but the Freedmen's Bureau did report such figures on an irregular basis during the first five years after the war. In July 1867 the state superintendent estimated that the freed people had contributed $3,500 per month toward school construction and teachers' salaries, compared to the bureau's monthly appropriations of $2,000 and the northern societies' $5,000 for the same purposes. Two years later, the blacks' monthly expenditures for tuition alone amounted to more than $3,000 monthly. (It should be kept in mind that only 5 percent of the state's school-aged black population attended elementary schools in any one year during Reconstruction.)[28]

Freed men and women also donated services and goods to sustain neighborhood schools. The northern teachers who arrived in Macon in December 1865 found that a group of black women had thoroughly cleaned their new home to ready it for their coming. In many villages, men helped to construct the school, and several communities supplied classrooms and teachers' lodgings with furniture. It was also common for congregations to offer their buildings free of charge for use as school buildings. During the summer the people supplemented teachers' salaries with fresh fruit and vegetables from their gardens. On Woodville Plantation in Morgan County, an elderly black man helped in his own way; he boarded nine children from the backcountry in his home so that they could attend a nearby school.[29]

In February 1868 an AMA teacher recorded the reaction of one of her older pupils when she gave him his first lesson in joining letters to form a word. He said to her, "I shall have to stand up and shiver first before I write it." These sentiments reveal the excitement felt by thousands of freed people all over Georgia upon learning to read and write. Teachers observed a universal enthusiasm for schooling. One expressed it this way: It was the blacks' "first act on coming to the surface, a kind of instinctive head-shaking, and clearing of the eyes, after emerging from the waters." Although poverty, work, logistical difficulties, and a statewide shortage of teachers served as barriers to regular school attendance, pupils of all ages and both sexes demonstrated their determination to learn. Teachers reported that some children walked several miles to school each day and then back home again; one AMA instructor called these youngsters "earnest seekers after knowledge" who had "mental cravings" for education. An Andersonville teacher marveled over her pupils who traveled long distances to school each day in the winter despite pouring rain and freezing temperatures. One day she tried to send her class home early because of the cold weather, but all insisted on staying in the icy building. She added, "None of us froze, though several were shaking with ague."[30]

Conservative figures (i.e., those based on the number of teachers who submitted monthly reports to the Freedmen's Bureau) reveal that about two hundred native black men and women conducted freedmen's schools in at least seventy Georgia counties from 1866 to 1870. A survey of federal manuscript census returns for selected Georgia counties in 1870, plus information gleaned from the archives of the Freedmen's Bureau and northern societies, provides a minimal amount of biographical information on these teachers. Males outnumbered females by slightly less than two to one. The women were very young, mostly in their teens and twenties, and unmarried. The men were slightly older, in their twenties and thirties, and evenly divided between those who were married and those who were not. About one half of all the single teachers lived at home with their parents, and the rest boarded with other families, presumably those of their pupils. Although half of the men were married, only a handful reported any personal property (no more than $800 worth) and none owned any real property, or at least any that they were willing to report to the census taker.[31]

Young black women, like their white counterparts in the North, evidently found teaching an attractive occupation before marriage. They could help to supplement the family income and sometimes (in the case of those who "boarded 'round") achieve a modest measure of financial and social independence for a short period. Black men who were literate probably decided to teach as a result of their commitment to advance the members of their own race or even to enhance their own status within the community. Except in the larger towns, teaching rarely afforded an income more stable than that derived from agricultural labor. Teachers received payment from a variety of sources, including tuition fees, money raised by local education groups, the Freedmen's Bureau or a northern society, or more likely, a combination of these. But few could count on a steady income from month to month. One black man urged the bureau superintendent to enclose a postage stamp with his monthly school report form because, he admitted, "sometimes i have not got the money to get it." A rural Decatur County teacher reported in September 1869, "I must try by sum other way for a living for I am suffering." He and many others also had to work in the fields to keep their families alive. Only those teachers in the largest towns or those who received northern support could in any way consider teaching a stable occupation.[32]

In dealing with Yankee administrators and school officials, black teachers often showed an acute sensitivity to their own shortcomings in terms of formal preparation. A Bibb County instructor wrote on his monthly report for April 1869, "I never went to School nor was I Ever taught a day in My Life—I hope my ignorance will be Excused." The difficulties under which many taught, including primitive facilities and an acute shortage of equipment and books, heightened their sense of frustration. It was not long before many of their students surpassed them in learning; some teachers tried to keep a step ahead of them by suspending school for a part of the year in order to attend classes in another town.[33]

A man from the village of Byron summed up the difficulties encountered by many black men who taught school in postwar Georgia when he wrote in the fall of 1874, "We have a school here which is well attended and the people are getting ahead of me in learning. . . . I expected to devote one half of this year to study, but had the misfortune to have my last year's crop of cotton destroyed by fire after gathering and preparing it for market which left me in debt and compelled me to work hard all this year to clear myself of debt." Still, these teachers persisted in their efforts, convinced that they performed a great service to their community. Anthony Wilson of Woodbine informed his AMA sponsor that he lacked textbooks and daily encountered opposition from native whites. But he added that he would never "think of leaving these people in their blindness." He named his school "Sunshine School."[34]

Incomplete but intriguing evidence indicates that, when presented with a choice, black parents preferred to send their children to schools taught by native members of their own race. (Proof is ample that they almost always scorned northern or southern white preachers in favor of their own religious leaders.) Although it is difficult to generalize about the quality of classroom instruction offered by southern black as opposed to northern white teachers, it is obvious that the Yankees had more training and formal experience, as well as better and more elaborate equipment (textbooks, maps, slates, papers, and pencils). The establishment of their own schools symbolized black defiance to planter authority. But larger questions remain: On what basis did they decide to support teachers from their own communities over those sponsored by northern freedmen's aid societies? Was it a decision based on color only?

A number of answers come immediately to mind. Respect for "double-headed niggers" persisted after slavery, and literate freed people who began their own schools immediately after the war often found it easier to gain their neighbors' loyalty than outsiders could. Sometimes the differences in tuition charged by two teachers was a determining factor; however, this could work against, as well as for, a black teacher in his or her effort to operate a school. Apparently, northern teachers early acquired a reputation for being strict disciplinarians. One black man recalled that he had received his "first schoolin'" from a Yankee and noted, "we were mighty surprised to find out that he wasn't very hard on us. We had to do something real bad to git a whippin, but when we talked or was late gittin' to school we had to stand up in the back of the schoolroom and hold up one hand." Finally, in a broader sense, the freed people might have been afraid of these whites and unreceptive to the strange ideas they brought south with them.[35]

In April 1866 AMA teacher Abbie Case told her superior of her brief and unpleasant experience in a small town near Savannah. She wrote, "There seemed to be a feeling of distrust toward all white people, teachers being no exception." Case's admission that she "found a great deal of difficulty in gaining the confidence of the people" because she was white points to the significance of initial encounters between blacks and northern whites in Georgia during the Civil War era. Evidence from a variety of sources strongly suggests that many slaves and freed people reacted out of both fear and resentment when confronted with their white "friends" from the North—whether they were soldiers, missionaries, teachers, or freedmen's aid society administrators.[36]

Although many owners tried to instill a dread of the Yankees in their slaves during the war, most blacks evidently understood that once the Union army appeared, freedom was not far behind. A daring few took the initiative and made good their escape to Union lines. Yet black people often reacted to their "liberators" out of disgust as much as gratitude. As Eugene Genovese suggests, this is to be expected when "troops from a racist culture . . . are turned loose on defenseless civilians of an ostensibly inferior race." In Georgia, Yankee intentions came into explicit focus early on the Sea Islands, where military officials forced refugees to work cotton fields, and, later in Savannah, where Sherman's men captured slaves and impressed them into Union service "to dredge out the river and harbor . . . , to hew timber, make roads, build bridges, and throw up batteries." Individual slaves were terrorized by the federal army; specific examples of soldiers' atrocities against blacks are too numerous to mention here. Mrs. Mary Jones recorded in her journal during the winter of 1864–65 that marauding Yankees had taken "whatever they wanted" from the blacks on her coastal plantation—even "Gilbert's knife and watch and chain, July's pants and blankets, George and Porter's blankets and clothes, the women's pails, piggins, spoons, buckets, pots, kettles, etc., etc." When a black woman hid from them, they called her a "damned wench" and threatened "to shoot her damned brains out." Blacks as well as whites suffered when Union soldiers confiscated food and destroyed plantation buildings. Through it all, children hid in crawl spaces and behind trees, "mortally afraid" of the white men who set fire to fields and screamed profanities at their parents.[37]

Encounters with Yankee clergymen and teachers who came on the heels of Sherman's army proved less traumatic but nevertheless often provoked apprehension among blacks. All these northerners were missionaries in the sense that they hoped to convert blacks to a certain religion or way of life considered superior by the whites to that of the former slaves. Thus the Yankees represented a threat to black people who wanted to listen to their own ministers and teach their own children. In the ensuing local and statewide conflicts, battle lines were tightly drawn between northern whites and southern blacks, who represented respectively the values of industrializing New England and those of the rural slave community.

"A colored man is never in a hurry," declared a Savannah AMA superintendent in exasperation. Indeed, the ideas of blacks and northern whites differed fundamentally about the ways time must and could be "used." To a New England farmer, a day's hard, steady work yielded a certain level of material gain; the more strenuous the labor, the greater the reward. Evangelical Protestants used agricultural metaphors to stress the importance of spiritual growth. They also encouraged the cultivation of good habits, the nurturing of the seed of goodness within one's self, and reaping the benefits of piety:

> The time is short!
> If thou wouldst work for God it must be now—
> If thou wouldst win the garland for thy brow—
> Redeem the time.

Work, win, redeem the time. Middle-class northerners stressed personal achievement, lofty ambition, competition, and mastery (especially over one's own passions) as the necessary ingredients to a moral life.[38]

The future had held little promise for black people under slavery. They worked hard, or rather were worked hard, but they never shared in the fruits of their own labor. Planning, saving, accumulating—these concepts had little meaning to a people who owned no material goods. They would have to pass on to their children something less tangible than land or money, a way of living that would enable their descendants to resist oppression in a spiritual, if not physical, sense. Thus emerged the slave "community."[39]

Georgia slaves fused the heritage of Africa and the reality of America into a unique folk culture that was both the product of and a response to slavery. On plantations and in cities, slaves created their own networks of emotional support through nuclear families and extensive kin relationships. The tenet of individualism was worthless, rarely if ever rewarded by the master class and potentially threatening to group solidarity. The slaves' religion was one of joy and collective hope, not self-denial and personal guilt. From family and faith they derived the strength not only to survive but to create a rich musical and oral tradition also.

After the war, evidence of "racial exclusivity" among the freed people indicated that they wished to adhere to those customs that had served them well under slavery and would be equally important to their new life in an old world of prejudice and injustice. This is not to suggest that they eschewed the values of hard work and individualism. Given a chance, the former slaves labored mightily to provide for their own families and advance their personal, as well as collective, economic self-interest. But the white teachers lacked a basic understanding of the dynamics of the Afro-American community and the people's desire to free themselves from all white influence. The specific ways in which the northerners incorporated the ideas of capitalism and evangelical Protestantism into their various social welfare programs for the freed people will be discussed in chapters 5 and 6. At this point, it is necessary to note only that Yankee schooling and religious instruction were culture-bound, and that the freed people at times (and in the case of religion, almost always) rejected offers of white benevolence.[40]

In a very real sense, the eighteen black teachers hailing from New England sponsored by freedmen's aid societies found themselves suspended between North and South, white and black. Little direct evidence exists concerning the relationship between the freed people of Georgia and their brothers and sisters from the North. William Steward's comment that the blacks of Americus were "enthusiastic over a Northern colored teacher" remains a tantalizing exception. But the men, especially, faced a dilemma. On the one hand, demonstrating a high degree of racial consciousness, they regularly pointed out to their white superiors the lack of political justice for blacks in Georgia. Hezekiah Brown taught Savannah freed people guided by the conviction that "we are an oppressed and despised race, as well as poor and in need," and, he said, "My heart is in the work, and my head, and my hands." Steward's Georgia experiences convinced him that these "depressed, downtrodden, abused and abased people" needed help and that "none can do it better than ourselves."[41]

But most of these men also served as representatives of a northern Protestant denomination—either Congregational, Presbyterian, or Methodist. Few Georgia blacks responded to the straitlaced worship services of northern churches, and it mattered little whether the proselytizer's skin was white or black. Even a native like Floyd Snelson, first black to be ordained as a Congregational minister in Georgia by the AMA, found it difficult to gain the trust of people of his own race. Writing about his disappointing results in coastal McIntosh County (he was a native of the Piedmont region), he reported, "The chances are much better for you in such a case, if you are raised with them than if you are a stranger." And yet Snelson clearly understood the political situation in Georgia, and worked at the local level to increase black political power; "I am laboring very hard to get thoroughly established and to recover all the rights and privileges that are due my people," he wrote. At issue was not his sincerity but his style.[42]

The attitude of white northern officials toward blacks was one of paternalism. When they began to work in Georgia, northern teachers and superintendents had preconceived notions about the role freed people should play in the overall education effort. They believed that black teachers lacked the formal training to be effective instructors and that enlightened white men and women must assume major responsibility for establishing—and to a great extent teaching in—black schools throughout the state. Representatives of freedmen's aid societies intended to oversee all aspects of black education. At the same time, few northerners felt inclined to provide substantial aid to local black communities without evidence that the people were able to raise a certain amount of money on their own.

These ideas illustrated two basic impulses: the northerners' desire to control black schooling on the one hand, and their demand that the people actively support their own institutions on the other. The two goals eventually proved contradictory, if not self-defeating. In rural areas, poverty-stricken communities were unable to make large cash contributions for the maintenance of schools. As a result, northern societies assumed that they had an insufficient appreciation of formal instruction and gradually withdrew aid from almost all rural areas. But, when blacks successfully established their own schools, as they did in some towns, northerners were shocked and offended at this lack of appreciation for white benevolence.

Specific examples from Georgia during the period 1865 to 1870 reveal this ambivalent attitude toward black education efforts on the part of the AMA. It was willing to sponsor native black teachers, but only if they could meet the same standards expected of its middle-class northern white instructors. In most cases the association insisted that prospective teachers belong to an evangelical church, teach five or six hours a day and in night school, spend Saturdays and spare time visiting families, and conduct prayer meetings and Sunday school classes. Georgia blacks who wished to acquire an AMA commission had to send New York headquarters a letter of application, a statement concerning church membership, and personal testimonials. In establishing these criterian the AMA was "non-discriminatory," for it required the same of its northern applicants. But in effect it severely limited the number of native teachers who could ever hope to receive aid.[43]

Most of the blacks supported by the association taught in the country, where the societies had little interest in sending Yankee teachers. (This policy fit in well with the group's plan to "secure greater economy of expenditure," for it paid all black teachers—male and female—fifteen dollars per month, the same amount paid to white women, but ten dollars less than white men.) However, in the towns, where black schools at times successfully competed with northern operations, officials candidly expressed their doubts about independent teachers who proposed to open rival schools. The first Freedmen's Bureau education superintendent in Georgia wrote to an association officer in 1866, "Although there is much to commend in the negroes, under the difficulties which they labor, I am becoming daily more impressed with their total unfitness to assist in the moral and mental elevation of their own race." But the freed people were sometimes willing to make a financial sacrifice to patronize schools taught by their neighbors. An AMA official lamented that same year, "Many (or rather I would say some) parents now prefer to send their children to col[ored] teachers and pay a dollar a month for Tuition than to send them to our schools free." This greatly irritated association teachers and administrators alike.[44]

Through their local education associations, country people also exercised a degree of selectivity in choosing their teachers. In the absence of literate blacks who wanted to run a school, they were grateful for northern teachers. But rarely did they agree to support a native white if they were suspicious of the man or woman's professed sympathy for their cause. One AMA teacher observed, "The colored people are very much opposed to southern teachers—I believe they would not be taught by them." Some native white Republicans managed to gain the confidence of black communities by contrasting themselves with "Rebel teachers." Still, the freed people made the ultimate decision concerning whom they would support to instruct their children.[45]

Despite these particular and general examples of black commitment to education, northern aid society policies proved restrictive and obtuse on the local level. In rural areas, the amount of money earned from the year's harvest had a direct impact on the quality and extent of local school operations. Thus a poor growing season one year meant no school the next without help from outside the region. Yet the AMA rarely took into account hardships stemming from bad weather, plagues of caterpillars, or the people's indebtedness to white landowners in its decision to withdraw all aid from a community that failed to fulfill an informal agreement concerning teacher support.

The association reasoned that it had a limited amount of money, and that it should enforce rigid standards in allocating what little it had. On a southern-wide basis this policy made some sense; the demand for money always exceeded the amount the North could supply. But, applied impartially without an appreciation of local conditions, these guidelines ignored the extent of a community's efforts in previous years. In a sense, they were self-defeating, for the societies would only help those people who could help themselves. Freed people who wanted to start a school but could afford to contribute little or nothing in the way of cash often received no northern support.

The early history of freedmen's work in the city of Savannah brings together these themes of black solidarity and northern benevolence. The Savannah case is by no means typical of other Georgia communities, but it does illustrate the extremes to which both sides would and could go in carrying out their own strategies for schooling. The AMA considered Savannah—the Christmas "gift" presented by General Sherman to President Lincoln in December 1864—of major symbolic significance to its educational work in the South. AMA representatives entered the city right behind the conquering army and immediately decided to claim the town as association "territory" in its long-standing war with the American Freedmen's Union Commission (AFUC) and MFAS. However, black leaders had different plans for their children's schooling. The dispute over who should teach Savannah's children immediately after the war left deep wounds in black and northern white relations that never healed.

The busy port, located on the Savannah River a few miles from the sea, possessed an exceptionally well-developed and cohesive black community during the antebellum period. Of the city's total population of 22,000 in 1860, 7,712 of the blacks were slaves and 705 were free. Skilled artisans worked as carpenters, blacksmiths, mechanics, and coopers. Other blacks made their living as longshoremen by loading boats with cotton at the end of the harvest season. They nearly dominated the field of industrial transportation through their work as porters, draymen, drivers, and boatmen. Some women found jobs as peddlers, and a few seamstresses and laundresses operated their own successful businesses. Black grocers, among the most prosperous of their race in Savannah, provided an additional source of employment for persons of all ages.[46]

Added to this diversity of occupations, the cosmopolitan atmosphere of the port city, and the existence of a small but significant group of black entrepreneurs was the predominance of a well-defined leadership class within the black community. The social and political life of blacks centered in the churches, especially the Baptist. Savannah blacks had founded the First African (Baptist) Church in 1788. By 1865 a total of three separate congregations claimed 3,500 members: the Andrews Methodist and the St. Augustine and St. Stephens Episcopal churches. The Savannah ministers provided a nucleus of articulate, aggressive leadership.

As John Blassingame has shown, all these factors in an urban setting combined to produce among Savannah freed people "a sense of unity and the will and the economic means to fight against white oppression." The black population doubled in the fifteen years after the war, and in 1880 the community had a total of fourteen churches and almost two hundred different clubs and protective associations. Businessmen bought property, and thousands of young and old men and women deposited more than $150,000 in the local Freedman's Savings Bank between 1866 and 1874.[47]

Black leaders were especially militant and outspoken. The Reverend James Simms founded the *Freemen's Standard*, a paper unequivocal in its stand on civil rights. He represented Chatham County in the state legislature during Reconstruction. James Porter, also a state assemblyman and active in Savannah education affairs, played a key role in organizing the Georgia Equal Rights Association in 1866, and led a city-wide campaign against segregation on public streetcars in the early 1870s. Aaron A. Bradley's blunt pronouncements on the evils of white supremacy earned him the enmity of northern as well as southern whites; Blassingame notes that this lawyer, often armed with pistol and Bowie knife, was "probably arrested more times than any other politician" in the nineteenth century. The Reverend Henry M. Turner, former Union army chaplain who figured prominently in Georgia religious and political affairs after the war, also made no secret of his disillusionment with the state's Republican party, and worked actively to increase the independent voting strength of black people. At the freedmen's convention held in Augusta in January 1866, Turner declared, "We want power; it only comes through organization, and organization comes through unity."[48]

The Reverend Tunis G. Campbell established a series of self-governing black agricultural colonies in the coastal region during the mid and late 1860s. Extremely active in Georgia politics (he was one of the black legislators expelled from the General Assembly in 1868), this New Jersey native denounced the new order under which "no matter what might be the moral worth or respectability of a mechanic or laboring man, his interests or rights must not stand in the way of the wishes of the capitalists or property holder." He later claimed proudly that Georgia Democrats kept their hands on their guns whenever they heard him speak.[49]

These men believed that Georgia blacks should rely on members of their own race for leadership in politics, religion, and education. But only in urban areas did the freed people have the economic strength to strive for this sort of total independence from whites. Even then, practical limits restricted their determination. Scattered throughout the city and a minority compared to white voters, blacks in Savannah could not achieve any real power in municipal government. And, though armed with a fierce desire to operate their own schools, they lacked the financial base to establish a comprehensive system of education free from white interference. For example, in 1872 blacks were forced to bargain with the new city school board for buildings, teachers, and equipment. By that time, they had learned very well some of freedom's lessons as taught by Yankee reformers.[50]

A few days after Sherman entered the city, a committee of black clergymen formed the Savannah Education Association (SEA). Its constitution provided for the funding of elementary schools through voluntary subscriptions. An executive board of nine men soon began to examine teaching candidates; within a week it had hired fifteen instructors and acquired buildings for use as schools, among them the Old Bryan Slave Mart. By January 1, 1865, Savannah blacks had raised $800 to support about five hundred children in school without charging any tuition fees. Louis B. Toomer, who had taught a clandestine school before the war, served as the fledgling system's "principal teacher."[51]

The SEA provoked astonishment among northern education officials who had recently arrived in the city. Commenting on the flurry of activity generated by the SEA, the Reverend John W. Alvord (soon to become head of the Freedmen's Bureau educational operations) remarked in wonder, "The interesting fact in this whole organization is that it is wholly their own. The officers of the Assoc. are all colored men. The teachers are all colored." On the first day of school, the children met in one of the churches and then marched en masse to their assigned schools. A representative of the American Missionary Association, the Reverend William T. Richardson, watched the procession with one of his coworkers, S. W. Magill. Richardson, thrilled with the sight, later exclaimed, "This army of colored children moving through the streets seemed to excite feeling and interest second only to that of Gen. Sherman's army. Such a gathering of Freedmen's sons and daughters, that proud city had never seen before."[52]

The euphoria of Richardson and Magill, both of whom had been asked by Alvord to assist in the operation of SEA schools, soon faded. Assuming that the freed people would welcome aid from their northern friends, Magill quickly formulated plans to incorporate white teachers into the all-black SEA teaching staff. He complained about the blacks' inexperience: "now however good men they may be, they know nothing about educating," he wrote AMA headquarters.

But he was startled to learn that, in a spirit of "exclusiveness," Savannah blacks adamantly insisted on opposing his efforts to involve whites in either the teaching or administering of their schools.[53]

Magill, enraged at the blacks' apparent refusal of northern white (and especially AMA) help, fired off several letters to his superiors. Detailing his objections to the SEA policies, he contended that most members of the executive board were barely literate. The blacks had told him that, if white teachers came to Savannah at all, they should serve as assistants to the black instructors. However, they were willing to accept AMA financial contributions, provided no strings were attached. In sum, declared Magill, "the whole thing . . . is preposterous." He felt particularly troubled because the AMA had entered the Georgia city hoping to find a "clear field" and instead encountered this "radically defective organization," which proposed to run its schools its own way and to use northern money if it possibly could. As another northern official put it, "What they desire is assistance without control."[54]

By late February 1865, Magill had made some inroads into the SEA, probably with the threat that the AMA would withhold all financial assistance from the organization unless it made provisions for white teachers and administrators. He considered it "a great point gained that they are convinced by their experience, that they are not sufficient of themselves." That spring the Reverend E. A. Cooley arrived from Massachusetts to assume charge of AMA operations in Savannah. He immediately set about trying to install white teachers over black assistants (formerly teachers), and Magill began to maneuver for a federal appointment as "Director of Education among the Colored People for the District of Savannah," a position he suggested the military create.[55]

The educational situation in Savannah had grown substantially more complex by the middle of the year. The two AMA representatives, Magill and Cooley, managed to start several classes taught exclusively by white northern women commissioned by their organization, but they continued to encounter resistance from the resilient SEA. Indeed, some Savannah blacks demonstrated overt hostility toward "all white people," whether they hailed from the North or South, observed Magill in June. As Cooley began to make preparations for the 1865–66 school year, he complained that the blacks were "very jealous of any interference on our part with their plans and operations," and he even reconsidered employing the freed people in any capacity in AMA-sponsored classes. The arrival of teachers from the New York and New England branches of the AFUC greatly increased the antagonism among all groups while each vied for money from the newly created Freedmen's Bureau.[56]

In July Alvord attended an end-of-term examination conducted by teachers of the SEA and pronounced himself delighted with the pupils' progress. He reported that the organization had raised more than $2,000 to support its schools since the beginning of the year and that—contrary to the overeager assessments of Magill and Cooley— it had a debt of only $100. By the end of the year, he had arranged for the federal government to relieve the SEA of its indebtedness. But Cooley had already made plans to absorb its classes into AMA schools, which now instructed about 250 pupils. The AMA official reported that he had to work fast to counter the "seditious harangues" of Aaron Bradley, whom he called "a very insolent and pestilent fellow." Bradley had just begun a political campaign urging blacks to vote as a bloc in all city, state, and national elections and warning northern interlopers not to meddle in Savannah affairs. Cooley was certain that the AMA could have taken over the SEA several months earlier had not Alvord's misplaced generosity and Bradley's rhetorical encouragement helped to sustain the group.[57]

Cooley's persistence paid off around the end of March 1866, when the SEA was forced again to apply to the AMA for financial aid. In attempting to provide some five hundred children with an elementary education, the group had overestimated the extent and stability of its patrons' resources. It planned to continue operations if it could receive outside help. But Cooley insisted that the AMA would contribute funds only if he could play a major role in deciding how the money should be spent. The SEA, faced with accepting either compromise or defeat, finally acceded to Cooley's demands. In April Cooley, while declaring that he planned to employ all twelve black teachers as assistants, triumphantly announced: "The field is now virtually our own and another year we can enter it with a great vantage ground in having a house, school buildings, and no opposition." Apparently G. L. Eberhart, the Freedmen's Bureau state superintendent of education, had awarded a large grant for Savannah education to Cooley rather than to the SEA and thus sealed the group's fate. As a group, Savannah blacks were no longer able to support a public school system. Economic dislocation caused by the war, coupled with a huge refugee population and an attendant smallpox epidemic, had disrupted the economic stability of the city's black population.[58]

The SEA left an enduring legacy to Savannah education. By 1867 the AMA had effectively discouraged all other northern freedmen's aid societies from conducting classes in the city, but found the people's bitterness a much more powerful threat to its work. The Reverend Ira Pettibone, who had assumed the superintendency of AMA schools in the fall of 1866, told of the difficulties that all his successors were to likewise encounter. Comparing the blacks' attitude toward the AMA with the rebels' feelings toward the North, Pettibone observed that the failure of the SEA had created a barrier of mistrust and suspicion between blacks and northern whites: "They cannot appreciate thorough drilling in education but if a col[ored] teacher will promise to teach them Arithmetic, Geo[graphy], English, History, Grammar, Dictionary, Philosophy and 'a *heap*' of other things then these are the schools which they prefer." In 1870 another AMA superintendent reported Savannah blacks still felt that the "colored people are competent to manage their own affairs in their own way." He added that some regarded a recent hike in AMA school fees as a "Yankee trick to get their money." Consequently, the northern-sponsored schools in Savannah were attended primarily by children of the poorest families, and private schools operated by blacks continued to thrive among the freedmen who could afford them.[59]

The SEA, the most impressive of Georgia's local black education groups, received little in the way of moral support from the AMA. Theoretically, the SEA fulfilled the AMA's most stringent requirements for financial aid. It represented a strong, collective effort on the part of the city's black citizens, who liberally committed their time and money to the venture. But it violated one of the AMA's most basic, though rarely articulated, policies—that any black group desiring northern aid must agree to relinquish control over school operations to its "benefactors." The AMA's guidelines lacked flexibility in the face of varying local conditions. More significantly, they left little opportunity for freed people to control all aspects of schooling from administration through teaching—on their own through trial and error, independent of white paternalism.

In 1869 a black teacher from the North wrote of his reception among the freed people of McIntosh County: "I cannot express their joy and gratitude at my coming. Their former masters were and are very much against their having a school." Throughout the South, going to school—or building, supporting, or teaching in a school— became a political act for black people. Like the newly formed churches, schools represented both the institutionalization of Afro-American community life and defiance to white authority. But there are few accounts of heated debates among whites over the desirability of blacks attending their own religious services, and there are no recorded instances of angry mobs burning black churches to the ground in Georgia during the years immediately after the war. Why did many whites react so much more strongly to the building of schools than to the building of churches?[60]

In New England, public education enjoyed the strong support of political and cultural elites who hoped it would promote social stability in the midst of rapid industrial and population change. However, their southern counterparts perceived no such imperative, for, in a sense, the purposes of common-school reform and the slave system were mutually exclusive. In the South, the institution of slavery served as a rigid social framework ordering relations among the different classes and two races. Additional forms of state intervention to socialize nonelite groups were unnecessary. Moreover, the white population of the antebellum South was relatively homogeneous in terms of religion (Protestant) and ethnicity (British stock). The region's economy, though growing, was not undergoing dynamic or rapid structural changes comparable to those in the North. Thus the preconditions for common-school reform were absent in this area of the country before the war.

Emancipation destroyed the legal basis of the southern social structure, and the early years of Reconstruction marked a period of intense struggle between blacks who wanted to assert themselves and whites who hoped to regain social as well as economic control over their former slaves. Enter the Yankee schoolteacher, committed as she was to black civil rights, and the stage was set for an explosive drama that made the neighborhood school a political and cultural battlefield. Throughout the state of Georgia, white people associated black education not only with the revitalization of Afro-American life, but with the abolitionist heresy of "social equality" imported by large numbers of zealous New England schoolteachers.[61]

The schoolhouse served overt political functions that escaped the notice of few white Georgians. Black leaders took advantage of cornerstone-laying ceremonies to deliver political speeches. The use of schools for Union League meetings heightened the perceived connection between black education and the Republican party. Consequently, former Confederates feared that the Yankees and their dupes, black politicians, had transformed the school (where children merely learned their three Rs) to a meeting place for Radical Republicans. Moreover, Yankee teachers taught "things not found in books"—ideas about black self-worth, the importance of voting, and so forth—that directly threatened the southern "way of life." In short, many southerners believed the black school was as potent a force for social change as black suffrage.

And yet there existed no one consistent "white" reaction to freedmen's education in Georgia. In fact, although a few whites ambushed children on their way to school, others received commissions from northern freedmen's aid societies and taught in black schools. The vast majority of whites responded in ways that fell somewhere between these two extremes. To suggest that opinion on the subject can be correlated with class and political loyalties is an oversimplification of the issue. Still, it provides an appropriate starting point for a discussion of three separate groups and their perceptions of black schooling: native white teachers of the freed people; planters and other community leaders; and, finally, the largest segment of the population, whites who had never owned slaves.

During the five-year period after the war, at least 150 native white teachers (50 of whom were sponsored by northern societies) taught black children in about one-half of all Georgia counties. The number of men was more than double that of women. Judging by the large number who signed "Mrs." to their Freedmen's Bureau monthly reports, most of the women were probably widows. Some of these teachers, like the Reverend John H. Caldwell and Mrs. Harriet Hart, professed religious, political, or personal ties with the North and shared with the New England teachers a strong commitment to black education. Caldwell received a commission from the MFAS to open a school in LaGrange, and later claimed proudly that he was "the first white citizen of Georgia to take a public stand in favor of the Congressional Plan of Reconstruction." He helped to found the Georgia Equal Rights Association, and served briefly as a Freedmen's Bureau agent and state representative in the General Assembly. During one particularly troubled period after the war, he predicted, "It will not be many years before the freedmen will be in a worse condition than when they were slaves." Because he condemned the "white trash" under the control of the "old slavecrats," it was not surprising that Caldwell's white neighbors considered him just as despicable as the most rabid Yankee abolitionist. Moreover, his argument that blacks should learn to read and write so that they could better "detect the numberless methods by which they are defrauded out of the fruits of their industry" gained him few friends among Troup County whites.[62]

Born in Bombay, India, in 1819, Harriet Atwood Newell Hart was the daughter of a Presbyterian missionary to that country. At age twelve she came to the United States with her parents, and nine years later moved south (presumably to Georgia) to teach school. She eventually married a McIntosh County planter. When he died in 1866, he left her with a large debt on the plantation. Penniless, she converted the parlor of her house into a schoolroom for the freed people who worked the surrounding land. She received two or three years of financial support (twenty dollars per month) from the northern Presbyterian Committee on Missions for the Freedmen. Of her pupils she wrote in 1870, "If they have but one leaf to a spelling book, they will bring it, and go over it, till they do better. They have set their heart to learn, and they will learn in spite of everything, and it won't be long before the whites see it, and acknowledge it, but it will be a bitter pill for them to swallow." She hoped someday to pay off the farm mortgage and sell the land to the blacks she taught to assist them "in their efforts to rise from their present condition." Other whites in the area made no secret of the fact that they believed she "ought to be drove out of the County" if she persisted in teaching the "black dogs."[63]

Employment possibilities for whites as well as blacks were severely limited at this time in Georgia, and many white teachers apparently sought to take advantage of possible financial support from northern societies or even the freed people themselves. Widows who had no other source of income sometimes found that teaching school could bring in just enough money to ward off starvation. Of course, this was not a decision calculated to make any woman popular in her town. "A *white* lady has applied for a black school!!!" exclaimed an Oxford MFAS missionary in 1866. Possibly, financial considerations were a primary motivating factor for many native whites. One AMA teacher reported from St. Mary's in 1868 that she had overheard a white man say, "our only way is to take the school into our own hands. We may as well get the negroes money as to let these *foreign* Yankees." And yet the fact that blacks often refused to send their children to schools taught by "Rebel teachers" indicates that few whites who were unsympathetic to the black man's cause could eke out a living this way.[64]

Some white newspaper editors and clergymen declared that black schooling per se—that is, the acquisition of literacy skills—was less reprehensible than Yankee education, which carried overtones of Radical Republicanism. A few argued strongly that persons loyal to the Confederate cause should assume the responsibility for teaching blacks. This was the "true friend" argument. The editor of the Baptist *Christian Index* condemned the Yankee teachers who came south to foment discord between the races, but he acknowledged that the freed people should receive some formal schooling: "It is in our inter-

est to do it; it is in the interest of the blacks that we should do it."
(This line of reasoning echoed the call of New England reformers for
schools taught by "moral" and "responsible" women and men.) These
were the community leaders who would later give their support to a
statewide system of public education and speak in favor of segregated black schools taught by native whites.[65]

It is difficult to generalize about the former slaveholders' reaction
to black schooling. Most tended to link the question with two other
crucial issues: their own political power and the need for a steady
source of tractable labor. These considerations formed the core of
their dilemma after the war. For example, whatever tie existed
between the schoolhouse and the ballot—whether bureau agents
registered blacks to vote there, or teachers encouraged their older
pupils to participate actively in the political process—rubbed raw
the nerves of whites who wanted to maintain their own hegemony
in southern society. Among planters, the sentiment against the en-
franchisement of blacks was as universally hostile as that against
northern freedmen's teachers. A Columbus teacher observed in 1868
that, although the "most intelligent whites" approved of black education, they united with other segments of the white population in
opposing schools taught by Yankees.[66]

On the other hand, as James Roark and Leon Litwack have pointed
out, concern over the "Negro problem" swept the south after the war
as landowners became convinced that they would have to compel
blacks to go back to work. In Georgia many black people left their
owner's plantation once freedom came and then refused to work as
hard as they had been forced to do under slavery. Labor agents
canvassed the state encouraging laborers to migrate to the Southwest, where wages were higher and possibilities to buy land were
better. As a result, some planters left the country altogether in
disgust, certain that they would never be able to grow cotton profitably after emancipation. Others considered importing large numbers
of immigrants—Chinese primarily—to replace "shiftless" blacks.[67]

One white resident of Griffin wrote in 1870, "give them schools
with us and they will remain here [instead of going to the 'Great
Valley']; they will become more useful to themselves and us." His
words indicate that some white employers believed a schoolhouse
on their property would help them to attract and keep a supply of
black workers. These landowners implicitly recognized the freed
people's great desire for schooling. Like the sharecropping system,
schools built by white planters amounted to a "compromise" between
the races in reestablishing economic relationships after the war.

Through their control of that precious resource, labor, black people as a group were not entirely powerless.[68]

On the whole, however, majority public opinion in Georgia was decidedly hostile to any form of common schooling for freed people. One Freedmen's Bureau official in fact suggested ("not in a profane sense") that *"our Lord and Saviour* could not please . . . these rebellious individuals if He were to assume control of a colored school." Like their wealthier neighbors, poor whites in Georgia regarded collective action on the part of blacks with fear. Another less frequently articulated source of antagonism toward Yankee educational activities on the part of this group was envy. The state of Georgia had had no public education system before the war, and poor children unable to afford private schooling only rarely had the opportunity to attend charity institutions. Postwar political confusion hindered the establishment of public schools (except in the largest cities) until eight years after the war. And so it is understandable why some parents resented the massive (or at least highly publicized) infusion of money and teachers for the express purpose of aiding the freed people. Wrote an MFAS teacher from Griffin in 1866, "the [white] people accuse us of partiality to the colored and say we do not care what becomes of the poor white children." The AMA superintendent in Atlanta noted in March 1866 that the educational work of the Pennsylvania and New Jersey Union Commissions among that city's indigent white children tended to "soften and allay the antipathy against the Colored Schools and teachers." Although all northern societies operated "integrated" schools (i.e., ones that were open to all children regardless of race), few parents risked public censure in order to take advantage of the opportunity. A freedmen's teacher in Camden County regretted that a white mother, after inquiring at the school, had decided against allowing her children to attend because "she consulted her friends and they were not willing." Apparently most of the handful of white pupils who did attend Georgia black schools were the children of northern teachers and superintendents.[69]

The ways in which white Georgians expressed their resentment over black education make up a separate story that is as long as it is dismal. The efforts to prevent teachers and children from going to school defy simple categorization; they were planned and spontaneous, initiated by individuals and groups. The lawyer who obtained an injunction against the building of a new school and the arsonist who destroyed one differed in tactics but not in purpose. Some whites pelted black schoolchildren with stones, others evicted Yankee teachers from their rented quarters, still others scribbled obscenities on classroom blackboards at night. Carriage drivers declined to transport school superintendents around town and postmasters and bank tellers refused to perform routine services for them. Tax officials levied inordinately high assessments against school buildings, employers threatened to fire all black workers unless their northern-sponsored teachers left town, creditors promised to recall mortgages if white farmers allowed schoolhouses to be built on their property.[70]

Confederate diehards rarely settled for verbal abuse and idle threats. It is beyond the scope of this discussion to list cases of physical violence toward the freed people during this period, but the reports of northern teachers and journalists, individual blacks, and white Georgians themselves all testify to the pervasive use of terrorism in discouraging them from voting, acquiring property, and going to school. As early as the fall and winter of 1864, bands of "Negro shooters" roamed the cotton belt, and in 1866 "a murderous crew . . . known as the 'Black Cavalry'" blackened their faces and rode about "at night on purpose to murder unoffending or industrious Negroes," according to John H. Caldwell. By spring 1868, the Ku Klux Klan had already achieved well-deserved notoriety as a result of its violent tactics, large membership, and extensive support among a cross section of the white population. The group claimed responsibility for burning schoolhouses and for sending written threats to northern teachers (Appendix H). One male AMA teacher was successfully "Ku Kluxed" out of Greensborough in the fall of 1869.[71]

Whites treated persons connected with freedmen's schooling in a selective manner, according to their race and sex. Male black teachers were whipped and murdered, but white men from the North received only threats—a frightening event for many, but one that did not involve physical danger. Black pupils were sometimes attacked, but northern female teachers suffered no violence to their persons during this period in Georgia. At least two pairs of women (stationed in Cuthbert and Andersonville) encountered some late-night harassment, but, again, these incidents proved to be emotionally nerve-racking rather than physically harmful.[72]

Given the strength of the Georgia Klan, the prevalence of racial violence, and the antipathy that whites harbored against Yankees during this period, it is surprising that northern teachers themselves suffered so little in the way of bodily harm. Perhaps whites considered the freed people, male and female, as more appropriate targets because of their vulnerability and alleged racial inferiority. A different standard existed for northern whites, especially white women. It is possible that even "country 'roughs' and crackers" (as one AMA superintendent called them) hesitated to stoop so low as to harm a white woman. To black women, of course, they extended no such courtesies. Despite some beatings and even murders of native white Republicans in Georgia, communities might have avoided "outraging" northerners in particular for fear of drawing national attention to the state. In the end, scare tactics often served the purpose of forcing northern teachers to head back home, or at least to seek refuge in a society-sponsored mission home in one of the larger towns.[73]

For the most part, federal troop occupation failed to discourage Klan activities and other forms of violence. Republican Reconstruction Governor Rufus Bullock (1868–71) hesitated to commit troops to trouble spots; he relied instead on local law enforcement and judicial procedures to deal with vigilantes. In any case, northern teachers frequently expressed their doubts about the use of outside troops to quell disturbances. Federal military officials usually felt no personal responsibility for the welfare of the freed people, and some capitulated to bribes—of varying degrees of subtlety—to remain inactive in the midst of the most flagrant cases of intimidation. At best, troops provided only temporary relief for persons active in black education, especially in rural areas. The violence of this era derived from ingrained prejudice and fear rather than sporadic impulses toward lawlessness. As one teacher observed in December 1868, the "hateful spirit of slavery" still reigned in the hearts of many southern whites. Neither military defeat nor federal troop occupation could erase this "spirit," which pervaded the state of Georgia after emancipation.[74]

Few northern teachers went south expecting white people in Georgia to welcome them with open arms; as neoabolitionists, they were fully prepared to encounter opposition from Confederate sympathizers. But although white hostility managed to thwart the educational effort in various ways throughout the state, it actually served a purpose for the teachers, who measured their own moral commitment by the violence of reaction they provoked among members of the white community. In other words, the more the teachers offended native whites, the more they became convinced that they were engaged in a great and holy task. As a result, few teachers felt inclined to depend on white approval of their work, and many were suspicious of any show of support from their former enemies. As one teacher expressed his feelings about the whites in Athens four years after the end of the war, "if they let us alone we feel glad." Predictably, the northern societies expended little time and energy attempting to make converts among their white brothers and sisters of the South.[75]

The teachers had also begun their Georgia work expecting that black people would be eager to attend school, and, in this, too, they were not disappointed. However, freedmen's aid society administrators were taken aback to discover that some blacks preferred to teach in and operate their own schools without the benefit of northern largesse. These initiatives on the part of the black community threatened the reformers' attempts to control the entire education effort in the state. It would be wasteful to allow the former slaves to expend northern funds on their own, according to white benefactors, who had great compassion for children learning their ABC's but little patience with people trying to learn how to operate their own schools. The northerners felt that in the long run these black efforts were inefficient; too much needed to be done in too little time to make education in postwar Georgia a joint venture between black and white.

CHAPTER IV

The Missionary-Bureaucrats and Freedmen's Education in Georgia

In October 1869 an American Missionary Association (AMA) superintendent wrote to New York headquarters and explained his recent decision to buy "a central lot in a very good part of town" (Bainbridge) in behalf of the group. William L. Clark, who also served for a time as a Freedmen's Bureau agent in Georgia, feared he had "acted beyond" his authority in making the purchase. But he declared, "I prayed hard and often concerning this matter—and I say not irreverently—that I believe our prayers saved to the Ass'n. or ourselves, or the work, hundreds of dollars." Clark's efforts to invoke the aid of the Almighty and strike a bargain for the AMA revealed a fundamental compatibility between missionary zeal and a keen business sense in freedmen's education. Aided by the Freedmen's Bureau, all northern groups active in Georgia sought to use the most economical means to educate the largest number of blacks in the state. The result was an educational bureaucracy impressive for its complexity, if not for its longevity.[1]

Established by an act of Congress in March 1865, the United States Bureau of Refugees, Freedmen, and Abandoned Lands was responsible for administering federal programs for southern blacks during Reconstruction. The head of the Bureau, General Oliver O. Howard, was strongly committed to freedmen's education and believed the agency could best use its resources by cooperating with private groups in building schoolhouses and paying teachers' salaries. The bureau offered a variety of additional forms of aid to the northern societies—including construction materials, cash, and discounts on transportation for teachers and supplies—but its chief source of influence lay in its effort to coordinate a uniform system of black schooling throughout the South.[2]

Faced with a chronic shortage of funds and a huge number of potential students to reach—in Georgia alone almost one-half million black adults and children—the freedmen's aid societies welcomed the bureau's efforts to oversee all educational activities. Complex state systems directed by dual hierarchies of government and society officials emerged between 1865 and 1870. The strict chain of command, enormous amounts of paperwork demanded of officials and teachers, and rigid specialization of individual responsibilities caused some Georgia workers to complain of the "red tape" involved in teaching. But northern agents remained convinced that centralized control over several hundred teachers, principals, and superintendents yielded the most efficient returns on their money.[3]

The societies encountered no existing structural framework on which to graft their freedmen's schools in Georgia. Although some localities maintained "free" or charitable schools in the antebellum period and though tentative steps were taken to establish a public school system right before the war, Georgia had no statewide system of tax-supported education in 1861. The war itself resulted in the suspension of most educational activities. Within three years after the fall of the Confederacy, the fledgling Republican party had incorporated a call for free schools into its platform; *"Relief, Homesteads and Schools* for the People" served as a catchy party slogan but little of substance came of it. The state's Reconstruction Constitution of 1868 included provisions for public education, but Georgia whites and blacks had to wait for Redemption, or the return of Democratic control, before they received money from public coffers to help support their schools. Responsibility for the delay rested squarely on the shoulders of Republican state officials who, torn by political and personality differences, remained distracted from the issue of education during their brief and stormy reign in the late 1860s. Although they expressed a rhetorical commitment to the grass-roots organizing of the Georgia Education (formerly Equal Rights) Association, most party members were more interested in this group for its political support, rather than for its efforts to establish schools at the local level.[4]

Finding a veritable vacuum of educational activity in Georgia, the northern groups concentrated on building a state school system based upon their own needs and opportunities. They did not include Georgia whites in this grand design. The AMA and other societies often mentioned loyal southerners in their discussions of persons deserving aid after the war, and northern-sponsored schools were officially integrated—that is, open to all whites who wished to attend them. But even native whites who approved of freedmen's education recoiled from the prospect of sending their own children to school with blacks, and the reformers showed no interest in going out of their way to appeal to this segment of the population by establishing separate facilities. Consequently the small, but well-organized, system established in the state in 1865 existed almost exclusively for the benefit of the freed people.[5]

The societies had a clearly defined model on which to base their southern enterprise. Beginning in the third and fourth decades of the nineteenth century, New England schoolmen had called for the systematization of common education on the state and local levels. Tremendous increases in population, especially in northeastern cities, produced formidable pressures on existing facilities. Newcomers, primarily poverty-stricken immigrants, could contribute very little in the way of financial support to public institutions. Schoolmen hoped to provide these immigrants, many of whom were Roman Catholic or non-English speaking, with a basic moral (Protestant) education as well as elementary instruction in literacy skills.

Moreover, the reformers believed that uniform educational systems throughout the country would guarantee increasingly mobile Americans access to similar types of schooling, whether they lived in eastern cities or western frontier towns. Common schools, by muting local ethnic and religious distinctions as well as transcending political rivalries, would serve as a dynamic force of national integration. To these ends, the administrators worked to increase public financial support of the schools and to build standard systems of education both within towns and throughout their own states. They called for uniformity of books, curricula, grading procedures, and teacher qualifications. They became obsessed with conformity in the name of "efficiency," and the educational bureaucracies of Boston and New York City became monuments to their ideas and influence.[6]

In their nationalistic fervor, the northern freedmen's aid society officials closely resembled the urban schoolmen. And, like their antebellum counterparts, they believed that the schools should reach as many children as possible and, by necessity, as economically as possible. The challenge for each group was to devise a "machine" in the form of a "system" so that "communication between North and South would be direct and supplies regular and unfailing." In the South, the various groups active in freedmen's education pooled their resources and formally agreed to submit to uniform guidelines relating to school operations. Their objective was a "system" of education that would avoid duplication of effort and waste of money. For example, in 1866 the American Freedmen's Union Commission (AFUC) called for "a more perfect organization and a more systematic division of labor" to promote "a permanent self-sustaining and growing system of popular education" in the South. This plan would provide black children in each state with a standardized common education, and the largest towns would serve as centers of higher learning where exceptional students could attend high school, normal school, or college.[7]

In Georgia, the AMA, the AFUC, and the Methodist Freedmen's Aid Society (MFAS) attempted to stay out of each other's "territory" while organizing their schools the same way and reporting to Freedmen's Bureau state education officials. Infrequently, two or three societies found themselves at work in the same area. This led to rivalry on the one hand and a pressure to "harmonize" their activities on the other. Bureau officials tried to mediate between the two parties, but the results were mixed. For example, in 1869 Augusta bureau agent Egbert B. Bingham finally induced both Baptist and Methodist superintendents in that town to make their schools conform to AMA standards in terms of admissions, grading, tuition, and discipline. But Bingham had originally gone south under the auspices of the association, and he was perceived as an agent of that group, even in his official capacity as bureau representative. Consequently, he had to spend much of his time (as he put it) "battling" with the other societies; intergroup suspicions and jealousies remained a major obstacle to systematization on a local, much less state, level.[8]

And there was never enough cash. In addition to performing routine duties related to educational administration, local superintendents also had to house and feed large groups of teachers. Thus discounts were vigorously sought on railroad and steamship fares, tracts, textbooks, and desks from sympathetic merchants in the North and even the South. The superintendents kept painfully detailed record books, and constantly searched for ways to consolidate operations here, cut back on expenses there. As missionaries wholeheartedly devoted to the cause of freedmen's education, they feared that lack of funds would block the fulfillment of evangelical dreams. Field Secretary Erastus M. Cravath urged his Georgia staff on to even greater heights of "economy" when he reminded John A. Rockwell in the spring of 1866, "If we can save expenses this summer we will have so much more to begin with next fall."[9]

Early in their Georgia work, the largest societies began to concentrate their efforts in the cities. Several basic considerations led to this decision. First, the northern groups could establish a hierarchy of schools—from elementary grades through college—only in population centers; such a program was totally impractical in rural areas, though 80 percent of Georgia blacks lived outside towns during this period. The AFUC affirmed in August 1865 that it aimed "to keep up a high standard so that the school system shall worthily represent New England,"—"at least in the large cities." By 1870 the AMA's educational complex in Atlanta was providing elementary instruction for two thousand children each year plus normal- and college-level studies for lesser numbers.[10]

A second reason for this urban bias involved the need for economy. In the cities, a smaller number of teachers could reach a greater number of children. (The rural population was so scattered that most instructors conducted classes for less than thirty children.) This way, the societies could also concentrate on school-construction projects, make more acceptable provisions for the boarding of teachers, and receive mail and supplies more efficiently than in outlying areas. Finally, they hoped to exert a more lasting influence over black communities by focusing their operations in the towns. The denominational groups established churches alongside their mission homes. An AMA field secretary explained in 1868, "Our policy is to get a part[icular] hold on a place by owning the school premises and putting up a mission home and as soon as we can a chapel and gather a church." All the societies considered the construction of large and impressive buildings as a wise investment in their southern work.[11]

The Freedmen's Bureau gave official sanction to this method of operation. As early as June 1866, the bureau's superintendent of education in Georgia, G. L. Eberhart, singled out the five largest towns in the state, listed their potential student populations, and suggested to the northern societies that they devote the bulk of their resources to these areas. During the next school year, northern teachers taught a total of 5,630 pupils, or almost 50 percent of the state's school-going black population, in Savannah, Augusta, Atlanta, Macon, and Columbus (Appendix E). (Not coincidentally perhaps, these were also centers of political support for the Republican party among both whites and blacks.) Between 1865 and 1870, the groups made a total of about five hundred teacher assignments in fifty different Georgia towns. More than 70 percent of these assignments involved the largest cities, which ranged in size from six thousand (Columbus) to twenty-four thousand (Savannah) but represented only 15 percent of the total black population in Georgia. The AMA exclusively controlled Savannah, Macon, and Atlanta, and shared Augusta with the Baptists. Columbus remained the domain of the AFUC. Only the Methodist society, more concerned with winning black converts away from its own southern denomination, avoided the largest cities in favor of medium-sized towns like LaGrange and Waynesboro.[12]

The attempt to create a uniform, efficient system of education was consistent with missionary goals. However, some freedmen's workers felt constrained by the necessarily rigid definition of roles and responsibilities which such a tightly coordinated effort implied. For example, the northern societies consciously relegated female teachers to an inferior position within the bureaucracy by paying them lower salaries than men and by denying them any administrative authority. But the missionary-bureaucrats soon discovered they could not "systematize" the women's evangelical fervor. The teachers took seriously their professional duties, and some of them offered explicit challenges to their superiors on a whole range of issues. Within the context of benevolent enterprise, these clashes highlighted the tension between male and female, administrator and teacher, superior and subordinate.

The work in Georgia represented only a small part—in statistical terms, roughly 10 percent—of the national freedmen's education effort. Between 1865 and 1870, thirty-one northern societies spent about fifteen million dollars in cash on schools in eighteen southern and border states and the District of Columbia. By the last year of Freedmen's Bureau operations (1869–70), these groups cooperated with the freedmen to instruct 149,589 pupils in 2,677 day and night schools taught by 3,633 black and white teachers. The coordination of educational work in Georgia alone presented an enormous problem during the five-year period after the war. Four major northern societies sent as many as 140 teachers to the state in one year. Schools sustained by the freedmen themselves, though scattered in rural areas, employed an equal number of teachers annually. During the 1868–69 school year, 13,263 (or about 5 percent of the state's black school-age population) received instruction in 232 day schools from 139 northern and 113 native teachers. In that year alone, all parties involved spent more than a hundred thousand dollars for school construction, teachers' salaries, and textbooks (Appendix E).[13]

The Freedmen's Bureau state superintendents of education (G. L. Eberhart, 1865–67; Edmund A. Ware, 1867–68 and May to July

1870; and John R. Lewis, 1868 to May 1870) assumed responsibility for overseeing all black schools in the state. General Howard
made explicit this objective in August 1865; he declared that the
bureau did not plan to "supersede the benevolent agencies in [the
work], but systematize and facilitate" their operations. The Georgia
office spent as much as forty thousand dollars annually on freedmen's education, and, between 1867 and 1870, it built or repaired
schools in sixty towns throughout the state. But the goal of a complete system remained illusory. Like the northern society officials,
all three bureau superintendents discovered they had far too much
work to do and too little money with which to do it. The mountain of
statistical reports and official correspondence produced by these
men and their tiny staffs over the brief five-year period testify both
to their bureaucratic expertise and the hopelessness of their task.
The Freedmen's Bureau educational archives contain no descriptions of classrooms or children; they consist of vouchers, receipts,
requests for money, monthly report forms, circulars, and compila-
tions of statistics.[14]

The willingness and even eagerness with which northern officials
cooperated with the state bureau superintendents accounted for
many of the bureau's achievements in the field of freedmen's education. In Georgia, distinctions between federal and private efforts
blurred. Eberhart and Lewis expressed full agreement with the
evangelical goals of the northern societies and cultivated close personal relationships with their leading officials. Ware, an "AMA
man," unabashedly used his position to promote his association's
work in Georgia. All three men corresponded regularly with northern society headquarters and informed them of specific localities
that needed schools and teachers. Although the other groups expressed some resentment over the AMA's preeminent position in
the state, they had nothing to lose and much to gain from a close and
"cheerful" cooperation with the bureau. The prime benefits included
money for school construction, discounts on transportation rates,
and a variety of supplies, from books and papers to stoves and rations. In addition, the agency showed no hesitation in allowing denominational groups to use bureau-built schools for religious purposes, on Sundays and during the week.

When he assumed office in the fall of 1865, Superintendent Eberhart had in his mind a comprehensive plan for freedmen's education
in Georgia. He began by taking a survey of schools to determine how
many were already in operation. The freedmen themselves supported fifty. Even though he feared most of these were "inefficient,"
Eberhart believed they served a useful purpose in providing rudi-

mentary instruction for illiterate adults and children. He expressed confidence that the northern societies, just beginning work in Georgia on a large scale, would provide a higher quality of education, and he hoped soon to "inaugurate a plan of normal instruction" for the freedmen in order to render them educationally "independent." This state system of education would soon "demonstrate beyond all cavil, that they [were] capable of appreciating and properly using, the blessings vouchsafed to them by an allwise Providence in the inestimable boon of freedom." In his support for a hierarchy of schooling and in his belief that education would serve to "uplift" and liberate the freedmen, Eberhart's approach closely resembled that of benevolent society officials. Yet he soon discovered, and his successors took for granted, that more mundane matters consumed all the superintendent's time.[15]

For example, Eberhart early vowed to make provisions for schools throughout the state to use uniform textbooks (he recommended the "National Series" published by Barnes and Company), but he actually had to devote most of his energy to matching northern teachers with black communities and appropriating money for salaries and school construction. By 1867 the bureau had exhausted all its funds for teachers' salaries, and within two years the money earmarked for transportation and supplies was gone. The last two bureau officials in Georgia concentrated on repairing schoolhouses, which they rented to northern societies for a nominal fee each month, and on distributing small amounts of cash, including some from a fund established by northern philanthropist George Peabody in 1867.[16]

The AMA, in particular, received immense benefits from the bureau at the national level and in the state of Georgia. General Howard maintained close personal relationships with AMA executive officials, especially former U.S. Sanitary Commission Agent Edward P. Smith. Between 1865 and 1870 the association was awarded more than a million dollars, or 20 percent of the bureau's total appropriations, for freedmen's education. In Georgia, Superintendents Eberhart and Lewis proved quite aggressive in obtaining property, buildings, and cash for exclusive AMA use, and Ware's primary loyalty to the association was, of course, never in doubt. The bureau authorized as much as ten thousand dollars for large city schools like Beach Institute in Savannah, and provided the society with such luxuries as normal-school buildings and small homes for teachers in rural areas. No other group received as much as seven hundred dollars to construct small schools in the backcountry. When the bureau ceased all operations except educational work in 1869, Howard agreed to sell a large number of bureau buildings to the AMA for one dollar each and pay ten dollars monthly per teacher. Still, there were limits to this preferential treatment. For instance, Lewis reacted angrily when he realized the Savannah AMA official had spent a large bureau appropriation on a mission home when the money was authorized only for the construction of a school, and New York headquarters had to assume responsibility for repaying the bureau.[17]

In late 1869 the national bureau education chief, John W. Alvord, rejoiced that his agency and the northern societies had achieved a "union of effort" marked by "harmony" and "earnest zeal." He gave evidence of this cooperation by stating, "our blanks are used by their teachers; their consolidated reports now correspond with ours, and thus we are able to act in general concert." These remarks indicate the importance placed upon data-gathering, an activity that preoccupied everyone from teachers and principals to superintendents, field agents, and district secretaries. The stacks of teachers' monthly reports and superintendents' financial accounts were comforting to state and national officials; the forms gave the illusion of order and served as ultimate proof of an educational "system." Predictably, field-workers had the least patience when it came to filling out elaborate reports. Teachers and local superintendents often rebelled in exasperation, and charged that the paperwork presented unreasonable demands on their limited time. Augusta Superintendent Charles H. Prince refused to comply with an AMA regulation that he keep records of each piece of clothing distributed to the freedmen. In January 1867 he wrote, "My time is so *thoroughly* occupied that I can not attend to matters of no consequence [sic]. I consider this one of the little things which need not take my time." An Atlanta matron considered the same order to be ridiculous in light of her difficulty in keeping up with that city's "floating population." All superintendents had trouble sending their financial accounts and education reports to New York on time each month. They could only apologize for their "criminal tardiness" in this matter and promise to do better next time.[18]

Despite Alvord's claim that bureau and society officials had consolidated report forms, Georgia teachers continued to fill out two separate blanks each month until November 1869 (the bureau expired just a few months later). They received a steady stream of instructions from a variety of agents: "Take special pains to have these papers go up regularly and correctly, and in a round plain handwriting"; fill out the forms on the last day of the month, and send them in no later than the second day of the next; and so forth. Moreover, the teachers were faced with a parade of ever-changing forms and reports for different purposes. Between 1865 and 1870, the bureau and northern societies devised a number of different consolidated report forms for AMA superintendents, five teachers' monthly report forms for AMA teachers, ten teachers' monthly report forms distributed by the Freedmen's Bureau, plus smaller numbers of miscellaneous blanks for specific purposes.[19]

The sponsoring groups used this information in different ways. The northern groups closed their smallest schools each year, and aggregate statistics were incorporated into annual reports to provide evidence of progress in the work. The bureau published detailed local, state, and national data on a semiannual basis. In 1868, when its congressional appropriations began to dwindle, the agency established qualifications for individual schools that applied for funds. In most cases, the bureau agreed to pay each society a small amount monthly calculated on the basis of its number of teachers, pupils, and school buildings. The little Peabody money available was also allocated on a per-pupil basis, according to teachers' monthly reports.

The northern aid societies and the Freedmen's Bureau devised independent, yet cooperating, administrative systems with parallel chains of command. Some men alternated between working for the bureau and the voluntary groups; this produced an interlocking network of personnel. The smooth operation of the bureaucracy depended upon a strict hierarchy of role assignments. There were five roughly equivalent levels of public and private officials: the chief policymakers of the respective groups; field agents based in the North who served as liaisons with Georgia workers; state and district officials; city and local superintendents, principals, and rural agents; and matrons, teachers, and missionaries (female social workers). Ordinarily, each level reported regularly to the one directly above it. Even within local administrative structures, teachers, missionaries, and superintendents were often reminded of their respective positions. Thus the letterhead on AMA mission home stationery listed names of workers in ranked order: first, the city superintendent and the school principal (the men), followed by the home matron, missionaries, and teachers (the women).[20]

Corresponding secretaries of the various freedmen's aid societies and the Freedmen's Bureau commissioner of education in Washington served as policymakers and administrators for their organizations. They had primary responsibility for the operation of the southern education effort at the highest levels; they approved structural changes in the system and set national goals on the basis of financial considerations. Their unceasing communication with each other produced a flood of correspondence among Washington (the bureau), New York (AMA), Cincinnati (MFAS and the regional office of the AMA), and Boston (New England branch of the AFUC).

Most of the nuts-and-bolts administrative problems devolved on the district, or field, secretaries of the societies, who were each in charge of several southern states. Stationed in the North, these officials made decisions concerning the establishment of schools, teachers' assignments, and shipping of food and supplies. They corresponded with local agents and individual teachers. The three AMA field secretaries were located in New York, Cinncinati, and Chicago (the Cinncinati office was transferred to New York City in 1870). During most of the period 1865–70, Georgia came under the jurisdiction of the Midwest Department, which was headquartered in Cincinnati and headed first by Samuel Hunt, then Edward P. Smith, and, finally, Erastus M. Cravath. In a similar manner, western Georgia and Alabama constituted an MFAS "Middle Department," administered from Cincinnati.[21]

Through infrequent visits and regular correspondence, Hunt, Smith, and Cravath attempted to oversee all AMA operations in the state of Georgia during their respective tenures. Local superintendents checked with the field secretary before assigning teachers to "outposts," building or repairing schools, transferring staff members, purchasing large quantities of staples for mission homes, and trying to settle personality disputes. The secretary goaded all workers under him to conform to the strictures of the bureaucracy, sent south elaborate instructions for the filing of school reports and vouchers for supplies and travel expenses, and insisted that each person acknowledge correspondence from the district office immediately (Appendix F). Maintaining a keen interest in the work of other groups in the South, he encouraged local superintendents to keep rivals out of especially promising "fields." But, as the "commanding officer," he rarely saw active duty on the battleground. Although the lowliest "privates" (the teachers) wrote him long, detailed letters about every aspect of their experiences, he could not afford to take too much interest in the specifics of their work. Indeed, the teachers were rather pathetic in their efforts to maintain close contact with this high official in the North, for they received little in the way of comments or helpful suggestions in return. If a secretary thought a particular letter held some intrinsic interest for readers of the *American Missionary*, he sent it along to the journal editor to consider for publication, but rarely wrote a personal reply.[22]

The Georgia assistant commissioner, the highest ranking Freedmen's Bureau official in the state, appointed the superintendent of education. Like the societies' district officials, the bureau superintendent experienced little or no direct contact with pupils, though he resided in Georgia. Eberhart, Ware, and Lewis depended upon local agents to carry out their orders. Each major town had both a society superintendent and a bureau assistant superintendent (sometimes called subassistant commissioner) of education. One person often filled both positions. He was responsible not only for the freedmen's schools within his own town, but also for those in nearby areas, which might include as many as twenty-five counties. He hired construction workers, assigned teachers, set tuition rates, and opened and closed the schools. As a society official, he had the additional duties of operating the teachers' mission home and, in some cases, serving as a school principal. The superintendents stationed in the five largest towns wielded the most influence in terms of daily school operations. Their range of duties was so wide—from coordinating end-of-the-year exhibitions to repairing the school furnace to suppressing feuds between quarreling workers—that it was little wonder few men managed to stay in the position very long. Most resigned because they felt overworked, unappreciated, or beleaguered by hostile subordinates. Only one man, the indefatigable Edmund Ware of Atlanta, persevered for the whole decade after the war (and, indeed, until his death in 1888).

The state Freedmen's Bureau officer also relied on agents scattered throughout the countryside for information and assistance. Although charged with a variety of duties, most of which bore no direct relation to schools, rural agents were officially responsible for reporting monthly on educational activities within their districts. Predictably, these local agents showed much diversity in their commitment to freedmen's education. Some ignored the issue of schooling altogether, and others made brief, perfunctory reports merely as a part of their routine duties. A few agents, notably Douglas Risley on the coast and George Wagner in the western part of the state, assumed an aggressive role in local educational affairs. These men helped freedmen to qualify for bureau educational funds, visited neighborhood schools, and participated in community association meetings. Both maintained close ties with AMA representatives. Of course, those AMA and MFAS superintendents who also served as bureau agents, whether in towns or rural areas, always took their educational responsibilities seriously. For example, John H. Caldwell (MFAS), in western Georgia, William F. Eaton (AMA), on St. Simons Island, and William L. Clark (AMA), in Bainbridge, taught schools themselves in addition to coordinating all educational work in their districts.[23]

Although most of the men occupied positions of authority within the Georgia freedmen's school system, most of the women served as teachers. Their position was somewhat anomalous. The teacher interacted with the freed people directly on a day-to-day basis. She was responsible for seeing that children in the classroom learned to read and write. In effect, the heavy weight of institutional machinery existed to enable her to do her work; she and the pupils were the system's raison d'être. And yet her role within the bureaucracy was an inferior one. Paid less than her male counterparts and prevented by society guidelines from ascending the hierarchical ladder to the position of principal or superintendent, she enjoyed little opportunity to make policy decisions on the issues that affected her directly in the area of school operations. This discrepancy between role and status of female freedmen's workers was to have serious implications for the Georgia school system.

Despite her lack of official power, the teacher ultimately served as the financial life-source for her society's work. The northern groups depended heavily upon voluntary contributions, and much of their creativity in sustaining an educational bureaucracy involved devising new strategies to coax and wheedle funds from the pockets of apathetic New Englanders. The teachers played a prominent role in fund-raising activities. Indeed, the societies operated under the assumption that personal contact with the freed people and their teachers would serve as the greatest inducement for individuals to contribute money to the cause.

Denominational groups, especially, felt rather defensive about their incessant calls for more of that commodity rhetorically described as the "root of all evil." The AMA assumed a discreet posture in 1865 when it proclaimed, "we are not beggars, but the 'Lord's collectors.'" But the fact remained that evangelical enthusiasm accomplished little without the financial backing to spread and sustain it. In December 1866 the association outlined an ambitious program of freedmen's education for the coming year. Of the points it stressed, the last was the most straightforward and compelling: the group required a minimum of three hundred thousand dollars to carry out its plans. Eventually the AMA discarded subtlety when it found itself sinking deeper and deeper into debt. By 1868 pleas for contributions had reached fever pitch as the major freedmen's aid societies scrambled for pieces of the ever-shrinking philanthropic pie.[24]

A vast network of local auxiliaries supported each national group. For example, the New York branch of the AFUC boasted 452 societies in July 1866. The AMA also depended heavily on individual

Congregational churches and Sunday schools in its efforts to raise money. Although these groups were encouraged to donate books and supplies, the parent body urged the largest and wealthiest to concentrate on raising enough funds to support at least one teacher annually. Amounts required for this purpose ranged from three hundred to five hundred dollars. Ideally, the auxiliary would sponsor a young woman from its own town and keep in touch with her while she taught in the South. The assumption was that personal ties would create an enduring financial and emotional commitment to freedmen's work. The New York branch of the AFUC assured its member groups that they could nominate "a devoted, competent, Christian lady, whom you know, and in whom you have confidence."[25]

To reach areas where no local group existed, all the societies kept professional collecting agents on their payrolls. Freedmen's teachers vacationing in the North during the summer served as enthusiastic and successful canvassers; fresh from the rigors of southern work, they brought to the task a sense of immediacy, if not emergency. The AMA also organized traveling fund-raising programs that featured freed people as speakers and members of singing groups. For instance, in the early 1870s, the Fisk Jubilee Singers and a musical group from Hampton Institute made the rounds in New England. While scouring the North for donations, each group took pains to stay out of each other's informally designated "territory." They also needed to publish frequent disclaimers concerning the solicitations of imposters who found posing as society agents very rewarding, in a literal sense.[26]

By far the most significant propaganda tool—in terms of the amount of time and money invested in it—was the monthly freedmen's aid society journal. The AMA had its *American Missionary*, the New England branch of the AFUC the *Freedmen's Record*, the New York branch the *National Freedman*, and AFUC Washington headquarters the *American Freedman*. The AMA attributed 50 percent of its annual income to contributions received in direct response to appeals published in the *Missionary*. Distributed at low cost (fifty cents to one dollar annually for subscribers), the journals served as vital links between the societies and their supporters, actual and potential.

Detailed letters from the freedmen's teachers accounted for more than half of the material published in these magazines. But editors were not satisfied to publish just any description of a Georgia classroom. AMA Corresponding Secretary George Whipple stated the matter succinctly in an 1866 letter to a Georgia superintendent: "In presenting the cause of the freedmen we are concerned not with inquiries after facts. People of the North have become fully acquainted with the general condition of things at the South. What they want and need just now are special and particular incidents illustrating everyday life among the freedmen." Whipple suggested that the teachers emphasize spectacular occurrences, including "cases of terrible suffering" and "deeds of hatred and violence on the part of the whites toward the colored," under the assumption that the "recital of one particular case of misery [as opposed to mere statements of fact] will move them [the readers] to tears." Obviously field-workers labored under considerable pressure to produce well-written, dramatic letters. Wrote one Augusta teacher of Whipple's high expectations: "should I fail to write them, he will be disappointed and I shall be mortified."[27]

Society officials showed no hesitation in editing letters—and that included composing whole new passages—for publication. Georgia teachers and superintendents alike took a dim view of this practice. Yet, once they placed a letter in the mail, it belonged to the sponsoring association. In deciding which letters to use and how to change them, editors walked a fine line between presenting an overly optimistic view on the one hand and painting an exceedingly dark picture of freedmen's work on the other. Contributors wanted some assurance that the blacks appreciated schooling and that northern money was put to good use. Yet society officials sought to impress upon journal readers the black man's "degraded" position in southern society and his total dependence upon northern support. This dilemma became especially acute around 1868, when the societies appeared torn between boasting of their successes and bewailing the dramatic decrease in annual receipts. Eventually, the result was a form of paralysis among some long-term workers. For example, a veteran superintendent who clearly understood the limits of freedmen's work wrote that "Those who have been longest in the field hesitate the most about writing. If we give *facts* as we see them, our northern friends either entirely discredit us, or we are told we make the picture so dark that the churches are discouraged and the collection of funds hindered. True, we find much that is encouraging, but then, we think that the churches should know something of the obstacles and discouragements of the work: else how can they appreciate its importance and difficulties." The editors had their work cut out for them.[28]

Letters of Georgia teachers contained in the archives of the AMA provide specific examples of editing by society officials. S. W. Magill's discussion of the Savannah Education Association (SEA) and its "spirit of exclusiveness" against northern whites never found its way into the magazine's columns, though other portions of his letter did. A Macon teacher's misgivings about the effects of piecemeal charity in the midst of "abject poverty and wretchedness" sounded a bit too depressing for the *Missionary*'s readers. By the late 1860s the teachers had learned to specify what they did and did not want printed. In 1869 one woman sent along this plea with a detailed letter describing her work in Atlanta: "Do what you please with it—except chop it up—I mean burn it or publish a part of it but *please* don't cut pieces out."[29]

On a more personal level, the Georgia teachers wrote thousands of letters to groups and individuals in the North as part of the AMA campaign to raise money. Most teachers received specific assignments so that they could provide regular accounts of their work to northern congregations and Sunday schools. In addition, they corresponded with their local sponsors and acknowledged donations of food and clothing with letters describing the freedmen's thankfulness. From AMA headquarters came a firm command: "It is very important when you receive boxes of goods that you acknowledge them *at once* to the *Donors* by a warm and hearty letter that will call forth a second donation."[30]

As the freedmen's aid organizations became larger and more complex, the need for steady sources of income grew apace. At the same time, the sheer size of the voluntary educational system threatened to eliminate the close personal contacts that were so effective in attracting supporters. Consequently, the teacher's role in raising funds assumed heightened importance. She had the responsibility to "excite" active sympathy on behalf of the "degraded masses," and also to sustain interest among those whose names were already on the societies' mailing lists. This institutionalized system of letter writing thus served as a creative response to the problems usually associated with large bureaucracies. Personal, detailed descriptions of life and work in the South gave ultimate meaning to the mass of reports and regulations that sometimes threatened to overwhelm the whole operation.[31]

Despite their commitment to a unified statewide system of black education, northern officials encountered a variety of obstacles to "harmony" among the different groups, as well as within their own societies, in Georgia. Most of these problems were inherent in the nature of the enterprise—a joint public and private effort dependent heavily upon volunteers and financial contributors. Foremost among the forces preventing cooperation stood intergroup rivalry. The societies apparently saw no contradiction in persistently calling for "unity" while fiercely guarding their own bailiwick and trying to expand at the expense of competitors. These divergent impulses coexisted in society agents and led, as one observer suggested, "occasionally to forms of self-seeking strangely at variance with the heroic self-sacrifice which the same individuals were constantly making." Underneath all the interdenominational rhetoric, these men considered each other dangerous rivals in fund raising, securing the "most promising fields of labor" in the South, and courting favor with the Freedmen's Bureau. Even the AMA, by far the most powerful group in Georgia, suffered from a generous dose of paranoia. In 1869 Edmund Ware, at the time head of the extensive educational complex in Atlanta, expressed fears that the northern Methodists and Old School Presbyterians would "gobble" up bureau Superintendent Lewis and turn him against the association. "If we are going to hold our ground here in Atlanta," he warned ominously, "we have got to be wide awake. The Methodists are on the watch here, and will get all they can." But, when he heard that the Baptists accused a local bureau agent of showing favoritism toward the AMA, Ware responded indignantly, "It is really strange that people claiming to be Christian will *be so*."[32]

From 1865 until 1870, the bureau received a barrage of complaints charging its agents with undisguised preference for the AMA. The Methodists, in particular, perceived real abuses. For example, in April 1869 the Reverend D. W. Hammond of the MFAS reported that the state bureau superintendent "positively refused to give one cent of money" to his group for their work in Atlanta. Lewis replied to this charge in a lengthy letter, in which he provided the standard explanation for favoring AMA schools in such cases: "in my opinion it was unwise to establish two or more weak institutions of that kind in this city, but rather concentrate all into one Strong and vigorous one." The AMA, long entrenched in Atlanta, had won the right to "occupy" that field. At the same time, correspondence between the bureau and AMA representatives reveals that Lewis and his colleagues indeed often went out of their way to aid the association, surreptitiously at times.[33]

Policy differences among the groups served as a less dramatic, but important, divisive factor. In Georgia, salary scales remained unequal. Individual societies devised their own school calendars, which featured different holidays and vacations. The Methodists considered schooling primarily a means of drawing freedmen into their churches; this approach differed from AFUC and AMA emphasis on common education. Of course, the northern societies always commissioned and paid their own teachers; they would never consider relinquishing these duties to a central agency.

Besides overt conflicts and jealousies, rapid personnel turnover plagued the effort at all levels during the five-year period after the war. The societies contracted with their teachers and superintendents for one year at a time; because participation in freedmen's work was purely voluntary, people left at will. Each year, the groups faced a new staff situation as teachers and superintendents left the work or were transferred to different parts of the South. For the most part, only northern-based administrators in Cincinnati, Boston, and New York stayed in the same place on a long-term basis.

In order to maintain a smooth-running and efficient organization, society and bureau officials recognized the need for constant communication among all parties. The archives of the major groups and the bureau bulge with thousands of letters, all handwritten, from Georgia during this five-year period. Correspondence followed both vertical and horizontal lines; top administrators and superintendents communicated with each other as well as with persons beneath them. Yet the thousand-mile gulf between agents based in Georgia and the North made the whole communication process a frustrating one. Letters, which traveled by steamship, took about a week to go up or down the East Coast. Sooner or later, almost everyone had to resort to a telegram in order to obtain vital information quickly. For example, when he wanted to purchase a brick building, a Macon superintendent cabled in September 1872, "Shall I take it answer today." Supplies from New York took much longer than letters to reach Georgia—up to one month in most cases.[34]

Teachers and local superintendents, in particular, often expressed dissatisfaction with the cumbersome communication network linking them to the North. They found it difficult to present an accurate picture of their work exclusively through written correspondence. Most had an opportunity to talk directly with society officials only twice a year, at the beginning and end of the school year when they visited "the Rooms" in New York. Some gave up the effort to explain their feelings on such issues as transferrals and dismissals because of the difficulty in writing about such delicate matters. Rather than argue with one official about her decision to remain in the South during the summer of 1866, one teacher merely wrote, "It would take too long to state upon paper, the reasons which presented themselves to me. ... I say, that if you were *here*, you would see the matter differently." This inability to commit to paper subtle aspects of a situation also proved annoying to the Savannah superintendent who wrote his superior at one point, "I wish I could explain the state of things in this field . . . I cannot do it by letter."[35]

Competition among different groups, checks lost in the mail, neglected monthly report forms, and communication difficulties took their toll on the ideals of systematization and efficiency. But few problems unnerved the missionary-bureaucrats more than those presented by teachers who resisted taking orders from their superiors. Although it often appeared as if the bureaucracy had assumed a life of its own—based on "official" status designations and regulations—opportunities sometimes existed for teachers to circumvent this formal structure and either ignore or usurp the power of men above them. At least at the lowest levels, the hierarchy of roles was a fragile creation, easily disrupted by persons who refused to conform to certain institutional strictures linking sex with status.

Historians of nineteenth-century common-school reform have noted that the feminization of teaching meant expanded professional opportunities for women, but within a limited social and economic context. Schoolmen like Horace Mann seized on the rhetoric of sentimental womanhood and declared that teachers should consider themselves mothers-away-from-home. Writers and reformers alike emphasized women's nurturative qualities—gentleness, patience, and kindness with young children—and glorified the function of female "moral influence" in the purification of the home and nation. But, despite this inflated rhetoric, women teachers received less pay than their male counterparts, and they were denied positions of administrative authority in local and state school systems. Based on both morality and "efficiency," the argument for female teachers was a powerful one; by the late nineteenth century (earlier in New England), unmarried women dominated the common-school teaching force.[36]

How did the freedmen's teachers maintain a belief in the intrinsic value of their work and yet accept their inferior status within their societies' educational bureaucracies? Did they deal with the situation philosophically (their superiors urged them to eschew "selfishness") or did they show signs of resistance and protest? Male officials sought to operate an efficient Yankee educational bureaucracy in which women occupied the lowest positions, but they failed to anticipate the determination of teachers who were imbued with a sense of "womanly" purpose. The teachers themselves were torn between their roles as professionals and as submissive missionaries. Most of them had a keen sense of professionalism; they had received some type of higher education (at a normal school, female seminary, or

Oberlin College) to prepare them for classroom instruction. Many had taught at least a year before going south, and they filled their letters to society headquarters with wonderfully intricate descriptions of their attempts to employ the latest pedagogical techniques in their southern schools. Although primitive facilities and a host of other problems limited their success in this area, the teachers demonstrated the type of self-confidence that comes from both specialized training and practical experience.

However, the evangelical emphasis of the AMA only served to reinforce prevailing attitudes toward women as highly emotional, sensitive, and religious beings, who, by virtue of their maternal instincts, were specially suited to teach young children. The association's call for "self-sacrificing" young females implied that these women should put the interests of "the work" above their own petty interests. On a more practical level, the society, always pressed for funds, paid female teachers less than men who did the same work. It opened no leadership positions to women in its New York City headquarters, New England and Midwest regional offices, or southern freedmen's schools, and rationalized its position by stressing that teaching was missionary work. The women who wanted to join the cause should not seek financial reward or personal aggrandizement, nor should they disobey their superiors. As religious workers, they were supposed to concentrate on "moral reform" and leave administrative matters to the men.[37]

But the teachers' idealism and firm conviction that they had a "great work" to do produced among some a self-conscious, self-righteous zeal that exacerbated the whole problem. Their sense of mission encouraged them to act with deliberation and speak out with conviction. As nineteenth-century female reformers, they sought to express themselves within the boundary of benevolent activity and, more precisely, the womanly function of teaching. But, as Nancy Cott has suggested of female missionaries in general, "religious commitment . . . proposed a submission of self that was simultaneously a pronounced form of self-assertion," and therein lay one source of conflict between men and women in freedmen's work. This tension inspired a variety of group and individual responses on the part of the women, including demands for salaries equal to those of male teachers and refusals to obey guidelines that infringed on their ability to run their own classes as they saw fit. The themes here are diversity and ambivalence (rather than incipient feminism), for the women reacted according to their own temperaments and the possibilities inherent in their individual teaching situations. A number of specific incidents involving Georgia teachers suggest they found opportunities for self-expression despite the limits of their formal status as defined by male bureaucrats.[38]

In December 1869 a twenty-five-year-old teacher of the Georgia freedmen submitted an eloquent letter of resignation to the AMA. Anna Snowden, a native of Norwalk, Connecticut, was protesting the AMA's policy of paying women teachers lower salaries than men. She suggested that "in this day of the discussion of human rights, work and wages, it is well to look into things." Another Atlanta teacher, Amy Williams, expressed a similar concern in July 1872, when she told the association's New York office that "the great disparity between the salaries and privileges of the men and women in the work is enough to arouse the indignation of any woman who has one particle of spirit or the sense of justice about her." Like Anna Snowden, Amy Williams highlighted the discrepancy between the responsibilities and salary ($800 per year) of a male superintendent and the exhausting duties and little pay ($135) of, as she put it, "the women who worked under him." The issue transcended the "equal pay for equal work" argument, for women did "a much greater amount of work" than their male superiors, she contended. Evidently, AMA officials failed to gauge the extent of teacher discontent on the matter. Snowden concluded her letter with the assertion, "I am not speaking for myself, but for my sisters," and Amy Williams assured the AMA that "I complain or feel no more intensely than almost every teacher you have in the field, all the difference being that I go to headquarters with my grievances instead of to my co-workers."[39]

The two Atlanta superintendents who worked with Snowden and Williams showed little sympathy for the women or their arguments; Snowden's final communication was ridiculed as a "smashing letter," and, in 1872, Amy Williams was informed cooly that no true Christian missionary would ever exhibit such an obsession with financial matters. Williams belied that charge by continuing her southern work until she retired. She finally achieved some recognition for her considerable teaching and administrative talents during the difficult transition period when the AMA turned over its black schools in Atlanta to the state-sponsored system in the mid-1870s.[40]

Another Georgia teacher, Julia Shearman, frequently condemned the AMA policy against female superintendents during her three-year tenure in the South. Well-meaning but inexperienced and incompetent male administrators offended her, and she declared that she and other women should have the chance to fill their places. An outspoken woman who evidently commanded the respect of both male and female freedmen's workers, she finally left the field when the association agreed to grant her only informal authority over its operations in Augusta.[41]

If few other teachers discussed the issues of "human rights, work, and wages" in letters to their superiors, many showed little or no hesitation in openly criticizing decisions from above that they considered unfair or ill considered. New York administrators as well as Georgia officials found the teachers a headstrong and opinionated lot, certain of their abilities and determined to resist the erosion of what little authority they already had. Teachers who were suddenly reassigned without prior notification or who found their integrity impugned if they complained about the AMA's nonchalant attitude toward sending out salary checks on a regular basis, responded with letters full of rage and sarcasm. Requests that they do extra work, such as correspond with additional northern Sunday schools, sometimes brought flat refusals. The teachers, who realized they were already overworked (entire staffs sometimes succumbed to illness or physical exhaustion), resisted further demands from New York headquarters.

Yet contradictions between style and substance lingered. A defiant letter often ended with an apology, implicit admission that the writer had temporarily stepped out of her sphere as obedient "daughter." After informing an association official of the various personality conflicts that plagued the Atlanta mission home in 1867, one teacher remarked that she felt she had a right to discuss such matters with him, but concluded by saying, "You may be assured that instruction and kind reproof I shall ever receive with gratitude and thankfulness." Four years after the initial controversy over the pay scale, Amy Williams was still writing letters full of suggestions for operating the schools in Atlanta, yet she, too, had to assure her superiors that she "certainly mean[t] no disrespect to the higher powers."[42]

If a teacher considered her supervisor remiss in his duties, she sometimes notified society headquarters directly rather than confront him over the issue. Apparently a gulf based on age and position created communication difficulties between teacher and principal. Some women might have wanted to avoid the unpleasantness of a quarrel in an effort supposedly characterized by Christian love and benevolence. One teacher sent her suggestion for revision of the Savannah school tuition policy to Erastus Cravath in New York and requested that he mention the idea to her principal without divulging its source. A group of teachers who gradually came to lose all respect for their superintendent (they wrote that "he signally fails to meet the duties of Beach Institute and . . . is of very little service as a whole") chose to present New York with a formal petition to that effect. In this particular case, as well as several others concerning teacher dissatisfaction with male leadership, the man's lack of professional educational qualifications seemed to be a major issue. One AMA official described the ideal principal as "a man of some age and experience to give him influence with the teachers." Julia Shearman, always sensitive to power relationships, provided a vivid illustration of the problem in her description of an Augusta school principal. She acknowledged that he possessed a pleasing personality but noted that he was "not quite enough of a *head* and I know that the teachers, *the best* teachers feel it."[43]

The women made an issue out of incompetence at the supervisory level despite the continual pleas from officials in the North for "harmony" among all freedmen's workers. The teachers were sensitive to the warning that conflicts within the educational system would hinder the cause in the sight of blacks and native whites alike. Nevertheless, they at times believed their professional responsibilities in the classroom demanded priority over public-relations considerations. Nor did they shun a weak administrator during the day and return to the mission home in the evening prepared to follow the dictates of the same individual in "family" matters. Perhaps they were too consistent in their efforts to effect "moral reform," the desire that had impelled them into freedmen's work in the first place.

The teachers accepted the schoolmen's argument that women's special, innate characteristics peculiarly suited them for work in the classroom. But, in the South, they supplemented notions of their own moral superiority with a strong sense of professionalism to produce forthright challenges to their male superiors in the fields of both educational policy and mission-home management. Their successes and failures alike indicate that formal role categories based on sex were not always accurate indicators of actual behavior.

Unlike the life span of northern state educational systems of comparable size, that of the freedmen's education system in Georgia was extremely short. By 1869 the effort had reached its peak. From 1867 on, the bureau and northern aid societies regularly announced new measures to cut back existing programs and curtail expenses. In fact, Superintendent Ware discovered that his duties consisted almost entirely of rejecting appeals for aid from all over the state. At the beginning of 1868, the bureau called nervously for "another year at least of vigorous work," but the end was in sight. The AFUC, declaring that it had accomplished its mission, ceased operations in 1869 (the New England branch continued to support some schools as late as 1876). The AMA withdrew its aid from most rural areas, and cited a debt in excess of fifty thousand dollars as the main reason for its decision to concentrate on institutions of higher learning and the urban elementary schools. The Freedmen's Bureau managed to sustain a skeletal educational staff in Georgia until mid-July 1870, and Superintendent Lewis worked until the last possible minute repairing schools and turning over to the AMA its leases on buildings. Ware regarded the closing of the bureau with great sadness, especially because he thought Lewis was just beginning to get "more and more out of patience with Methodists, Baptists, and O. S. [Old School] Presbyterians in their attempts to do School work in Georgia." The AMA had lost a valuable ally and benefactor.[44]

Despite its brief existence, the system successfully combined evangelical reform commitment with at least a minimum of bureaucratic efficiency. The operations of each northern group demonstrated that the more zealous the missionary, the louder the call for "economy." In their frantic efforts to put together a workable bureaucracy that would accommodate up to thirteen thousand pupils annually, society officials proved themselves as adept at educational administration as school reformers in the North. They failed in their attempts to create a uniform system of schooling throughout the state, and they stubbornly refused to tap a major source of professional expertise—the women who served as teachers. But the bureau's work represented the federal government's pioneer, if fleeting, venture into education at the state and local levels. And the societies' cooperation resulted in a unique combination of public and private effort previously unmatched in the nation's history of social welfare institutions.[45]

CHAPTER V

Schooling

In their attempt to transplant the northern common school to southern soil, the freedmen's workers assumed that the institution would serve the same function in Georgia as it did in New England. In the first place, they believed that all black people should learn basic literacy skills to prepare them for life and work in a democratic society. Secondly, they felt that the school should supplement the family in providing a broad education, consisting of the rudiments of citizenship training plus a distinctive brand of Victorian-Protestant "moral instruction." The long-range purpose of schooling, in this view, was the intellectual and moral growth of responsible individuals who recognized their duty to God, country, family, and self.

In Georgia, teachers and administrators struggled to duplicate as nearly as possible the northern classroom experience under the assumption that form and structure, as well as content, had intrinsic importance. If the school were to have the same salutary effects in the South that it had in New England, it would have to operate like a Yankee school and follow similar standards of physical configuration, grading procedures, curriculum, discipline, and pupil attendance. Likewise, the freedmen's school year would have to conform to the northern educational calendar, and parents would have to accept teachers as equals in the process of socializing their children. Elements of Yankee schooling were adopted in Georgia classrooms with varying degrees of success. But, if the teachers often felt discouraged, they rarely reexamined the central premises under which they labored. The wider significance of schooling became lost in a maze of everyday worries and details.[1]

The teachers and their sponsors adhered to a vision of an egalitarian society free of political discrimination and racial prejudice, and they were proud that they offered the same kind of instruction to southern blacks that white children received in the North. At the same time, freedmen's workers evinced a self-righteous moralism that rendered them exceedingly narrow-minded on matters of religion and personal behavior. Lewis Perry suggests, "Their goal was social order, and their rationale was the long understood duty of true converts to meddle and control." As paternalistic (and maternalistic) "culturalists," they sought to recast southern society in the image of New England, and their profound didacticism marked them as the standard-bearers of mid-nineteenth century evangelical Victorianism. In the words of one historian, the teachers were self-righteous because they belonged to "a culture that believed they knew God well."[2]

They had a clear notion of what and how pupils should be taught. For example, during the first few months of schooling the children should be introduced to (or strengthened in) habits of self-control and obedience that would both make the learning process smoother and provide lessons in character development. Pupils should learn to practice in the classroom those virtues that would serve them well in the larger world: honesty, politeness, temperance in speech, consideration for others, respect for authority. They should gain some understanding of the places and people around them so that they could have a better sense of their relation to other persons and the wider concepts of state and family. Above all, the children must learn to assume responsibility for their own behavior. One of the greatest evils of slavery was that it had forced individuals to relinquish this responsibility to another person.

Like most middle-class northerners of the time, the teachers assumed that a free man was the master of his own destiny. The strength of personal character and determination went a long way in explaining who was successful in life and who was not. "Success" was measured primarily not by the accumulation of material goods (though that was surely a component of it) but by the ability of a person to lead a productive and worthwhile existence. In early Victorian New England, work was at the "core of moral life," and the gospel of industry gained a certain amount of credibility within the context of an expanding northern economy. Not everyone could become rich and successful, but at least a few people did, and others took heart. Daniel T. Rodgers points out that keepers of the New England moral conscience faced a dilemma by the mid-nineteenth century, when the factory system began to challenge their assumption that each man owned his own labor and would benefit from it accordingly. In the South, a similar situation pertained among blacks; as dependent agricultural wage workers, they could exercise but little control over their own work situation. The teachers, of course, recognized this problem, but avoided confronting it directly by encouraging the freed people and their children to save money and cultivate other habits of self-discipline so that they might eventually buy their own land.[3]

Two major forces in the South blocked the educators' efforts to produce "ebony Puritans." The first was the freed people themselves, for their resistance to northern schooling (at least moral instruction) reflected both political and cultural considerations. The great sacrifices blacks made to establish schools for their own children soon after the war was a type of institution building that symbolized their spiritual independence from whites at long last. On a more fundamental level, black parents wanted their children to learn to read and write, but they would not and could not yield them up irrevocably to the northern teachers. Economic factors precluded the sustained school attendance that the Yankees insisted was so crucial to their plan of moral development. Moreover, the northern curriculum in general was based on values that were alien to the former slaves in Reconstruction Georgia. For example, the great stress placed on "punctuality" as measured by a timepiece had little meaning to a people whose work schedule had been and still was shaped by the movements of the sun. The second force, the combined weight of southern tradition and racial discrimination, meant that black people in Georgia would have precious few of those personal "opportunities" that formed the practical foundations of Victorian ideology. The teachers intended not to create these opportunities for blacks (which, in any case, would have necessitated a massive restructuring of southern economy and society), but to enable their pupils to advance by means of their own willpower. Few teachers ever came to grips with the realization that hard work and Protestant morality were not always rewarded, at least not on earth.[4]

Teachers in Georgia began to divide their classes into grades according to pupil advancement in the fall of 1865. In November of that year, the Savannah superintendent assigned children attending American Missionary Association (AMA) schools to one of two grades on the basis of their ability to read. The result was three "schools," two consisting of 120 pupils each who had just started classes, and one of 45 children who had advanced to the second reader. A separate teacher conducted music lessons and general exercises in each school. A night school for adults and industrial classes rounded out the Savannah school program.[5]

Gradually, each freedmen's school followed the Savannah lead, and, depending on its size and resources, systematized its classes according to a northern system of grading. In rural areas where no school had been established previously, all pupils were abecedarians and attended classes together. But, in the towns, pupils moved through several grades as they mastered the fundamentals of reading and writing. These grades (sometimes called "schools") included subprimary, primary, intermediate, lower grammar, and grammar (or "advanced"). Theoretically, they consumed eight years of schooling; pupils spent three years in the primary grades, two in the intermediate, and three in the grammar. (However, only a small number of children ever completed such an extensive program in Reconstruction Georgia.) Superintendents created combinations of these classes to meet the needs of their school populations. For example, in 1868 the Augusta system operated seven day "schools," including two primary, two combination primary and intermediate, two intermediate, and one grammar.[6]

Because few of the children who entered school immediately after the war had enjoyed formal education or would have an opportunity to prolong their schooling, the primary classes received the most attention. Children were first instructed in classroom decorum, basic concepts such as left and right, and the alphabet. After these preliminaries, they moved on to reading, writing, spelling, and arithmetic. Children sufficiently advanced in reading studied geography.

The experiences of two teachers illustrate this progression. On the first morning of school in October 1865, Esther Douglass found in her rural schoolroom "120 dirty, half naked, perfectly wild black children crowded on the floor," all from nearby plantations in Savannah's Ogeechee district. They had so much difficulty understanding her that she engaged the help of an elderly black woman in order to determine their full names. They readily gave their first names, but not until the "old aunty" said, "Chillun, tell de ladies your Pa title" (surname) did they respond to the teacher's full satisfaction. During the next few days, she taught the children that the ringing of her hand bell signified silence, and that they were to repeat after her as she read from alphabet cards on the wall. She noted that "their progress was wonderful," and by the following June reported that they had all learned to read words (some of five syllables) from the cards. They sang hymns, repeated Bible verses, and "had learned many things about right conduct which they tried to practice," she told her superiors in the North.[7]

During the 1865–66 school year, Mary K. Colburn had charge of a hundred primary pupils in Andrews Chapel, Savannah. Like Douglass, she devoted the first weeks of instruction to lessons on cleanliness and discipline. At first sight of "the array of untutored little ones, moving about so uneasily on their benches," she almost despaired, but soon managed to divide the group into smaller classes, or "recitations," according to their reading skills. The least advanced children began with the alphabet and went on to read in the *National Primer*, a standard New England textbook. The pupils who could already read a little concentrated on the *Pictorial Primer*, and received instruction in spelling and verse memorization. The quickest group mastered the *Sanders' Speller* as well as the *First National Reader* and advanced to the next book in the Sanders series. In addition to these three reading classes, Colburn and her assistants conducted a geography and an arithmetic class (Appendix G).[8]

Guided and encouraged by their administrative superiors, Douglass, Colburn, and their coworkers tried to employ pedagogical techniques based on the latest theories of child learning currently espoused in western Europe and New England. Initially, they believed these theories could be applied with equal degrees of effectiveness in all teaching situations, regardless of the pupils' race, class, or cultural background. In this sense, the teachers took south with them an enlightened, egalitarian system of pedagogy. But gradually some of them came to realize they had very definite ideas about the effects of a child's race and culture on the schooling process, and this realization forced them to confront their own prejudices toward black people in general and the Georgia pupils in particular.

The northern societies insisted that their teachers have some familiarity with current standards in teaching methods. The AMA considered a New England clergyman's evaluation of its Macon teachers the highest compliment when he wrote after a visit in the South: "Intelligent, refined, thoroughly capable, [they] teach with enthusiasm, and adopt the latest and best method of imparting instruction in vogue in the common schools of Boston and Worcester." (As in all AMA schools, a contract-renewal system allowed superintendents to weed out teachers "of the old school.") This glowing description, published in an 1868 issue of the *American Missionary*, represented an ideal attained by few freedmen's schools in Georgia (including, perhaps, those in Macon).[9]

Although not all teachers taught with the same degree of proficiency and self-confidence, they did share a basic educational philosophy that influenced their performance in the classroom. In terms of mid-nineteenth century educational standards, the teachers were adherents of the Swiss reformer, Johann Heinrich Pestalozzi, and considered themselves pedagogical "soft-liners" committed to "faculty psychology." For educators of this period, the theory of faculties provided a coherent, comprehensive approach to the learning process that had practical application in the areas of curriculum, discipline, and the construction and equipping of classrooms. Advocates of this relatively benevolent philosophy believed that each child possessed innate capacities called the intellectual, moral, and physical faculties. For example, the intellectual faculty enabled children to use their powers of perception, conception, discrimination, judgment, comparison, and memory. In very young children, the faculties lay hidden or undeveloped until the teacher cultivated them through discipline and exercise. Although the communication of information played an important part in this process, the good teacher sought to encourage each child to think for himself rather than to "pour" vast quantities of facts and figures into his head or demand that he memorize long passages. True learning took place when the teacher aroused a child's curiosity and interest and enabled him to pursue learning on his own.[10]

This educational philosophy had major implications for everyday classroom procedure. Obviously, the "modern" teacher tried to appeal to her pupils' best instincts, rather than rule them by fear, and conducted her class with a mild, but firm, hand. Assuming that the children appreciated a routine, she demanded punctuality in attendance, maintained a daily schedule of exercises, and insisted on quiet at all times except during recitations. Shunning any system of prizes, awards, and "emulation," she realized that each child would do his best if she performed her own duties well. The conscientious teacher chose spelling words from reading lessons rather than arbitrary lists so that her pupils could familiarize themselves with each word's meaning in context. She emphasized the study of geography, and used globes and maps to provoke the children's interest in distant lands by teaching them first about their own town and state. She applied principles of the new "object teaching" whenever possible so that each child could use his own powers of discovery —his five senses—to learn quickly and with pleasure.

For northern aid societies, this educational ideal was as relevant to freedmen's schools as it was to those in New England. In fact, many northerners in the work believed that the "degraded" condition of the black population as a whole made even more imperative the need for highly skilled, up-to-date teachers. One superintendent declared in 1867, "It is a mistaken idea that *almost any one* will do to teach these ignorant ones in the South. I would say send the *best* or none." A colleague agreed that each Georgia town needed "a good thorough efficient school taught in the New England style." The importance of freedmen's work admitted of no halfway measures, no shoddy techniques or old-fashioned teaching methods.[11]

Evidence of the emphasis accorded Pestalozzian educational theory within freedmen's schools comes from a variety of sources. The relatively large number of teachers who had recently received formal training in New England normal schools suggests that many of them had been introduced to these new ideas and concepts shortly before they embarked on their mission to the South. In handwritten letters and printed guidelines, northern officials and Georgia superintendents and principals provided teachers with specific objectives for the classroom, in which the women were exhorted to combine gentleness of demeanor with firm discipline. As a matter of policy, both the AMA and the American Freedmen's Union Commission (AFUC) forbade the use of physical punishment except in extreme cases, and both encouraged teachers to become familiar with modern pedagogy as discussed in handbooks such as "Teachers' Motions" by Horace Mann. Some mission homes even boasted extensive educational libraries on curriculum, object teaching, and methods for governing the classroom. Yet the proof of the success with which these ideas were put into practice comes not from orders handed down from New York, Boston, or Cincinnati, but from firsthand descriptions of everyday procedure provided by teachers, visitors, and the children themselves.[12]

Freedmen's teachers did their best to incorporate the tenets of faculty psychology under less than ideal conditions in the classroom. For example, almost all of them supplemented instruction in the fundamentals with lessons in geography, even at the primary level. This subject enjoyed widespread popularity in elementary schools during the nineteenth century. According to educational reformers, children were most interested in the things closest, or most familiar, to them. The teacher was to take advantage of this inherent curiosity and encourage them to think about the nature of their geographical region. Next, she could expand their interest to other parts of the United States and finally to foreign countries. Teachers of the freed people defined geography in its broadest sense, including elements of history, political science, botany, and anthropology. In addition, they turned geography lessons into other kinds of useful exercises. Texts provided interesting material for reading and spelling. The drawing of maps tested the children's skills and patience. The teachers' frequent requests for charts, globes, maps, and special textbooks indicate that geography was an important part of the curriculum.[13]

This technique of supplying the children with materials they could see or touch extended to other aspects of primary schooling also. Letter, word, and motto cards as well as phonics charts were used to teach children how to read. Pictures made even arithmetic easier to study. One teacher thanked her superior in the North for sending her new arithmetic books, and added, "the pictures in it are enough to make the scholars willing and anxious to study it." A coworker used block geometric figures to illustrate mathematical principles and relationships. Another teacher provided her pupils with a treat by introducing them to the stereopticon, on which were shown views of Niagara Falls and other famous scenes in the North. The blackboard was such an indispensable item that one woman appropriated a couple of pine boards from the ceiling of her school-room to serve that function.[14]

The teachers valued all types of visual aids because they considered the problem of getting and holding the children's attention a crucial one. The division of classes into recitations meant that as many as a hundred or so children needed to be kept busy and interested in their studies while a small group met for its own reading or arithmetic lessons. Julia Shearman observed of her Augusta class, "to rule 170 children with the stick, making them sit still with nothing to do for four or five hours, while I drudge through a recitation with a class of 20 is a style of teaching that will never suit me, though with our present system, it is the best that can be done." Teachers tried to occupy nonreciting pupils with exercises to be performed on individual slates and with lessons provided by the most advanced students, who served as teaching assistants (another method favored by pedagogical reformers).[15]

In letters to their superiors, the northern women justified their own work in particular and the efforts of their societies in general by congratulating themselves and their students loudly and often. They knew that the most dramatic stories of classroom success would not only find their way into their society's monthly journal, but would also serve to solidify their own place within the local educational bureaucracy. This is not to suggest that these reports and letters were entirely self-serving, or that the teachers had a cynical view of the standards by which they themselves were to be judged. But descriptions of the children's performances are so glowing, and so predictable in both style and content, that they are rendered highly suspect as true reflections of the educational process.

The following examples from four different teachers are typical: "The pupils do try, and work like beavers. . . . I see improvements in general ways, improved aptitude on so many points, ability to study even in the freshest material." "My pupils are making good progress in their studies and are improving very much in behavior and punctuality. They read quite well. . . . I have one class of 15 in geography that would compare favorably with the classes in our Northern schools. Their answers are prompt and correct and their lessons are thoroughly understood. The difficulties I meet with are those that teachers find everywhere." "In seven years of teaching at the North, I have not seen a parallel to their appetite for learning, and their active progress." "I never knew scholars—North or South—to make more progress than these have."[16]

A variety of other Reconstruction sources indicate that black children and adults embraced schooling enthusiastically after emancipation, and it can be assumed that those who attended classes with any degree of regularity acquired basic literacy skills quickly. But indirect evidence provided by the teachers themselves reveals that the women encountered many difficulties in teaching that left them bewildered and frustrated. When they wrote rosy accounts of their schools, they might have told the truth, but it was not the whole truth.

In at least a few cases, possibly the teachers themselves were surprised by their pupils' intellectual capabilities, and thus tended to exaggerate their progress in learning to read and write. Some teachers went south with preconceived notions about black people and their ability to learn, though of course they never revealed "their own strong prejudice on account of color" during the application process. The few who confessed to such feelings in letters to their superiors felt free to discuss them only after experiences in the South had changed their minds. In a letter to AMA headquarters, one teacher wrote approvingly of her Augusta pupils and then admitted, "once I would not have believed I could have been so content and *happy*, far away from friends and in a *colored school*," and added that she now realized black people were "human beings like ourselves the only difference being a *darker skin*." A school principal spoke in similar terms after a few months' work in Atlanta: "I had some feelings about *color*. I feared it would be unpleasant to teach colored people. But it is a *pleasure*. I love them as much as I ever did any pupils. They are as *smart* as any." And various other guilt-ridden teachers confessed to the same kinds of initial fears and biases.[17]

The problem went deeper than skin color, and it would be inaccurate to suggest that the teachers went south as racists and then underwent a change of heart when they saw how well their pupils learned. In fact, the case might have been nearly the reverse, given the teachers' frustrating experiences in trying to morally "reform" the black population en masse, both in and outside the classroom. Most of the women joined the work believing that they could teach their black pupils the same way they taught northern children— that the same assumptions about what a preschooler did and did not know, for example, applied in both cases. But, before long, they realized they were dealing with a new kind of pupil in the South. Unfortunately, it is difficult to state with any certainty where the teachers' racial prejudices left off and where their sensitivity to differences of class and culture began. Hailing from small rural towns in New England and the Midwest, most of them had previously instructed the sons and daughters of middle-class Yankee professionals and farmers. These were children raised in a culture that valued literacy, a society that presumed all youngsters would spend at least a couple of years in school to learn how to read and write and do simple exercises in arithmetic.

Black abecedarians, on the other hand, had no familiarity with certain concepts that most teachers took for granted when instructing elementary-school children. They did not understand the terms "country," "state," and "nation" (this made even simple geography lessons quite difficult for them), and often did not know their own age. Many of them had never seen artifacts of everyday middle-class life, including clocks, books, pens, paper, and newspapers. The women also observed that the children were unaccustomed to remaining still for long periods of time because they had no experience in sitting through long, quiet church services or silent Sunday afternoons at home. They were "untamed animals" or "frolicksome young zebras" who were unacquainted with "the restraints of the school-room." These were the "dirty, half naked, perfectly wild black children" Esther Douglass encountered on her first day of school, and the "untutored little ones, moving about so uneasily on their benches" who so unnerved Mary Colburn.[18]

Black pupils were not "just like" white pupils after all. Moreover, the teachers recognized that slavery had left its mark on the children and conditioned their responses to white authority figures. The pupils deeply feared physical punishment, and even at tender ages possessed a keen understanding of the "deference ritual" as a way of behaving in the presence of whites. For these reasons, the teachers were forced to abandon at least some of their notions about first graders' intellectual skills and group behavior. It was not that black children came to school with no cultural baggage at all; rather, their baggage differed from that of their white counterparts in the North, and it was part and parcel of the conditioning imposed upon them by the system of slavery. Some teachers became confused and frustrated when they realized that their assumptions about young children in general did not pertain to this new situation. Still, most persisted in their belief that a minimum amount of schooling could bring black children up to a basic level of literacy and middle-class morality.

Because few of the Georgia freed people knew how to read and write in 1865, the women found themselves teaching abecedarians of all ages, another kind of pupil they have never encountered before. It was not uncommon for teachers to have persons of forty to fifty years of age in their night classes. This fact of age—though obvious and predictable from the nature of night school—had a profound effect on the teachers who were younger than their pupils. A harmony between age and authority prevailed in the day schools; the teacher was an adult and the pupils were children. But, at night, the women had to temper their style out of consideration for the special needs of their elderly pupils. An Augusta teacher summed up the dilemma when she described her reaction upon instructing a "venerable old man" in reading: "I confess I felt some delicacy at correcting the old gentleman for the misplacing of a letter or two, or the disregard of the commas and periods. . . . I almost felt as if I were offering an insult to his grey hairs."[19]

The freedmen's teacher was unprepared to deal with the factors that made her new pupils different from the ones she had taught in the North—their race, poverty, slavery background, and ages. Her superiors urged her to rely on familiar classroom procedures even under these new conditions. And so she continued in her attempts to make the southern classroom experience conform to her expectations. In the process, she often seized on one crucial fact of southern teaching—the chronic shortage of adequate facilities, including school buildings and equipment—and cited physical discomfort and inconvenience as the source of all her difficulties and disappointments. She came to believe that, once the children were situated in large, well-constructed rooms complete with modern teaching aids, her enlightened approach would ultimately be appropriate and effective.

The teachers were correct in their conviction that inadequate or poor classroom facilities, rather than modern theories, often shaped pedagogy in the freedmen's schools. Between 1865 and 1873, northerners assigned to Georgia taught under a wide variety of physical conditions and used various kinds and amounts of equipment. By the late 1860s, instructors in Atlanta, Macon, and Savannah taught in schools similar in size and convenience to the best in Boston and New York. But the first teachers to arrive in the state right after the war had to make do with far less elaborate facilities, even in the largest towns. Savannah teachers initially experienced difficulty finding any suitable school buildings at all; before the opening of Beach Institute, they had to settle for accommodations in the Freedmen's Hospital, church basements, and the mission home. In Macon, the AMA early located its schools in four different black churches, and the teachers soon discovered the problems in using sanctuaries for classrooms. Although readily available and cheap to rent, they were often poorly heated and lighted and, of course, contained no blackboards or desks.[20]

The facilities in Atlanta initially included a Confederate commissary transplanted from Chattanooga, Tennessee, which suffered from such inadequate insulation that teachers often were forced to dismiss their classes early on cold winter days. The description of another Atlanta structure used for school purposes in 1865 would have chilled the heart of any northern teacher preparing to embark for the South: a "very insecure and open wooden building, belonging to the colored Methodists, which had been demolished by the Twentieth Army Corps in order to secure surrounding buildings against fire." The principal reported that during the winter of 1865–66 he rarely taught in the building, which accommodated about two hundred pupils, without wearing his overcoat. Teachers in other parts of the state located their schools in deserted mansions, cotton-gin buildings, and old slave "praise houses." Children in Camden County marked the passing of the old order by learning their lessons in a cotton house where slaves had been whipped, and Andersonville teachers held classes in abandoned hospital buildings where thousands of Union soldiers had died as prisoners during the war.[21]

According to the teachers' frequent letters on the subject, the poor insulation and lighting in these structures affected the children's ability to concentrate on their studies. One woman spoke for many of her coworkers when she complained of the wretched condition of her rural school (formerly a chicken house); the room had no windows, "but if the light will not come in through the cracks sufficiently to illuminate its darkness, the air will, sufficiently to ventilate it most thoroughly." In a climate where the temperature dropped below freezing during the winter, even along the coast, such structural deficiencies severely hampered the learning process, especially for children attired only in thin and tattered clothing. Rural teachers vented their frustration over spending eight hours a day in these schoolrooms by providing the graphic details for their superiors in long, angry letters. They wanted to devote their time to the children, but had to spend an inordinate amount of energy trying to make old buildings safe and comfortable.[22]

During the first few years after the war, teachers also contended with extremely large classes, especially in the cities. A shortage of buildings and teachers as well as the emigration of freed people to urban areas produced classes of up to two hundred children per teacher. "For one teacher to govern and instruct 150 scholars is no small task," wrote the Augusta superintendent to AMA headquarters in 1866. Small schoolrooms compounded the problem.[23]

Although rural classes rarely exceeded a hundred pupils, makeshift arrangements often meant cramped quarters for the smallest of schools. Esther Douglass described her classroom at the Wild Horn Plantation near Savannah as follows: "Our schools are held in the parlors of the 'great house.' My room is 16 × 17 feet; in this I have often *packed* ninety five pupils of various sizes; for lack of seats about a score stand *huddled* up in one quarter of the room." She noted that the crowding hindered her from teaching "the proprieties of the school room," and presented more "discipline problems" than she would have had under more favorable circumstances. One of her coworkers observed that her own pupils sat so close together that "as a natural consequence" they constantly pinched and hit one another. Few teachers of the Georgia freedmen experienced the luxury of teaching small classes, and rural and urban teachers alike endured the headaches of teaching too many children in rooms too small.[24]

The combination of teacher shortages, a limited number of classrooms, and high attendance rates necessitated double sessions and staggered scheduling in the larger towns. A common arrangement consisted of primary classes from 8:30 or 9:00 A.M. to noon, intermediate or advanced sessions from 2:00 to 5:00 P.M. and classes for adults from 7:00 to 9:00 in the evening. Although most teachers were accustomed to the day schedules of either one long or two shorter periods, the additional hours spent in night school made their workday long and tiring. Many routinely taught eight hours, six hours during the day and two at night. Moreover, teachers often reported that their actual class time often exceeded the limits set by formal schedules. Hearing the last of daily recitations and answering questions posed by curious, excited children at times kept them in the school long after the last bell had rung. This rigorous and fatiguing schedule prompted some of the women to rebel against additional responsibilities by arguing that their effectiveness in the classroom would be sacrificed as a result. Harried and overworked, they hardly conformed to the image of the demure and poised teacher who always had her class under control.

Because most of the Georgia teachers needed to adapt their style to drafty and crowded rooms, many children never enjoyed the advantage of learning environments espoused by the educational theorists who influenced the teachers' methods and objectives. The physical surroundings proved distracting, at least, and in the case of very small and ill-constructed school buildings, even injurious to the health of teachers and pupils alike. Under these conditions, few children received personalized instruction designed to meet their own interests and capabilities. Teachers who had large classes and no books resorted to drilling their students on nonsensical exercises out of sheer desperation. (Lacking any kind of texts, one woman spent her time teaching a large class of abecedarians to read any number up to one billion!)[25] Teachers whose nerves were already jangled found their patience wearing thin after long hours each day in the classroom. Because they were acutely sensitive to this relationship between classroom conditions and pedagogy, it is not surprising that their concern for adequate facilities served to obscure more fundamental problems related to the suitability of the curriculum for black pupils of all ages.

"I am not satisfied to labor merely for the advancement of my pupils in the knowledge of books," wrote one teacher. She and her coworkers considered "moral instruction" integral to their education effort. The twin goals of morality and literacy became inextricably entwined; indeed, the teachers would have been unable—and unwilling—to separate them during the normal course of the school day. Reading lessons consisted of short stories about good children who loved God and obeyed their parents. Geography exercises contrasted the energetic North with the lazy South, and songs were hymns to patriotism. A rigid emphasis on classroom decorum was intended to encourage respect for authority and personal self-control. Theoretically, this type of instruction was nonsectarian, though it was of course grounded in the tenets of the Christian religion, and more specifically Protestantism. Unaffiliated with any specific denomination, the AFUC nevertheless joined with the AMA in assuming that certain values were universal among all "moral" persons—that lying, stealing, and cheating (under any circumstances) were bad, and that piety, industry, thrift, and temperance were good (at all times).[26]

Moral education involved the eradication of certain vices learned under slavery, and the implanting of new habits, plus a moral conscience, in each child. According to the freedmen's teachers, their pupils reacted to whites primarily out of fear. They lied when it suited their purposes, evinced little interest in keeping their promises, stole when confronted with the least hint of temptation, and lacked any sense of their own self-worth. They had no concept of themselves as independent human beings whose individual destinies could be shaped by their own character and effort. The teachers wanted to instill in the children a conventional sense of right and wrong, and increase their self-control to a point where they could eventually boast of moderation in all personal habits except the love of honest toil. When these children grew up, they would be able to provide for themselves and their families, and in the process achieve the satisfaction that came with being a responsible American citizen. This was classic Victorian ideology, which emphasized achievement, motivation, repression, and planning for the future. The teachers believed that these cultural values would serve the freed people well in their transition from slavery to true freedom.

Ironically, black children and their parents found they could please their white teachers in ways similar to their behavior under slavery. If their actions conformed to the whites' demands, they were rewarded. In the classroom, children won the praise of their teachers fairly easily. The northerners attached great importance to personal behavior and hoped that outward signs provided evidence of inner growth. William L. Clark judged his pupils not "by the number of books they have studied, or the pages they have conned, or the copies they have written," but by their "clearer eyes and clearer faces and clearer utterance, and more erect bodies, and manly and womanly appearance." If the children refrained from misbehaving merely because they feared they would get caught if they acted otherwise, the teachers felt this was at least a step in the right direction. Predictably, they believed that their pupils showed great progress by conforming to certain classroom strictures. Obedience and orderly deportment revealed visible changes in moral character.[27]

The problems of punctuality and discipline preoccupied the teachers. The children should report to school promptly in the morning. They must maintain perfect silence when not reciting, and obey the teacher's commands quickly and cheerfully. Some women reported they had model schools in these terms. Often they expressed their success in military training-camp metaphors and cited the "rigid enforcement" of rules of "Punctuality, Politeness, Order, Neatness, and Cleanliness" and the "subjection" of the pupils to northern classroom standards. One woman formed her class into an Ivy Company, each child a soldier in the daily war against infractions of the "Rules of Order." An observer from the Augusta *National Republican* lavished praise on an AMA school when he remarked, "the perfect obedience of the pupils, reminds one of a Prussian regiment on drill, compared with the raw militia."[28]

The teachers' obsession with order stemmed at least in part from antebellum stereotypes that portrayed blacks as victims of an indolent (southern) way of life. The efforts to enforce bourgeois expectations in this area met with some unanticipated difficulties. Perceptive teachers admitted their demands for punctuality were unreasonable in light of the freed people's limited experience with daily schedules regulated by clocks. Indeed, few freedmen owned or needed timepieces. School bells proved useful, but northern principals and teachers frequently found themselves in the embarrassing situation of trying to enforce time standards when they themselves lacked watches and no clocks were available in either schoolrooms or mission homes. This was often the case during the first few months of work in a particular location. As late as 1867, Savannah schoolrooms were unequipped with clocks and the house had no bell; moreover, none of the teachers had watches. The problem was particularly acute in rural areas and small towns. One Andersonville teacher reported despairingly: "we are *so* troubled to 'collect our faces' in time: The colored people having no time pieces and no guide but the sun are often, yes *usually* behind time." The issue remained an important one for many teachers while they taught in the South. The item on teachers' monthly report forms "Number always present and always punctual" increased their sensitivity to this problem. In addition, the shortage of timepieces seriously impaired their ability to conduct recitations on time and otherwise follow a set daily routine.[29]

Although they often claimed the children were surprisingly "tractable," most teachers encountered problems in governing their pupils. They noted that youngsters attending school for the very first time required extra patience. Crowded classrooms always encouraged whispering, giggling, and pinching. Children forced to amuse themselves for hours at a time while their classmates recited naturally became restless. Teachers often observed special problems during the first few weeks in each term, when pupils gradually returned to school, new ones arrived for the first time, and the process of grading upset normal classroom routine. An Atlanta instructor reported that her pupils exhibited "mirthfulness and want of order"; once she initiated them into the rigors of classroom discipline (i.e., "got them into the harness"), "it was difficult to keep them there, and what made it more so, was having new recruits every morning." Her school, which had 70 pupils on the first day of classes, consisted of 200 by the end of the first week.[30]

Nineteenth-century common-school discipline often consisted of physical punishment, especially feruling, or hitting the palm of a pupil's hand with a ruler. However, antebellum educational reformers argued that the teacher should appeal to the child's natural love of order, rather than fear of discipline, in governing the school and that she should use the ruler or the rod as a last resort. The New England branch of the AFUC uttered stern pronouncements on the undesirability of corporal punishment in freedmen's schools. AMA principals in Georgia also spoke out against the practice. Several suggested that the freedmen had already experienced too many whippings for this type of corrective measure to have any value in the classroom. General Howard, head of the Freedmen's Bureau, summed up the prevalent opinion when he declared, "whipping may do for slaves, but freedmen should do right without it."[31]

Principals and superintendents set guidelines and established policies, but ultimately the discretion of the teachers played a large role in determining modes of discipline. In some instances, they used the rod in freedmen's schools. In addition, other methods were applied that they felt fit the nature of the offense. One teacher treated her young offenders one of two ways: she either made them sit on the floor until they were quiet, or filled their mouths with paper to keep them from whispering. For older boys, usually considered discipline problems in both the North and South, suspension or expulsion were used in the worst cases. After their ejection from AMA classes in Augusta, two sets of brothers enraged the local superintendent by seeking and gaining admittance to a rival school operated by the Baptist National Theological Institute. This incident highlighted the fact that, in the larger towns, students who felt they received unfair treatment in one school could simply attend another—assuming tuition rates were the same. This situation might have had some impact on mitigating the severity of punishment administered in freedmen's schools.[32]

For most principals, a teacher's ability to maintain order in her classroom served as a gauge of overall teaching performance. This fact helps to account for most principals' dislike for older teachers, whom they considered too fragile to conduct a class firmly. By visiting individual classrooms on a regular basis, the administrators evaluated their staffs, and recommended to their superiors in the North whether or not teachers should be allowed to return the next year. A superior teacher was usually described in terms like these:

"a thorough disciplinarian," "governs her school well," or "succeeds in maintaining discipline and securing the respect of the school." Failure to enforce certain accepted standards of classroom decorum resulted in a principal's overruling a teacher and taking over her class or even discharging her. This type of intervention occurred rarely, but it indicated the importance attached to "governing" the classroom effectively. Discipline was a regular part of the freedmen's schools' "curriculum"; it provided general lessons in citizenship and self-control.[33]

Traditional schoolbooks reinforced the teachers' attempts to impress upon the freedmen the Yankee virtues of industry, thrift, temperance, patriotism, and piety. From *McGuffey's Reader* to *Webster's Dictionary* and the Davis *Primary Arithmetic*, black children in Georgia learned the three Rs from northern textbooks (Appendix G). Considered as a whole, these volumes presented an ethnocentric view of the world, in which New England was portrayed as the center of evangelical religion, local democracy, and social and political reform. Apparently only one text used by Georgia teachers, Lydia Maria Child's *The Freedmen's Book*, was specifically written for southern blacks. Long active in the antislavery movement, she sought to provide a special type of reader that would be more meaningful to the freedmen than old-style Yankee textbooks. It contained biographical sketches of heroes of black liberation that were meant to inspire pride and self-determination in the children. However, the book received only limited use in a few advanced classes in postwar Georgia. Certainly financial considerations played a role in the freedmen's aid societies' decisions not to take advantage of specialized texts, for they often relied on donations of traditional works from publishing houses and individuals. Still, most teachers and administrators felt the old books would do, that their lessons were suitable to the needs of the freed people.[34]

As a means of supplementing textbook materials, the teachers emphasized informal classroom discussions with their pupils. These talks often centered on political or moral comparisons between northern and southern society. In this respect, southerners' fears that the northern teachers "taught [the children] things not found in books" were certainly justified. Textbooks used in freedmen's schools extolled New England culture and deprecated the "aristocratic" pretensions of the South, but the teachers went further and instructed their classes on Union righteousness and rebel wickedness. The nonsectarian "moral instruction" offered in all schools made explicit the political and cultural assumptions inherent in the freedmen's aid societies' educational work.[35]

Teachers took pains to provide these lessons not only because they considered them of inherent value to the children, but also because frequent visitors to the schools enjoyed quizzing the youngsters on their understanding of the war and their own personal aspirations. Women who taught in the larger towns, especially, became used to performing in front of visitors. Potential financial contributors, representatives of various northern groups (not necessarily the sponsor of the school), and Freedmen's Bureau officials were among the honored guests. The children's ability to impress them might materially contribute to the success of the entire operation.

Thus, the Atlanta AMA community rejoiced over the performance of young Richard Wright in 1868 before a group of visitors from the North, including General Howard. After addressing Wright's class on the importance of education, the general inquired of the pupils what he should tell his friends about the Georgia freedmen when he returned to New England. Replied the youth, "Tell them we are rising!" This scene received wide coverage in AMA literature, and the Atlanta school gained national prominence as a result of it. John Greenleaf Whittier commemorated the event in a poem entitled "Howard at Atlanta," which the AMA gladly used in its fund-raising efforts.[36]

Teachers also planned and prepared for end-of-term exhibitions with an eye toward the expectations and standards of visitors. Conducted during Christmastime and again in May, these closing exercises served both evaluative and social functions. Although children did not receive a grade for their performance, exhibitions provided parents, principals, and dignitaries from both the North and South with an indication of the accomplishments of each class. Schools often broke the antiemulation tenet of the new psychology by awarding prizes in the form of books or medals to outstanding pupils. At least one teacher, however, adhered to the modern doctrine that her pupils "should be 'influenced by higher motives than recompense or reward,'" and kept her class out of a May 1871 school exhibition in Savannah.[37]

Open and free to the public, exhibitions often drew large crowds of parents, local officeholders (black and white), and curiosity-seekers, especially in favorable weather. The spring event represented the culmination of a year's work and was usually preceded by at least four weeks of frantic activity by faculty and students. Teachers drilled the children on individual and group recitations, practiced songs, and lectured them on the critical need to show other whites that blacks were capable of performing well. The school superintendent agonized over the order of exercises and tried to figure out ways to get up to four hundred children in and out of the lecture room in an orderly fashion The end of the program, which sometimes consumed six hours, brought sighs of relief from everyone—observers and participants alike. Parents' praises, self-congratulation on the part of the northern freedmen's aid society community, and favorable press reviews from the few friendly white newspapers in Georgia climaxed the school year.

In a limited sense, the exhibitions provided an opportunity for outside observers to judge for themselves reports on the pupils' educational progress. The northern teachers believed that these end-of-the-year affairs offered dramatic proof of what they had maintained all along—that the children showed a great eagerness to learn, moved rapidly through the fundamentals (even under adverse physical conditions), and possessed intellectual abilities equal to white children. In essence, they had used northern pedagogy and curriculum with the intention of disproving the white critic from Savannah who predicted, "those children learn only like parrots. The teachers will soon come to the bottom of their brains." But, in most cases, the teachers themselves had little idea whether the children had actually improved their intellectual abilities, for the exhibitions featured recitations based on rote memorization, and performance style was just as, if not more, important than content. The exhibition, then, was unreliable as a measure of success of freedmen's schooling, though the teachers hailed it as such.[38]

In their efforts to duplicate northern schooling conditions in the South, freedmen's aid societies followed a standard New England school year consisting of three terms: fall, winter, and spring. The schools observed traditional holidays and also suspended classes so the children could participate in community-wide celebrations marking the anniversaries of Lincoln's Birthday, Emancipation Day, and the ratification of the Fifteenth Amendment. Because the societies offered teaching commissions on an eight-month basis (October through May), they did not include summer school in their regular educational program. Northern officials stressed that teachers were to return home during the hot months for health reasons. Other justifications for closing down operations during the summer included the societies' inability to finance three extra months of schooling, the need to reorganize after each year, and the fear that the children would lose much of their interest in school if it were offered on a twelve-month basis.

In any case, it is doubtful whether many of the teachers would have agreed to stay in the South year-round, without any chance to escape the oppressive summer heat and visit with friends at home. Yet some did prefer to remain after May and conduct classes for at least part of the time. A few expressed reluctance to discontinue classes for a group doing exceptionally well in their studies. Others, who had arrived in Georgia late in the school year, felt they could not cover the material they planned unless they held classes past the normal closing date. A few were more candid in offering reasons why they wished to stay behind while their coworkers departed for a cooler climate. Teachers who dreaded and loathed the sea voyage home preferred to stay in the South rather than endure two passages within three or four months. And, for some, life in the South held more attractions than a summer spent with friends or relatives in the North.[39]

Northern administrators judged each request separately before allowing a teacher to hold classes over the summer months. Even though formal policy discouraged the arrangement on a wide scale, officials could cite compelling reasons to permit summer sessions on a limited basis. They believed it was desirable to have at least a couple of teachers remain in the larger towns in order to continue northern operations, even if on an informal level. This avoided the necessity of closing the schools and mission home completely and entrusting their care to a nonsociety member, white or black. Too, teachers could also help prevent the founding of rival schools that might attract children away from their own classes in the fall. In Savannah, the ever-watchful superintendent, E. A. Cooley, warned his superiors in the spring of 1866 that "The Catholics are starting a school among the Colored People. . . . I am not at all fearful of this doing much while our schools are in session but they will have the field too much to themselves when we go north on our vacation and we may find them too well rooted when we return next October." With characteristic missionary optimism, he could only hope that "we shall find truth mighty enough to prevail even if Error does have the territory to herself for three months." In order to keep the northern presence alive, society officials sometimes permitted teachers to conduct summer schools separate from their regular school-year work.[40]

While attempting to maintain a five-day week, eight-month annual schedule, the teachers encountered many disruptions that affected the schooling process at all grade levels. They had coped with some of these problems in the North. For example, bad weather, including rainstorms and very low temperatures, often resulted in the temporary closing of school. Illness sometimes kept a teacher herself at home. But the women had to contend with far more serious threats to an uninterrupted school year in Georgia than they did in New England. Lower tuition rates and competition offered by independent schools, southern white hostility, the contract work year, epidemics, and labor demands on the children meant that most pupils received schooling on a sporadic basis at best. Few enjoyed continuous classes with the same teachers during the school year.

Freedmen's education was a competitive enterprise because a number of northern groups and black and white teachers all tried to attract the same students, especially in the larger population centers. As a general rule, white teachers were at a disadvantage in areas where blacks operated schools. In Savannah, especially, an antiwhite feeling was always visible and manifested itself in several independent operations. White teachers in that city constantly bemoaned the fact that attendance in their own classes fluctuated according to the rise and fall in fortunes of the black-run schools. Furthermore, rival northern-sponsored schools could attract freed people disillusioned with certain policies; for example, tuition increases often resulted in wholesale defections from one school to another.

In some parts of the state, teachers discovered that any tuition charges often prevented children from attending school at all. In an era when most blacks just barely managed to eke out a living, schooling was a luxury. Laura Parmelee recounted an incident from her own education in the realities of postwar life when she wrote from Andersonville in January 1872: "Loss of wages and sickness among the stock are the reasons for boys and girls leaving school. When some of them told me they must stop coming 'because the cholera had killed fathers' hogs' I smiled forgetting that bacon was the staff of life in this country." Thus the state of the local economy directly influenced school attendance; a ruined crop, poor harvest, epidemic among farm animals, or drop in the price of cotton were all factors that influenced the continuity of local education efforts. After 1868 most schools charged tuition, and the normal rate of one dollar a month per pupil loomed large in a family budget when the household head was lucky to break even at the end of the year.[41]

Some teachers found themselves in empty classrooms because their pupils were afraid to come to school. This problem was most acute in rural areas around election time. One woman accounted for a suspension of her Bainbridge classes in December 1870 by reporting, "It was thought unsafe to teach during the three day election." In Athens, white hostility toward another northern white teacher threatened to drive her out of her small school in 1868. She noted that if Grant failed to win the presidential election she would "very likely have to *clear out*." Intimidation had resulted in low attendance at her school and she counted on continued Union troop occupation to keep classes in session. A more general, year-round problem was the white harassment of black children on their way to school.[42]

Teachers attempting to operate their Georgia schools on a three-term schedule encountered another unanticipated difficulty in the form of Freedmen's Bureau labor-contract policies. Initiated in 1866, the system dictated that blacks should contract with their employers each year on January 1. As a result, a massive shifting of the black population took place annually in December, when freed people moved in search of better employment opportunities—a movement that affected life in the cities as well as rural areas. The Christmas celebration, the longest and most joyful of holidays for blacks each year, added to the general disruption of school activities. Because preparations for the festivities began in mid-December and because many freedmen were not settled in their new jobs until the middle or end of January, teachers raised their voices in an annual chorus lamenting that the one-week end-of-term vacation (from December 25 until January 1) in reality amounted to a four- to six-week suspension of classes. More than one instructor noted that payday (December 31) created opportunities for diversion more attractive than schooling to adults and children for weeks to come. Moreover, in January teachers usually had to adjust to entirely new classes, often either much smaller or larger than their first-term groups. An employer's labor practices—the wages he offered, his fairness in dealing with his workers—all affected the nature and size of local school-aged populations.[43]

These drastic rates of pupil turnover severely limited the effectiveness of teachers trying to provide an uninterrupted year of instruction on the northern plan. Laura Parmelee, who never reconciled herself to the end-of-the-year dislocation during her five years of work in Andersonville, expressed her frustration over this uniquely southern problem: "The shifting of the people from place to place makes wretched work with *classes* and *reports*. Our hardest and most *discouraging* work comes from this constant disorganization of our school," she wrote in December 1869. She knew it curtailed her overall effectiveness. Of the 112 pupils then enrolled in school, only 20 had attended classes on a relatively continuous basis since 1868 (when the school was opened), and one-third had never gone to any school before. "You see how little chance we have to attain a high scholarship," she wrote to the AMA field secretary.

That official's constant concern with up-to-date and accurate statistical records of school attendance only served to intensify her anxiety over the matter.[44]

The basic problem was that the northern school year in Georgia failed to correspond with the work year. Great population movements marked the end of each calendar year, and the summer months (when the teachers returned north) were less busy for the very young children of agricultural workers. A native white teacher sponsored by the AMA pointed out the contradiction in a letter to a freedmen's aid society official in September 1870. She conducted classes during the summer months and found that the highest attendance rates came in July and August. In September, enrollments dropped because "every thing here must comply with the demands of King Cotton" during that month. It is difficult to say whether the agricultural cycle and labor-contract negotiations or the teachers leaving during the summer months produced more of a disruptive influence on schooling.[45]

The teachers realized that serious personal problems for which the children could not be held accountable resulted in a majority of the absences from school. The major reasons for individual absenteeism were illness, lack of warm clothing, and work. (Indeed, absence was the norm, attendance the exception.) The high incidence of sickness among refugees after the war plagued schools all over Georgia. Epidemics of measles, smallpox, malaria, and scarlet fever kept many children out of school. Teachers excluded from classes any youngster who came from a family where one member was contaminated. In rural districts, where schoolhouses were poorly insulated, they preferred that the children remain at home rather than sit in drafty rooms wearing ragged clothing. But the problem occurred in cities too. One teacher wrote of her Atlanta class in January 1866: "Many [pupils] have been sick and others have not clothing to make them comfortable[;] many come without shoes or bonnets and of course cold and wet days they cannot come." A large number of children went barefoot to school year-round, even in freezing temperatures. For these reasons, the northern women considered their attempts to provide pupils with warm clothing a vital part of their teaching responsibilities.[46]

The most frequently cited cause of individual and group absenteeism was the parents' need for their children's labor. Schooling necessarily took second place to work during particularly busy seasons and when older family members became ill and the children were needed to replace them. Black children in Georgia worked in a number of different capacities; besides the common task of watching younger brothers and sisters while their parents labored in the fields, they planted cotton, corn, and rice; kept birds from eating the seedlings; hoed weeds; and helped harvest the crops. Even very young children could be used all these ways. One black instructor noted that spring sowing along the seacoast required the labor of every child who was able "and those that are not have to stay home to take care of the babes while the others are laboring all day in planting rice and other grains." According to another teacher, all children "large enough to take a three or five mile walk in the field" were considered old enough to work on plantations.[47]

Urban employment was less seasonal, but no less disruptive of the schooling process. Parents in the cities often withdrew their children from school so that they could help with a trade or the operation of the household. One Savannah teacher described the composition of her class this way: "I have Cooks, Washers, and Ironers, Cigar Makers, cotton pickers, Nurses, Milk carriers, toters of water," and also, as if they constituted a separate group, "playful girls and boys." She reported that her working pupils often fell asleep in class.[48]

These frequent interruptions in the school year revealed the fundamental conflict between schooling and economic advancement during the lean years of Reconstruction. Although teachers claimed that formal education would enable the freed people to improve their economic status, they failed to realize that sustained school attendance could actually hinder a family's efforts to survive on a week-to-week basis. Families who advanced above the poverty line (and these were few) could usually do so only by sacrificing their children's education. One teacher observed that destitution was widespread in the town of Athens but that about fifty black families in the area had managed to acquire homes in the five years since the war's end. She added, "doing this has been quite a serious effort on the part of many so that they have felt obliged to withdraw their children from school and place them at service." Another instructor revealed the irony of the situation in Frederica in September 1869 when she predicted exceptionally good attendance for the first term in her school. Caterpillars had destroyed the region's entire cotton crop "so they [the children] have no work to keep them from school." Of course, this natural disaster meant severe economic hardship for the area's black population.[49]

Although the teachers entertained little hope of changing southern society in a fundamental way, it is clear that, at least in a limited sense, the freedmen's aid society schools served to symbolize the dream that some day all Americans would live in a more humane and just society. This hope was dramatized in both private and public situations. For example, on a personal level, ties of affection grew between teachers happy in and committed to their work and children eager to learn. The white women seemed to be the primary beneficiaries of any emotional satisfaction derived from the classroom experience, but the children apparently responded to the most sensitive teachers with warmth and appreciation. It is only possible to speculate whether these brief contacts had any lifelong impact on the pupils. "I am strongly attached to my pupils and they to me," wrote one teacher in the spring of 1866, but her words provide no clue as to the larger significance of these "attachments."[50]

Some children tried to cope with the high turnover rate among the women who came south by writing letters to society headquarters requesting the return of popular instructors. "We are a band of Scollars decidedly attached to our dear teachers," began one letter. Other classes formulated petitions asking teachers to remain in the South: "We have been with you so long and now if you go off you'll leave we's to we *dry* selves." Correspondence helped to sustain these relationships and keep teachers vacationing in the North informed about the children's summertime activities and their eagerness to start school in the fall. One pupil concluded his July letter to a teacher with the words, "I had no idea that I should miss you so much as I have. I should be happy if I could see you once more sitting at your table." One little girl had her father, Floyd Snelson (he also attended school), write a letter to their teacher, who had resigned to get married: "Nancy says please send her some of the pieces of your wedding [gown] and other garments." This note also contained news of the pupil's family, including the sad report that Snelson had broken his temperance pledge not to consume whiskey "on account of having the disease that required such a remedy."[51]

Over and beyond the affection growing out of the normal teacher-pupil relationship, the children and northern women at times shared feelings of closeness unique in the history of American schooling. It is true that the southern classroom retained an authoritarian atmosphere because of the use of northern-style pedagogy; the teachers' role left little doubt about who was in charge of the class. In spite of the Pestalozzian emphasis on appealing to the child's imagination and letting him develop according to his interests and capabilities, strict scheduling, large classes, and a constant concern for punctuality and order helped to eliminate flexibility and the element of personal freedom from the classroom. And yet the wider political situation encouraged the growth of close bonds between teachers and pupils, for the intrusion of southern white hostility into the school fostered a special feeling of urgency, or even solidarity, between them. The building itself sometimes served as a reminder of the immediacy of the slave past. Some Georgia children learned their ABC's in Savannah's Old Bryan Slave Mart, and others studied in sheds where slaves had been whipped not too long before.

On at least two occasions, AMA classrooms became scenes of interracial violence provoked by native whites. Both confrontations involved black youths who, pursued by white assailants, sought refuge in the school, and before the horror-stricken children and teachers were forced to engage in either a fistfight or gun battle. In June 1868 Floyd Snelson (who later became an AMA missionary in Georgia) wrote a letter to the AMA field secretary requesting that the two Andersonville teachers who had just left for the North be sent back the following September. He explained, "get them if you please to come back again; we know that you all is the only friend we have save god."[52]

But in only one learning environment did the northern teachers enjoy the opportunity to get to know their students well and oversee their personal and intellectual progress on a regular basis. This was at the advanced level, and more specifically at schools where young people boarded during the academic year. These institutions of higher learning accommodated few Georgia blacks (probably fewer than five hundred in any one year in the decade after the war), but they served as the most efficient means of instructing the freed people in Yankee values and habits. Boarders were under constant supervision from teachers, who established strict guidelines in every area of personal life—from prohibitions on drinking and smoking to dress codes and chapel attendance. At the same time, the schools provided a unique opportunity for close personal contact between blacks and whites.[53]

Established by the AMA, Atlanta University was perceived as the crowning achievement of freedmen's work in Georgia. Although idealistic northern teachers often dubbed an intermediate school a "university" in the hope that it would become one some day, Atlanta University just about lived up to its name. As one faculty member pointed out during the first few years of its existence, it offered courses of study inferior to those at good New England colleges but superior to western or southern schools at the same level. Under the leadership of Edmund Asa Ware, founder and first president, the school had a classical curriculum, including courses in Greek, Latin, history, geometry, algebra, natural philosophy, and forensics.[54]

The student boarders did contribute to the maintenance and operation of the physical complex, but Atlanta bore no resemblance to an industrial school. It prepared young black men and women to become teachers and clergymen, not manual laborers. Indeed, the faculty of the school, though rugged in its own way, consisted primarily of experienced female teachers and ministers trained in New England; they hardly qualified as instructors in the industrial arts. Regardless of the "practicality" of educating young black people for professional careers in a society that severely limited their opportunities, the AMA sought to provide its university students with the same type of formal education offered to whites in northern schools. Although enrollments rarely exceeded fifty students per year during Reconstruction, the school demonstrated the association's commitment to provide future black leaders with a rigorous Yankee-style higher education.

The high point of the institution's early history came in June 1871 when a committee of white southerners, headed by former Confederate Governor Joseph E. Brown, examined the students and showered them as well as the faculty with accolades. This incident received a good deal of press coverage, both in the North and in Georgia. The *American Missionary* carried several articles on the episode in the summer of 1871, and the Atlanta *New Era*, Atlanta *Constitution*, and Augusta *Georgia Republican* all covered the story. The review board, appointed by Reconstruction Governor Rufus Bullock, visited the school because it held the status of a public institution (it received a small amount of public financial support each year). The final report, released after three days of examinations, discussions with faculty members and students, and inspection of the school plant, gave unqualified support to the teachers, curriculum, and school organization.[55]

The ultimate source of the AMA's "great joy and victory" lay in the difficulty of the exercises performed proficiently by the normal and preparatory students. Members of the board could scarcely conceal their amazement as the young men and women confidently recited passages from Caesar, Virgil, and the *Anabasis* of Xenophon; answered questions in geometry and algebra; and engaged in rhetorical exercises. In their report, the southerners admitted that a majority of their group had "heretofore entertained that the members of the African race [were] not capable of a high grade of intellectual culture," but that afterwards all agreed that the students' academic achievements would "do credit to members of any race." The board recommended that the state continue its support of the school. (The fact that it did until 1888 indicates that the curriculum did not pose an immediate threat to the system of race relations that prevailed in postwar Georgia.) The AMA considered the students' performance a tremendous educational accomplishment and a confirmation of its fondest hopes for the system of black education. The students, neatly and modestly attired, had recited in a variety of difficult subjects with no trace of the "peculiar 'lingo' for which the Southern African is noted." Six short years after the Civil War, these young people, from fourteen to eighteen years of age, stood before a group of astonished former Confederates and demonstrated the effects of their Yankee schooling.[56]

Classical studies represented only one part of the education offered by the AMA at the higher level. In boarding schools, the behavior of the young men and women had to conform to the strict standards imposed by the northern missionaries; for the time being, at least (i.e., while the students attended classes), "moral instruction" was a successful element of the curriculum. Thus AMA higher education in Georgia represented the culmination of the larger purposes of the freedman's societies as they applied to personal character reform. But this type of schooling significantly affected the growth of the state's black community as well. From a nineteenth-century northern viewpoint, Atlanta University provided appropriate instruction for its students; the clergymen and schoolteachers who received an education there were eminently qualified for professional service on behalf of their own people. Like other comparable institutions established throughout the south during this period, Atlanta contributed substantially to the emergence of an educated black leadership class in the late nineteenth century. The northern societies partially filled a huge educational vacuum that otherwise would have remained empty, for the freed people lacked the resources and the white Southerners lacked the will to establish such schools of higher learning.[57]

The Yankee program of freedmen's higher education sparked a heated debate among historians. Carter G. Woodson was one of the first scholars to suggest the shortcomings inherent in this type of curriculum for southern black students. In his book *The Mis-Education of the Negro*, published in 1933, Woodson affirmed the "sincerity" of whites who established, paid for, and taught in black schools; their goal was, he wrote, "to make the Negro conform quickly to the standard of the whites and thus remove the pretext for the barriers between the races." But, in the process, he argued, white teachers denigrated Afro-American culture, stripped black students of their "race consciousness," and left them in psychological and social limbo—estranged from their own people, ashamed of their heritage, and yet barred from full and equal participation in American life.[58]

Since the time Woodson offered this perceptive critique, other historians have tended to emphasize one side of the issue or the other—either the teachers' racial egalitarianism (their "sincerity") or their convictions of white cultural superiority. Considered separately, both points are accurate but insufficient to explain the historical significance of freedmen's education. Taken together, they offer insight into the tragic implications of Yankee "benevolence."[59]

In evaluating the northern educational effort, it is important to distinguish the very limited, specialized program of higher education from mass common schooling. Overall, the northern teachers had only a marginal impact on the Georgia freed people. They reached but a tiny minority of the state's population each year; most blacks remained isolated in rural areas far from schools of any kind. Those children who did manage to attend classes did so on an irregular basis, and classroom conditions were often not conducive to learning. Still, despite the hearty self-congratulation and praise on the part of the teachers, they clearly did provide the rudiments of an elementary education to the pupils they reached for any length of time. In the cities—where attendance rates were high (perhaps as much as 50 percent of the school-aged population in Atlanta and Savannah), less susceptible to the vicissitudes of the seasonal planting cycle, and more stable from year to year—the teachers achieved more with greater numbers of children. A slight drop in the overall black illiteracy rate from 1860 to 1870 suggests that schooling provided by native black and white northern teachers did have some tangible effect (Appendix I).

However, the goals of black "uplift"and "elevation" proved to be elusive for the teachers. Freed people in postwar Georgia were unfamiliar with the concepts that were central to the northerners' style and purpose of teaching. The slave community had encouraged self-help and solidarity; its members thought in terms of day-to-day survival, not progress along a vague continuum to "success," defined in terms of money and moral behavior. They derived feelings of pride and self-respect from their religion and relationships with kinfolk and friends, not from the work they performed for the benefit of a white owner. Hope for the future was expressed in religious imagery, the winning of freedom through salvation and the liberation of the soul; material rewards had no place in their hierarchy of social values. Furthermore, the moral imperatives of an industrializing society had little relevance to the lives of most blacks—even after the war. The vast majority of freed people in Georgia had been, were, and were destined to remain unskilled agricultural laborers. The irony inherent in the teachers' attempts to instill the Protestant work ethic in persons who had literally slaved their whole lives for other people is self-evident today, though it was not to the teachers in 1865.

Their preoccupation with order and obedience in the classroom put a premium on conformity, passivity, and deference to whites in authority. And yet the intentions of the instructors were not reactionary in a political sense. Most had to deal single-handedly with large numbers of pupils for several hours a day, and they enforced strict disciplinary procedures in an effort to prevent the whole situation from getting out of hand. Given the limits of contemporary pedagogical theory and the inadequacy of school facilities, it was impossible to offer instruction in a room where children got out of their seats, walked around, and talked to each other at will. So "order" was definitely a practical consideration.[60]

Still, black people learned these same kinds of lessons (to follow commands issued by whites) under slavery. On the surface, it would appear that the teachers merely tried to instill in their pupils habits of hard work, punctuality, and sobriety that would make them tractable workers for their employers. But the actual effects produced by schooling admit of no easy generalizations. The Yankee teachers (unlike their native white counterparts who taught in the public schools after Reconstruction) believed strongly that black people should vote and aspire to owning their own land (i.e., they should become truly independent citizens). Again, whether these exhortations had any long range impact is doubtful, but the teachers were clearly not dupes of the planter aristocracy.

Although they remained committed to the common school as a force for social change, few teachers who stayed in the work for more than a couple of years deluded themselves about the overall good they were accomplishing. As if they did not have enough problems in the classroom, at the end of the day they had to watch their pupils leave and return to what the women considered to be unhealthy and demoralizing living situations. Schools could never fulfill their intended purpose as long as parents and friends continued to exert "dangerous influences" over the children when they went home. Consequently, the teachers made an effort to extend the classroom outside the walls of the school and into the home and church to reach all members of the local black community.

CHAPTER VI

"To Teach Them How to Live"

"What a strange study these people are! Ever pleasing, disappointing, and puzzling us—Strange inconsistencies!" So wrote an American Missionary Association (AMA) teacher soon after she arrived in Savannah. In their personal behavior and religious beliefs, the Georgia freed people often baffled their northern benefactors. But the "inconsistencies" to which the teacher alluded stemmed as much from the reformers' own contradictory assumptions about the "nature" of blacks and the effects of slavery on them as from the actions of the former slaves themselves. The teachers walked a philosophical tightrope between their belief in liberty and restraint, individual responsibility and environmentalism, racialism and a "universal" human nature, the innate depravity of man and his potential for perfection. The web of charity and self-help programs devised by the teachers to aid southern black people represented the institutionalization of antebellum abolitionist ideology; because that ideology was a by-product of middle-class northern culture, it provided the teachers with only an incomplete understanding of the people they sought to help.[1]

According to the freedmen's aid societies, slavery had been an evil institution of "unspeakable corruption" that crushed its victims with the arbitrary physical force of the master. Now that the slave system was gone, the freed people were in a "plastic" or "elastic" state, and the teachers merely had to "mould them aright." If there was one primary idea that guided these social welfare efforts, it was the need to instill in blacks the virtue of self-control. The discipline to resist the ever-present temptations of sexual promiscuity, intemperance, and other forms of personal dissipation should come from within, not from an external source like the slave master. The conscience was the only reliable guide for moral behavior. Northern teachers wanted to assist the black person in increasing his or her own moral sense, which had long lain dormant under slavery; they would "sow the seeds" of righteous living that would bear "fruit" in the near future. As one teacher expressed it, "My great desire is to do them the most real good not to please and warm them for a day, but to sow seed for a good harvest." The teachers looked forward to the time when their own work in the South would be finished. Immediate relief measures were necessary because people who were cold, hungry, or ill often lacked the physical and emotional resources to lead a moral life. And self-help associations like temperance societies would serve as temporary props only to bolster the people as, childlike, they took their first steps as independent beings.[2]

Slavery had fostered a great deal of carelessness and immorality among its victims, but the blacks were not fully responsible for their own sinfulness, according to these neoabolitionists. Of the people's tendency to come late to meetings, one Augusta instructor exclaimed, "What can they know of the value of time whose time belonged to another? What wonder that when so much was *extorted* they kept back all strength and service possible?" Yet these reformers tempered their belief in environmental conditioning with a conviction that, whatever one's disadvantages in life, each person must ultimately assume responsibility for his or her own behavior. After their release from bondage, blacks could be provided with moral guidance and become as chaste, thrifty, pious, and honest as the most rugged Yankee yeoman.[3]

The teachers remained somewhat ambivalent about the nature of the black "character." Although rarely articulating this view, they apparently held that black people, though "equal" to whites in the sight of God and in their capacity for moral growth, were inherently different in their racial characteristics. The Georgia freedmen's workers believed that, beneath the surface characteristics produced by slavery, lay certain innate qualities peculiar to the black race. These included religious devotion, patience in the midst of suffering, emotionalism, and a fondness for music. The teachers expected blacks to retain these stereotypical characteristics, moods, and habits despite the educational process. As James M. McPherson and Ronald G. Walters have suggested, this component of abolitionist ideology is best described as racialism (rather than racism), though it often manifested itself in an arrogance that was akin to racial prejudice.[4]

It was in the area of religion that the teachers' contradictory perceptions of blacks stood out most dramatically. They were continually astounded by the ability of the former slaves to retain a steadfast religious faith in the midst of physical hardship. And yet the teachers were disgusted by the freed people's collective expression of that faith, and by the black preachers who helped to sustain it. The Congregationalist AMA teachers were accustomed to quiet, staid worship services conducted by well-educated ministers who considered the graceful explication of a Biblical text more important than heightened religious passions. Black "shouts" offended (and perhaps even threatened) whites primarily because the element of personal restraint was missing in them; the blacks were "fiery glad" in their religion, and their rituals testified to a spiritual release that stood in stark contrast to their earthly bondage. But the conflict was more than ceremonial. As Eugene Genovese has suggested of American black and white Christian traditions, "Beneath the similarities and differences of style lay a divergence of meanings, including some divergence in the very meaning of God." After the war, white clergymen from the North failed miserably in their attempts to convert Georgia blacks to a faith based on guilt.[5]

The teachers knew they had their work cut out for them; as one said of the people on an isolated plantation near the coast: "There is I think an almost total lack of any standard of morals in regard to purity of life and truth speaking. . . . I think the habit of long years of slavery stands in our way, years in which they were taught 'that a man might be a good Christian and lie and steal and commit Adultery.'" But what the northerners perceived as a "lack of any standard of morals" among blacks was actually a different standard from their own. Slaves had had a clear notion of what was right and what was wrong. However, their code of personal behavior was shaped by the need for personal and group strength, rather than overcoming temptation. Few slaves (Uncle Tom notwithstanding) were tortured by their own sinfulness when they drank whiskey on a Saturday night, broke a hoe on purpose, stole from their master ("Roast pig is a wonderful delicacy, especially when stolen"), or told him they were happy to be his property. The slaveholder had no rights that the slaves were bound to respect, yet they respected each other within the realm of community, family, and church life. These standards of conduct and priorities persisted among southern blacks after emancipation, but the teachers' own notions of morality were too absolute to tolerate any behavior among the freed people that they would have disapproved of in themselves.[6]

The clash between southern black and northern white culture occurred with varying degrees of intensity throughout the state. Women assigned to the Sea Islands or coastal areas discovered that the people's language (a Gullah dialect) and music remained relatively uninfluenced by whites. One teacher reported that the former slaves in Brunswick were "the most ignorant and degraded of all this ignorant and degraded race." They were "heathens," just like "raw Africans," she said. Most could hardly understand English. Another white woman reported that people in the back country near Savannah spoke a pidgin English that "was to us, a confused jargon." A coworker observed that the plantation hands she met "can truly be said to be (in this enlightened 19th century and living as they have all their lives in the midst of the chivalry) side by side with their brethren in the wilds of Africa." Thus, in extreme cases, members of the two groups could not fully understand each other's language.[7]

On a more general level, the encounter between teachers and Georgia freed people amounted to a meeting between a rational, nineteenth-century, middle-class culture and a traditional premodern one. Afro-American beliefs in spirits, ghosts, and fairies amazed the northerners. An Andersonville instructor attempted to "expose the absurdity of conjuring by animals" for her students. She reported that they understood the "physiological impossibility of frogs, lizards, and snakes running around in the body," yet still insisted that people could be "witched with lizards."[8]

Other cultural differences were not so dramatic as these African retentions. The teachers were fascinated by the songs their pupils sang "in such a queer time." Apparently the fascination was mutual. One instructor requested more singing books for her class because the children were "all very fond of singing and particularly the new songs that they have been learning. They say 'they are not like the songs we used to sing!'" Truly "Amazing Grace" and "Juba dis and Juba dat" were worlds apart in their lyrics, their rhythms, their meanings.[9]

In the cities, where a significant number of freed people were familiar with middle-class white culture, the situation was often quite different. The relatively large number of skilled black craftsmen and entrepreneurs—before the war either free men of color or hired-out slaves—meant that some already possessed or at least understood the values of independent workingmen by the time they came into contact with northerners. The whites' exhortations probably came as no surprise to these urban folk. And yet that did not necessarily mean that the teachers found an eager and compliant audience in the towns. In fact, the larger and more prosperous the middle-class black community, the more highly sophisticated were its religious and secular leaders. Savannah freed people made the Freedman's Bank branch in that city one of the most successful in the South, a sure sign that many artisans and businessmen were as thrifty as New England misers. However, the community resisted northern white influence; its educational leaders tried to operate their own schools, and at least one local ministerial association incorporated into its constitution the provision that no white clergyman ever be allowed to join.[10]

Lawrence Levine notes that "Freedom may have dissolved the homogeneity of slave culture, but it did not completely dissolve that culture itself." Most Georgia teachers stayed in the South only a short time, and were unable to observe any long-term effects resulting from their efforts. Initially, the teachers labored with high hopes for the future, though gradually the depth of their disappointment became proportionate to the loftiness of their goals. Few of the women perceived any tangible results from their social work in Georgia, and they often expressed feelings of inadequacy and despair in their attempt to improve the freed people's standard of living. They had intended to "plant the seeds" of morality in children and adults alike, but feared that they were not destined to witness the "ripening of the fruit" while they were in the South. And so a "harvest"—the emergence of a pious, economically independent black yeomanry—would have to wait for future generations; meanwhile, the teachers would have to content themselves with "sowing and with the evidence of life in the seed." Ironically, to convey their frustration, freedmen's workers often used the image of darkness, shade, and thunderclouds. In 1867 one Augusta teacher wrote hopefully, "better times are *sure* to come—we believe . . . we shall see light, even through our national darkness." In a sense, this sense of resignation was well founded, but it was created by the teachers' failure to fully comprehend the Georgia caste system as well as the black man's resistance to the white man's ways.[11]

The teachers never agreed among themselves upon the extent to which they should provide charity—that is, the free distribution of goods and services—for the freed people. On the one hand, the women saw horrible destitution among innocent and helpless people. But they feared that massive, gratuitous relief would discourage personal initiative. During the first four or five years after the war, these points were informally debated. Some teachers argued that unlimited aid was right and necessary, and others charged that lessons in "self-help" should begin immediately. In its official policy, the AMA tried to avoid both extremes. The teachers often used their own judgment in handing out goods.[12]

Proponents of charity pointed out that, before the blacks could learn how to provide for the future, they must be able to survive on a day-to-day basis. Because the people emerged from slavery with no cash, no property, and little experience in paying for supplies—let alone saving money—northerners could justifiably provide them with things free of charge. In requesting materials to start an "industrial school" (classes in sewing and cooking), one teacher observed in November 1865 that, though their ultimate goal was self-reliance, the blacks could not then "make bricks without Straw." Some instructors noted that the people bore no responsibility for their present wretched condition and therefore could not be held accountable for it. Indeed, Atlanta Superintendent Ware suggested that the North should assume guilt for the sin of slavery and provide relief to the victims cheerfully and freely; charity amounted to a temporary and well-deserved form of assistance. Others argued that postwar economic conditions, poor harvests, and racial discrimination spelled widespread poverty for the overwhelming majority of Georgia blacks. If required to pay for supplies, most would simply have to go without them and succumb to disease and starvation.[13]

But a few teachers considered northern aid in a different light. Cornelia Drake thought it better for the freed people to suffer rather than have their needs continually relieved by northern largesse. (Of course, only a tiny fraction of the Georgia population ever received any direct aid from northern teachers.) She admitted that her coworkers considered her attitude "harsh and unkind," yet she persisted by saying, "in a large number of cases, giving does more harm than *real* good." Although few of her colleagues supported her strongly on this issue—even her AMA superior later criticized her for these remarks—her fears reflected a concern on the part of many teachers for the implications of large-scale charity.[14]

Teachers and northern officials devised a variety of means to compromise on the subject of aid. Abbie Johnson, who operated a highly successful "Rag Department" in Savannah, charged low prices to those who could afford to pay for the clothing. She used the proceeds to buy bread, meal, and hominy for the old and hungry. But she did such a good "business," she actually turned over a profit to the AMA. She reported that she would "give more freely were it not that [Superintendent] Niles' better judgment bids me teach them *dependence* on *themselves*." To avoid duplication of aid, several teachers, especially those in Atlanta, kept scrupulous account books of each recipient's name and condition. Most missions maintained a system whereby teachers served as caseworkers and visited families to determine whether or not they qualified for immediate assistance. Those whose poverty met a standard of "worthiness" received tickets they could redeem for clothing at the mission home. This policy of screening applicants and using supplies as reward for "good conduct, neatness, and punctuality" gained widespread acceptance among teachers and superintendents alike.[15]

Regardless of individual misgivings about charity, the Georgia teachers sought to relieve the most obvious cases of physical suffering among refugees in the largest towns. Ill and hungry, living in rude huts or under cast-off building materials, they needed the most basic assistance. Teachers in Atlanta and Savannah agreed that these "half-clad, ragged shivering people" demanded immediate attention. For the neediest cases, the teachers used all their ingenuity to provide relief. Usually they distributed supplies received from the North and England (one instructor expressed the satisfaction she shared with her "begging" coworkers when she wrote, "I enjoy very much getting money out of people, especially those that are able or stingy.").[16]

Teachers received garments for both sexes and all ages by the barrelful. In one month during 1866, two Atlanta teachers disposed of a total of 3,183 articles, including 211 dresses, 213 skirts, 243 shirts, 297 pairs of stockings, 119 pairs of shoes, 210 coats, 639 hospital gowns, 57 caps and hats, 287 pairs of pants, and 44 overcoats, as well as vests, infant clothes, shawls, caps, and scarves. Several different northern freedmen's aid groups had contributed the clothing, which filled ninety-six boxes and barrels. This was apparently an unusually busy month for these two teachers, who worked together in relief efforts. While in the South, most individual teachers received at least one barrel of goods from friends or relatives in the North, but they sometimes drew on their own resources to provide cash for food and rent. In Columbus, Sarah Chase spent the living allowance provided by her well-to-do father to buy bedding, medicine, clothes, soup, and meat for widows, children, and elderly people. At one point, she made what she considered a considerable sacrifice by "parting with some underclothing which I thought someone needed more than myself—and that immediately."[17]

The teachers filled their letters to administrators, friends, and journal editors with detailed accounts of the current status and past misfortunes of aid recipients. These individual histories proved valuable in encouraging northerners to donate additional clothing and supplies. In their descriptions of suffering, the women often concentrated on three themes: the specific causes of the person's poverty, his current physical surroundings, and his gratitude for the aid (usually recorded in "Negro talk"). One teacher observed that, if her friends at home could but see and talk to the blacks themselves, they would demonstrate much more generosity. She and others tried to make their letters as interesting as possible by describing personal conversations and writing compelling descriptions of the people's wretched circumstances.[18]

The letters of Martha D. Ayres, published in the *American Missionary*, provide good examples of these anecdotes. For instance, in March 1867 she described the plight of a widow and her six children who had appealed to her for help. The black woman had worked on a plantation near Macon, but she received only food and clothing for herself in return. She resolved to go to the city in hope of better providing for her children. On the way, "relying on her honest purpose and her prayers," she felt too frightened for her children's safety to sleep at night. Arriving ragged and hungry, she finally obtained lodging in a single, tiny room and tried to find work as a laundress. Ayres gave her some clothes and bedding that she received "with unbounded gratitude." She used one quilt to cover all the children and the other as a rug for the dirt floor. The teacher concluded her letter by noting that "life has *darker views*" even "in this world of plenty, in which God so liberally scatters perfume, flowers, and sunshine."[19]

Besides distributing food and clothing, the teachers tried to provide medical care for the ill. In the process, they contended with predictable health problems engendered by widespread poverty and disease. Particularly devastating were the cholera outbreak in Savannah in 1865 and the smallpox epidemics in Atlanta and Columbus in 1866. The efforts of Esther Douglass to treat Savannah cholera victims according to directions in her "Homeopathic book" indicate both the teachers' heroic determination and the inadequacy of their skills and resources to aid the ill on a large scale. A missionary in the city found many sick persons when she visited the freed people's homes in 1866, but she felt powerless to help them; white physicians refused to prescribe medicines for blacks without payment in advance and even then they might not do anything, "so great is their hatred for colored people." She identified the needs of the ill: clean clothes to replace their "filthy rags," medicine (she specifically suggested "Humphrey's Homeopathic Specifics"), and nourishing food. She concluded sadly that no work had ever affected her so deeply: "It is so hard to turn away from positive suffering with no ability to relieve."[20]

Most women had never before witnessed personal hardship to rival what they found in the refugee camps. At least three had served in army hospitals during the war, but for many of the rest— young, middle-class schoolteachers—the scenes of destitution and disease were new and terrible. One teacher described her horror upon seeing the gaunt, pinched faces of a freedman's family. Huddled around a dying fire and shivering in their miserable rags, they subsisted on potatoes. She wrote, "You have no idea what scenes of degradation we witness, nor how crushing the life of a missionary must be." One can only imagine the emotional response of a Savannah teacher who stood by the deathbeds of five persons, including a child who starved to death, during the month of May 1867. For another woman, the sight of a hungry child gnawing on the head of a rat epitomized the horrors suffered by blacks after the war.[21]

Several teachers who had only words of sympathy and comfort to offer refused to make any visits at all unless they could provide tangible assistance. Even the most devout women at times felt that an offering of spiritual sustenance amounted to little more than an insult in the face of such misery. Martha Ayres, while pleading for more help from the North in the fall of 1866, threatened to cease her missionary visits altogether "as a knowledge of wretchedness which I cannot relieve is a constant burden which I feel unequal to bear." She said that Bible reading and prayers, without some sort of physical relief, amounted to nothing.[22]

It is one of the ironies of freedmen's aid work that in her charitable role the northern teacher resembled the antebellum slave mistress. Caring for the ill was the special province of the slaveholder's wife, and she also had the duties of passing out clothing and, in some cases, providing religious instruction to the bondsmen. Of course the analogy between the roles of these two women is imperfect; for example, no northern teacher ever subjected a black person to the kind of physical abuse that southern white women were well known and feared for. But the fact remains that, despite differences in attitude, method, and intentions, the teachers and their antebellum predecessors shared certain social welfare functions.

Apparently many freed people perceived this similarity. The northern women often encountered the "deference ritual" that blacks performed under slavery. Cries of "Oh! Missis! We'se glad to see you!", flattering remarks, wide smiles, and gifts of eggs served as typical greetings for both types of white women when they visited black quarters. It is difficult to determine whether the freed people persisted in this behavior after the war because they actually harbored deep-seated suspicions of the teachers as middle-class white women, whether they wanted to express genuine joy and gratitude toward them, or whether the short lapse of time after slavery merely precluded radical changes in the way they behaved in the presence of white authority figures. The teachers recognized and deplored overtly servile behavior, but curtsies, "pulling of feet," bows, and effusive professions of love all inspired delighted responses in the northern women.[23]

Immediate relief was a vital service in a time of great suffering. But the teachers hoped to exert a more permanent effect upon the lives of the freedmen by means of special classes, societies, and institutions that would instill Yankee virtues in the people. Personal contact between the former slave and the teacher was necessary, they believed, but more formal and structured group experiences would pave the way for "moral self-sufficiency." When the last teacher had left for the North, the blacks of Georgia would be able to rely on their own families, Sunday schools, temperance societies, and savings institutions as instruments of their personal and collective improvement.

In October 1867 the AMA sent to Atlanta a handwritten circular containing instructions for the preparation of photographs dealing with freedmen's work. It suggested that, in addition to a classroom scene, a photo showing a family gathered around a teacher-missionary would effectively convey the purposes of the association. The white woman should be "neatly, not fancifully dressed," and the background of the picture should consist of the "'dresser,' with the neat dishes, etc." In concluding, the circular stated that the AMA would rather wait a while than receive "an untasteful picture unskillfully executed." The image of a black family respectfully listening to a northern teacher read the Bible in their modest but orderly home represented an ideal among freedmen's aid societies.[24]

Whatever the frustrations involved in trying to instill a code of New England tidiness in poverty-stricken urban refugees or rural peasants, most of the teachers possessed a basic faith in the strength of the black family. Their accounts from Georgia in the two years after the war confirm the recent work of Herbert Gutman on this subject. Men and women hastened to make legal their long-standing emotional ties by getting married; people of all ages searched for loved ones from whom they had been separated years before (a Savannah teacher described the reunion of a father and son who had not seen each other in thirty-two years); elderly and poor people shared their meager fare with orphans; black men did their best to eke out a living for their families.[25]

The northern teachers were both Puritan and Victorian in their belief in the importance of the family. "Family influences" shaped individual character and eventually determined the moral tenor of the whole society. Wrote one Andersonville teacher, "I have visited a good many of these people in their homes, and am more and more impressed with the idea that they can never rise to take a position in the world until there is a great improvement in their homes." In making these calls, the teachers resembled pioneering social workers; they checked on applicants for aid, dispensed advice on home economics, encouraged regular school attendance among the children, and offered words of sympathy ("a word *kindly spoken* seems to take effect")—or sometimes reproof. An Atlanta teacher liked to follow her pupils home in the afternoon and "learn how they live"; in that way, she believed she could have "a greater influence" over their personal growth. During these visits, a wide variety of pamphlets sent south by groups like the American Tract Society, American Bible Society, and Western Tract and Book Society were distributed. Even though each woman devoted at least part of her time to this duty, it was a full-time responsibility for persons specifically designated as "missionaries" or "missionary visitors." For example, Cornelia Drake visited ninety-eight Savannah homes in June 1866.[26]

Special classes for women complemented visits in the teachers' attempts to improve the quality of home life. Conducted in a local church, school, or mission home, these sessions provided instruction in the responsibilities of motherhood for adults and girls. According to freedmen's aid groups, slavery had dishonored the black woman and emancipation held few triumphs for her. Denied suffrage and lacking a formal education, she wielded a potentially dangerous influence over the future of the black race. While her husband led the way in the political sphere, she must be taught to assume the central position in the moral and religious regeneration of the family. The AMA asserted as a "truism of political and social philosophy that in no age, among no people has the Race ever maintained a higher plane of morality than that occupied by its mothers, wives, and daughters."[27]

The classes amounted to combination sewing circles, prayer meetings, and discussion groups. A Savannah teacher, who stressed the duties of women as "wives, mothers, and housekeepers," called her gathering "Mothers' Meeting and Sewing Class." In her "Industrial School," another instructor taught cutting, shaping, and fitting of garments, plus advanced sewing for women and older girls. She depended upon donations of muslin, denim, calico, knitting yarn, thread, and needles to sponsor the classes, which were held twice a week and attended by fifty to eighty persons. An Athens teacher formed a society of young women (called a "Ladies' League") that was designed to cultivate in them a "literary taste" as well as teach them how to sew.[28]

The teachers' letters from Georgia (some that were published in society journals and many others that were not) focus on the value of family life to a people whose kin relationships had previously found no legitimacy in the eyes of the law. Freedmen's workers thus reiterated a prominent argument of the abolitionists: family ties among blacks had remained strong in spite of overwhelming odds. But, when it served their purposes, the teachers could find reasons to disregard the sanctity of the family and take children away from their parents. Professing a special interest in the welfare of pupils they considered particularly bright and promising, teachers used several means to free them from "demoralizing home influences." Of course, to a limited degree, the common school fulfilled this purpose by removing youngsters from their homes for a few hours each day and exposing them to cleanliness, neatness, and the teacher's benign influences. As one teacher remarked, each class was "a great family" unto itself.[29]

But sometimes the white women believed a child needed to break completely from his home and parents. When recommending pupils for Atlanta University and other boarding schools, teachers all over the state invariably included descriptions of each youngster's home life along with assessments of his or her academic potential. One teacher urged Atlanta President Ware to accept one of her male students because she thought "if he could be taken away from his home influences he might be safe from a life of sin." In a letter to the president of Fisk University, Sarah Stansbury wrote of a girl of thirteen, "It is desirable from the character of the Mother and Sister that the girl should remain from home several years without returning for vacation." The same teacher, when sending another pupil to Atlanta, stated that she was a good scholar and added, "Her home influences however are deplorable; her mother changes husbands as often as some ladies change their bonnets."[30]

A few teachers took the more drastic step of either adopting children themselves or sending them north to live. In most cases, but not all, these were orphans. Follow-up information on these children is practically nonexistent. At times the adoption process consisted of the teacher's caring for the child while she worked in Georgia and then finding him or her a new home when she returned to the North. Cornelia Drake, a Savannah missionary, adopted an orphan girl in 1868, but she also sought a family in New England to take care of the youngster. However, she was uncertain whether she could make the proper arrangements: "it would be a pity [the little girl] should be just put in somebody's kitchen with only servants for her associates." Her comment suggests the dangers inherent in placing black children in white northern homes to give them a new and "better" life.[31]

Aided by the Freedmen's Bureau and a northern philanthropist, the AMA established an asylum for black children in Atlanta a year after the war's end. Again, most, but not all, of the inmates were orphans. A teacher had reported in April 1866 that at least a hundred small children in the city lived without parents and subsisted on hardtack and saltpork. Many of their fathers had served as Union soldiers and died during the war. The association began to make provisions for the children in June, when it set up some tents near the mission home. A temporary structure erected that summer served as the asylum. Rose Kinney, its first matron, had charge of twenty-one children, aged three to twelve. All came from the nearby refugee camps. Kinney had her hands full caring for the sick (in August that amounted to half of the total number) as well as providing religious instruction for the older ones. She depended heavily upon Freedmen's Bureau rations and donations from the North to feed and clothe her charges. A high turnover rate became characteristic of the asylum population as parents claimed offspring who had been separated from them during the war, children found homes in other black families, and some became servants in white households.[32]

The next matron, Rebecca Craighead, concentrated on finding northern sponsors for as many children as possible. She corresponded with white friends in Ohio who "want[ed] girls." She preferred to send the children north, for there, she wrote, "they will be better cared for, and taught *how to live.*" In the late spring and summer of 1867, she sent several inmates to the Adrian, Michigan, orphan asylum, established that year by the AMA to accommodate southern orphans. Craighead proved so zealous in disposing of some of the children under her care (as many as eighty-five at one time) that she incurred a severe rebuke from AMA officials. Apparently she wanted to send the children to live in the Adrian asylum rather than return them to the homes of grandparents, aunts, and uncles who had placed them in the Atlanta institution when they could not afford to care for them. She declared, "My idea is that *they* have no further claim upon them, and that we have a right to find homes for such, just as much as though they had no relatives."[33]

In a move to save money, the AMA made preparations to close the Atlanta asylum in January 1869. Only twenty small children remained, and they were sent to another association institution in Wilmington, North Carolina. Atlanta Superintendent Ware noted that, as far as the older children were concerned, "there is a great demand for children who are large enough to do anything." Presumably, Atlanta had no shortage of white persons willing to accept responsibility for potential errand boys, servants, cooks, and laundresses. Visiting the booming city in the summer of 1869, representatives of the New England branch of the American Freedmen's Union Commission (AFUC) reported with evident satisfaction that Atlanta no longer needed an asylum for its homeless black children.[34]

Of all the social institutions established by the freed people, the church was the strongest and most basic within the context of community life. In their religious (unlike their educational) activities, the former slaves quickly achieved self-sufficiency and independence from white authority. They needed no assistance from northern or southern whites in supplying the main ingredients of church work: a strong religious faith, a preacher, and a place to meet (a brush arbor would do). Under slavery, black people had nourished a faith that blended elements of African folk religion and western Christianity. After emancipation, they formalized patterns of clandestine worship and publicly embraced religious leaders who provided them with messages of hope and spiritual liberation. White Protestantism, characterized by foreboding doctrines of original sin and predestination, offered them little solace. For these reasons, the northern teachers in Georgia attracted few black converts to their respective denominations, primarily Congregationalism and Methodism.[35]

The teachers entered the field with grandiose plans. Mental and moral education availed little without a revitalization of the spirit prompted by religious instruction and culminating in a conversion experience. The freedmen's aid societies were certain they possessed the basic raw material necessary to a successful proselytizing venture: the black person's honest faith in God and simple trust in Jesus. According to the teachers in Georgia, this "childish simplicity" and "simple faith" manifested itself in the people's "patience"; the most devout might become "perfect through suffering." One teacher lauded a very poor, elderly black man who saw "Jesus everywhere" and told her that many were in worse straits than himself. To her question of how he paid the month's rent came this reply: "Well . . . when de month's 'most out, sometimes I say, 'Lord, what shall I do? I'se got no money'; but when Master Jesus *says* he'll mind you, he *will* mind you, an' he sends one friend an' anoder, an' I make out. I'se satisfied." The white woman exclaimed, "Blessed trust! Happy poor yet rich man." This image of the black man as a

Christian child permeated the writings of the teachers, and bears a striking resemblance to that projected in Harriet Beecher Stowe's *Uncle Tom's Cabin*, which many of them had apparently read.[36]

But black worship services shocked the teachers. Genovese describes a ritualistic form similar to the one witnessed by white northerners in Georgia soon after the war:

> Typically, the preacher begins in a carefully measured way and steadily works toward a more rhythmical and intense delivery. As the rhythm, rising and falling, builds toward a climax, punctuated by groans, grunts, and cries, the preacher virtually breaks into a chant and then a song. In effect, he guides his congregation toward a musical response. . . . No two sermons can be alike, and each shows the marked influence of the spirituals and vice versa. Each sermon becomes a new poetic construction and a new combination of artistic elements.

Several aspects of this type of religious meeting deeply offended the teachers. They described the congregation's body movements—shuffling, peculiar gesticulations, swaying back and forth—as "animal excitement" and therefore indecent church behavior. Music had its place, but not the "weird songs," which combined religious and secular themes. One AMA official charged that Savannah blacks had "no conception of singing as an act of worship but are bent on a Banjo performance." And the lack of an intelligent sermon based on scriptural references rendered every black "shout" incomplete, and, according to the teachers, spiritually meaningless. Ellen Adlington complained that at a local Baptist church service she was "screamed at in a wild ignorant half rhapsody with not a word said of the commandments."[37]

It was no surprise then that the teachers reserved their harshest judgment for native black religious leaders, whom they condemned as drunken, adulterous, profane, and power-hungry men. Their performances in the pulpit hardly conformed to New England Congregationalism's standards of decorous spiritual leadership; one teacher could not tolerate seeing the preacher in Newton periodically spit in the fire during services. Representatives of the AMA in Georgia confirmed the presence in that state of "Uncle Cato," a stereotypical character depicted in an 1870 *American Missionary* article. Uncle Cato, probably a composite of the teachers' complaints about black clergymen, exhibited the familiar shortcomings of intemperance and illiteracy. But, even more importantly, the writer suggested that the old man "hates the school and the teachers, and opposes them in all secret and underhanded ways; not openly, 'for fear of the people.'" The teachers implicitly acknowledged the high status of preachers in the black community, and perceived these men as rivals in both their religious and educational work. These fears were not groundless, but only because the vast majority of blacks felt a strong commitment to their own religious leaders.[38]

The people's "childlike" innocence in religious matters testified to their potential as moral human beings, but it also made them more vulnerable to unscrupulous men and authoritarian religions, according to the teachers. In Georgia, representatives of the freedmen's aid societies viewed with horror any sign of Roman Catholicism, which they associated with superstition, ignorance, and feudalism. In some towns, especially Savannah, the Catholics contended with northern Protestants for influence over the freed people by establishing both schools and churches. An AMA superintendent estimated that several hundred Savannah blacks belonged to the two Catholic churches in that city in 1869 (though AMA paranoia usually led to exaggeration on this subject). A special teaching order from France, the Sisters of Mercy, conducted regular day schools; it is uncertain whether they used English or French as the language of instruction. Methodist and Congregational teachers reported Catholic religious activity in Atlanta, Macon, Columbus, and Thomasville during the eight years after the war. Still, the near-hysteria revealed in the *Annual Reports* of the Methodist Freedmen's Aid Society (MFAS) and the *American Missionary* bore no direct relation to the so-called Catholic threat in Georgia during this period. The long diatribes against this ecclesiastical "enemy of civil liberty and . . . friend of the oppressor the world over" served more as rallying cries for evangelicals than demonstrations of the Catholic presence in the state. The image of the papacy adding four million docile, malleable blacks to "the solid and obedient masses which it controls at the North" was a popular one in society journals. Evidently, for the black man, life as a Catholic would differ little from his former life as a slave.[39]

Convinced they had an opportunity to shape black religious loyalties in a "transition" period immediately after emancipation, representatives of the AMA and the MFAS engaged in serious proselytizing among the Georgia freed people. Methodists found themselves dealing with a different problem than did the AMA in its work. The former group concentrated on trying to convince the freed people already affiliated with the Methodist Episcopal Church (South) and the African Methodist Episcopal Church to "return" to the "true" Methodist Church. The rivalry among these three groups often reached a bitter intensity (one southern preacher implored God in prayer to "send the Yankees to Hell and to send them quickly"), yet northern missionaries always considered it an intradenominational fray. On the other hand, the AMA faced a more basic difficulty; the Congregational Church had little intrinsic appeal for blacks in terms of theology or ritual. They perceived the Church of the Puritans (unlike Methodism) as the embodiment of a whole new, alien religion. Although the Georgia church work of the MFAS rested on a solid foundation, the AMA had none. In contrast to the cajoling Methodists, Congregationalists considered all native black denominations, even the small Presbyterian group, as dangerous and unworthy rivals.[40]

These differences highlight the contrasting goals and methods of the AMA and the MFAS in their religious activities. The MFAS freely admitted that its schools served merely as an adjunct to missionary work; its main objective was to acquire new church members. Methodist missionaries showed no hesitation in encouraging traditional forms of black worship or in hiring native blacks to serve as lay preachers or exhorters. Competition among the northern, southern, and African groups often resembled a violent political game, in which schools and new church buildings were weapons and converted souls were prizes. At times, two of the groups would form a temporary alliance in order to eliminate the third from a town or area. In these ruthless, opportunistic struggles, doctrine played little part. Moreover, no group ever raised the possibility of racial integration as a serious option; that would have eliminated all white support immediately. By 1876 the northern Methodists had managed to wrest only 2,591 black members away from the two southern groups in Georgia.[41]

The AMA had even less to show for its religious work on behalf of Congregationalism. Church membership statistics—the denomination had established eight churches and won only 429 formal converts by 1873—reflect its insistence on theological rigor and institutional purity. The AMA placed strong emphasis on common schools because it considered an educated citizenry a prerequisite to serious proselytizing in the South. Although the association admitted in 1867 that few tangible signs of religious conversion were evident among the freed people, it added, "The REAL progress of religion among them will begin and keep pace, with their *Christian education.*" The Congregationalists shunned hasty or halfway efforts at conversion; they preferred to wait rather than gather in souls with unseemly haste. The long, elaborate training and ordination procedures for Georgia's first Congregational black minister,

Floyd Snelson, indicate that the AMA had serious reservations about supporting native black clergymen for the sake of political expediency.[42]

Yet association representatives persisted in sponsoring a variety of religious activities that supplemented their church work. Ministers and teachers conducted prayer meetings and Bible classes for adults and children, and offered lessons in theology for a few willing participants. As evangelicals, they encouraged revivals and protracted meetings that, though often attended by large numbers of interested persons, led to few Congregational-approved converts. For the most part, these demonstrations of religious "enthusiasm" appeared relatively calm, even unenthusiastic. AMA ministers described the most successful ones in terms similar to those used by the Reverend C. W. Francis in his account of the special religious meetings in Atlanta in 1868: "During the spring months we have been blessed with a quiet and thorough religious awakening. . . . The work was marked by the deep thoughtfulness of all brought under its influence, by earnest inquiring after the truth, by sincere convictions of sin and simple faith." Three years later, Superintendent Ware echoed Francis's observations in similar words: "The work is quiet but deep and thorough I think." One teacher contrasted the "gentle" AMA revival methods with those of the freedmen religious leaders, who hoped to "drive" souls into heaven instead of first winning their minds.[43]

AMA workers identified those "touched by the Spirit" in several ways. The use of the "anxious seat" was common in AMA-sponsored revivals. Men, women, and children who exhibited unusual introspection—indeed, a lack of consciousness of all worldly functions like eating and sleeping—evinced the outward signs of conversion. Francis, describing particularly "clear" and "satisfying" evidence of divine grace, cited a ten-year-old girl who came to school with a note she had written pinned to her dress. It read "Please don't talk to me today, and I won't talk to you, do the right, God sees you all." An old woman, addicted to smoking for thirty years, gave up her pipe as she went through a conversion experience. Gradual, inward, heartfelt changes, which sooner or later manifested themselves in visible ways, provided evidence of true faith.[44]

The teachers showed strong interest in the religious progress of their individual day-school scholars and a predictable zeal for Sunday school teaching. One Andersonville instructor, like her AMA coworkers, hoped that her Sunday school would produce some "visible work of grace" among her pupils. She reported proudly that her Sunday scholars "seemed quiet, eager, earnest." A Savannah teacher told one of her pupils that Sunday school was, "of all others, just the place to seek religion." As regenerate Christians, the teachers accepted this responsibility as part of their regular duties, though a few felt unequal to the enormous task of helping to lead a child to God. And denominational loyalties were always a prime consideration. Wrote one AMA worker upon hearing that some Savannah pupils wanted to be confirmed by a rival minister, "I am pleased to have them Christians but I am not in favor of putting our scholars into the Episcopal church."[45]

In December 1873 Savannah AMA Superintendent Alexander N. Niles warned his superiors in New York against sending a white minister to that area of Georgia because "The people have not yet risen so high in their conception of the proprieties of worship.—Nor in their experiences as to *desire* a highly cultured minister." Try as they might, AMA representatives could never seem to "get a hold on the people." The Reverend Frank Haley reported from Macon a few months later that "there *exists a strong prejudice against suffering white ministers to be pastors of colored churches.*" Especially in the larger towns, where the AMA presence was so highly visible, the freed people of Georgia expressed definite preferences in terms of their religious allegiances; they retained traditional religious practices and trust in ministers of their own race. The Baptists remained the largest black denomination after the war despite the feverish efforts of white Congregationalists and Methodists. Both white groups blamed their failure on the "ignorance" of the people. Although they recognized the disadvantages under which they labored in trying to attract converts, northern clergymen and teachers in general failed to comprehend the larger social significance of Afro-American religious institutions.[46]

According to the teachers, the way the freed people gave themselves over to wild abandon and sensuality during their religious meetings indicated a general vice encouraged by the slave system: moral laxness in all areas of personal behavior. The master had not been interested in the morality of the slaves per se. If it suited his purposes, he would bribe them to do a hard day's work by promising whiskey as a reward. He was not troubled by sexual promiscuity or foul language so long as it took place out of his sight and hearing. According to abolitionist ideology, the slaves, deprived of any real spiritual guidance, freely indulged in sinful activities without any pangs of guilt. What, wondered the northern teachers, would happen once these people were free and enjoyed even more opportunities to succumb to temptation?

The worst fears of many neoabolitionists were confirmed. In particular, Georgia teachers reported that freedmen, women, and children consumed vast quantities of alcohol in the day and at night, in their homes or on the streets. Even though these accounts were exaggerated, black people often did take advantage of the freedom to purchase liquor whenever they wanted and could afford it, and many (like their poor white counterparts) attached no moral stigma to drinking. "Whiskey wagons perambulating the country" and dram shops in the cities and towns did a booming business among blacks and whites alike, according to northerners touring the South. The teachers soon realized with dismay that persons of all ages indulged in this demoralizing habit. One woman described her frustration over the intransigence of a ten-year-old who refused to join her temperance group because he liked whiskey and did not want to give it up. The Reverend Robert Carter, a black man chosen by the AMA to further its religious work in Savannah, disappointed his benefactors by purchasing large amounts of whiskey—more than a dollar's worth each day—from a local merchant. Superintendent Niles noted that, when he asked the seller what Carter "did with so much whiskey as it was impossible to drink it all—he replied that his family all liked it from oldest to youngest."[47]

The pervasiveness of the problem astounded teachers who disapproved of the consumption of alcohol in any quantity, and they believed drunkenness was a major obstacle to the regeneration of all freed people. One woman complained that "tipsy men" often disrupted her night school and that she could usually find at least five or six inebriated students in her class. Another expressed regret that so many blacks in Andersonville apparently preferred to spend their meager wages on liquor and tobacco rather than improve the physical appearance of their homes. She believed her greatest task was to make them "*feel* the *need* of improving their temporal condition." The use of liquor thwarted all attempts at self-improvement and social responsibility.[48]

As a result of what they perceived as self-indulgence on the part of black people, the teachers enthusiastically promoted temperance (which they defined as abstinence from drinking, smoking, and swearing) through voluntary societies. They believed that the elimination of these personal vices depended upon the cooperative efforts of the offenders. According to this view, men, women, and children could most effectively reform themselves by admitting their weaknesses; publicly pledging to refrain from liquor, tobacco, and profanity; and then meeting regularly in groups to reaffirm their pledges and inspire one another (like modern groups of confessed alcoholics and gamblers who seek self-reformation by drawing strength from others with similar problems).

Variously called "Bands of Hope," "Vanguards of Freedom," "Morning Stars," "Lincoln Brigades," "Cold Water Societies," or "Excelsior Teetotallers," most of the groups used the *Band of Hope Ritual* as their guidebook. This pamphlet detailed the slate of officers, standards of membership eligibility, fees, rules, catechisms, and order of exercises for meetings. The societies made provisions for members' offenses (one cent for the first, three cents for the second, expulsion for the third). Songs extolling the temperance cause often compared alcoholism to slavery, and portrayed drinkers as "slaves," alcohol as "chains," and the temperance pledge as moral "freedom." Recitation of the "Pledge" constituted the high point of each meeting: "I hereby solemnly pledge myself to abstain from the use of all spirituous and malt liquors, wine or cider, as a beverage; from the use of tobacco in every form, and from all profanity." Those who felt moved to "take the pledge" received badges to wear at future meetings. The teachers allowed individuals to attack their problems incrementally by dividing the pledge into two parts, one dealing with alcohol and the other with tobacco. Temperance picnics as well as the distribution of almanacs, tracts, and magazines supplemented regular meetings.[49]

It is difficult to gauge the teachers' success in persuading the freed people to abstain from habits that many did not consider wrong. At least fifty northern-sponsored groups, whose members exceeded thirteen hundred, existed in Georgia during the 1868–69 school year. (These figures, taken from Freedmen's Bureau Teacher Monthly Reports, are conservative; for example, the Atlanta temperance association, whose members numbered more than three hundred, was not listed.) The teachers attempted to gain the support of local black leaders in their efforts; some of them served as guest speakers at meetings and as adult sponsors of clubs. However, the northern women were reluctant to let the blacks conduct meetings on their own. One teacher objected to the loudness of temperance meetings held in her schoolroom and the "rough enthusiasm" exhibited by some of the men. She hesitated to interfere on behalf of more sedate procedures, but observed that the members had "very much loosened the desks with their thumping."[50]

The teachers themselves rarely overestimated the degree of change in behavior wrought by their temperance agitation. Augusta children took the pledge eagerly, but only so they could receive badges, according to the superintendent in that town. Helen Leonard encountered serious obstacles to the cause in Milledgeville, where she and her coworkers were unable to convince the deacon of the local Baptist church of the advantages of abstinence from alcohol. Too, speakers at local temperance meetings tended to be rather unconvincing. The teacher persuaded a local northern-born planter to talk to her group on the evils of drink and tobacco. He urged his listeners to refrain from these bad habits, but admitted that he had no intention of doing so himself. Another teacher shared similarly frustrating experiences in Albany. The black owner of a general store there agreed to give up the use of intoxicating spirits "but *not* the traffic in them." When the white woman returned to the town after summer vacation in 1868, she discovered that the society she had started the spring before no longer existed; it had "died a *remarkably easy* death." It is possible that only within boarding-school situations, where the teachers could rigidly proscribe the use of alcohol and expel offenders immediately, did specific temperance preachments significantly affect black behavior—and then only because abstinence amounted to a prerequisite for staying in school. Still, patterns of saving among Georgia blacks after the war indicate that many were moved, probably out of economic self-interest rather than guilt, to forgo certain expensive habits.[51]

The teachers often argued that the money squandered on whiskey could be put to far better use. Specifically, they recommended that the freed people save as much as possible from their meager wages and patiently await the day when they could afford to buy a small house and piece of land. A savings account was the best "investment" that blacks could make, now that they had the opportunity "to *use* and *lay by* their earnings for their own benefit and improvement"; release from bondage meant freedom to save, not waste, their money. Like abstinence from liquor, saving entailed giving up momentary, petty indulgences for future gains.[52]

In 1865 northern freedmen's aid societies hailed the formation of a savings institution especially for southern blacks, the Freedman's Savings and Trust Company (often called the Freedman's Bank). It was a private business-philanthropic venture established by northerners sympathetic to the plight of freed people, white men who hoped it would promote hard work, regular deposits, and moderation in personal habits. The history of the four branches in Georgia (Savannah, opened in 1866; Augusta, 1866; Macon, 1868; and Atlanta, 1870) substantiates the findings of the bank's most recent historian, Carl R. Osthaus. In his book *Freedmen, Philanthropy, and Fraud*, he shows that the institution was "one of the significant forces" of missionary uplift among blacks in the South after the war. In its promotional literature, it echoed the pleas of northern teachers; in its daily operations, it received financial and moral support from the Freedmen's Bureau.[53]

Georgia affords a good example of a state where the AMA-Bureau-Bank "triad" was cemented with overlapping personnel. AMA Superintendents Edmund Ware and C. W. Francis of Atlanta and John R. Rockwell of Macon played an active role in establishing branches in their cities. Other AMA representatives, including Charles H. Prince (Augusta), Philip Cory (Atlanta), and I. W. Brinckerhoff (Savannah), served as bank cashiers. Bank officers (some of whom were also Freedmen's Bureau agents) frequently visited AMA mission homes, and two of them eventually married teachers they met in Georgia. AMA superintendents and teachers routinely carried out major financial transactions with the bank, depositing funds, securing loans, and cashing checks. The work of Rockwell in 1867 revealed the interrelationships among these three agencies of northern benevolence. Sent south by the AMA in 1865, he later received an appointment as assistant superintendent of education for the Freedmen's Bureau, and promptly located his office in "new and desirable quarters" of the Macon branch of the Freedman's Bank.[54]

As a result of these ties and circumstances surrounding the establishment of the bank, many blacks mistakenly believed it had a formal relationship with the Freedmen's Bureau (and, by implication, the federal government). Bank cashiers were often military men dressed in uniform, and many depositors thought that Congress controlled it through the bureau. The bank capitalized on these false impressions. The Reverend John W. Alvord, a Congregational minister who had served as an attaché in General Sherman's army, provided the initial impetus for the bank and obtained its congressional charter. Alvord was the Freedmen's Bureau superintendent of education from 1865 until 1870 and this fact, combined with congressional approval and enthusiastic endorsements of top bureau officials like General Howard, created an aura of respectability and permanence about the institution.

As corresponding secretary of the bank, Alvord toured the South promoting established branches and opening new ones. This duty corresponded nicely with his position as bureau superintendent of schools, and he held both jobs simultaneously for five years. He even asserted that, in the long run, the bank would prove more beneficial to the freed people than the common schools—an interesting opinion for the bureau's chief educational officer and one his own financial interest in the enterprise did little to discourage.[55]

Advertising booklets implied that savings accounts would help to eliminate all the injustices the freed people encountered in the Re-construction South. Sprinkled with quotations like "Tall oaks from little acorns grow" and "Despise not the Day of Small Things," these tracts listed "Reasons Why You Should All Put Money in the Sav-ings Bank": *"Because it is your surest way to get a start in life"*; *"Because, being your own master, it is your duty to provide for your settlement in life, for your families, for sickness, and for old age"*; and, *"It gives you character."* In the classroom, in churches, and in private conversations the teachers urged the blacks to save their money, and more specifically, to deposit it with the Freedman's Savings and Trust Company.[56]

Because of all this propagandizing, plus the desire on the part of many blacks to buy their own land, the deposits of the four Georgia branches totaled $333,053 in 1874. Osthaus's survey of Augusta bank depositors in 1871 indicates that two-thirds were male and about one fourth were literate. Artisans, farmers, cooks, domestics, and laborers all put their faith and money in the bank. A surprising number of them were very young; almost a quarter of the depositors were schoolchildren under fifteen. By that time, about 17 percent of all Macon blacks had opened accounts. Largely as a result of the demands of the freed people themselves, three of the seven men who served in the key position of cashier of a Georgia branch were black. Although the bank never granted any financial credit to its mod-est depositors (it did, however, make loans to notorious financiers like Jay Cooke), it served as a source of pride in the four Georgia communities.[57]

The missionary-superintendents and teachers knew little or noth-ing about the institution's irresponsible loan practices at the main office in Washington, D.C., from 1870 on. The bank had always suffered from poor bookkeeping and outright embezzlement on both the national and local levels. For stealing $8,000 worth of Augusta deposits from 1867 to 1874, Philip Cory earned the dubious distinc-tion of being the only bank cashier sentenced to prison (though he later received a pardon in return for agreeing to serve as an Indian agent in the West!). The failure of Congress to oversee the bank contributed to its problems, and in June 1874 it closed its doors, unable to meet financial obligations. The issue remained alive in the courts until 1910. In Georgia, at least 4,500 depositors collected dividends of $169,300 (about half of the amount due them) between 1875 and 1900, but that hardly lessened the pain for persons who received nothing, either because they were unaware of the dividends or because lawyers' fees consumed the little money that was due them. Most of the 50,000 individual depositors throughout the South had small accounts they had accumulated over several years of careful saving.[58]

The response of Georgia bank supporters to this debacle was predictable. Blacks reacted with outrage. Not surprisingly, the freed people's community in Savannah vociferously protested the bank's closing. A letter-writer to the *Savannah Morning News* pinpointed the horror of it all: "While poor men have become victimized," he charged, bank officials "have become fat by crime and false representations." A black clergyman in that city denounced the operation as a "company of robbers and thieves." AMA representatives were mortified by this episode in the history of northern "philanthropy"; lamented the Atlanta superintendent in February 1874, "the disgrace and shame of it is no small burden to carry here." An official in Savannah reported in 1874, "The closing of the Freedman's Bank is a terrible blow to the colored people here. The whites glory over it, and use it against all Northerners." The AMA had lost both money and face in the venture. However, embarrassment (no matter what the cost in actual deposits) was a small price to pay compared to one's life savings.[59]

Judging from its intentions and means, the Freedman's Savings and Trust Company represented the quintessential freedmen's aid effort. It combined the financial sensibilities of Republican businessmen with the evangelical fervor of Yankee reformers. That the bank profited from its ties with both the AMA and the Freedmen's Bureau was no accident. Its demise served as a lesson for the teachers and freed people alike. The reformers realized that the "right" motives and idealistic rhetoric could not compensate for the greedy mismanagement of "benevolent" enterprises. And it confirmed the suspicions of many blacks that northern goodwill had serious limitations.

If they lacked the sensitivity of modern cultural and social anthropologists, some northern teachers compensated in part with astute analyses of the effects of racial prejudice and the traditional southern economic system on black personal and group advancement. From firsthand observation they knew, to a limited extent at least, that white prejudice constituted an enormous barrier to their own plans for black "regeneration." A man might work hard and plan to save his money, but if he failed to receive adequate compensation— or any wages at all—his labor yielded little. A widow might try to provide for her children, but if she were charged an exorbitant amount for rent, she might have to relinquish responsibility for them. Even if parents recognized the importance of schooling, economic necessity might compel them to send their children out to work. A few teachers realized that, regardless of a black person's "moral character," white employers, merchants, and landlords could stifle his or her development simply by refusing to pay wages or by cheating in the marketplace.

Moreover, the informal, brutal effects of racism did little to further the black man's sense of self-respect. In 1866 Abbie Case, recounting the problems that prevented a destitute woman from adequately feeding, housing, and clothing her children, observed, "There seems little hope for better things, unless white men can be prevented from practicing the extortion they have been permitted to for the last two years." She continued by saying that when blacks could work on their own they fared well "but in nearly every instance where they have been under the whites they are wretched and destitute." Yet few teachers matched Case's precision in singling out white prejudice as the root of the freed people's degradation.[60]

In their belief that blacks needed more (or something different) than lessons in personal character reformation, a handful of society representatives turned to activities outside the mainstream of evangelical missionary work. About ten men became active briefly in Georgia local and state political affairs; two successfully won positions as Republican postmasters and another occupied the position of Revenue Officer for the Savannah District for one year. Superintendents Ware and Rockwell served as members of the Georgia Equal Rights Association. On an informal level, many teachers took an active interest in state and national elections and urged blacks to vote for Republican candidates, though they were often disappointed by the party's negligence in the areas of civil rights and state aid to public education.

Other teachers focused on the people's immediate struggle to become successful, independent farmers. In January 1869 Harriet Gaylord, writing to New York, apologized that "a lady should seemingly so far overstep her province as to write a letter on spades axes hoes etc." She explained that the laborers near Savannah desperately needed agricultural implements and suggested that the AMA might well use its resources to provide the tools free of charge or at nominal prices. She feared that the matter fell outside the province of the association but stressed that, if northerners "wanted to do the Freedmen a practical good," they could find no better way.[61]

Another teacher, Sarah Stansbury, initiated a unique effort to provide blacks with essential staples, groceries, and supplies and at the same time help them to circumvent the high prices set by white merchants. In 1869 she informed Field Secretary E. P. Smith that a black farmer in Cuthbert, Ruben Richards, wished to open his own grocery store in the town. A landowner, he had made a profit from the sale of his cotton during the previous year, and wanted to help his people by providing food and goods at low prices. Explained Stansbury, "I know of no better way to furnish pecuniary aid to the colored people. After working a whole year to raise a crop they are wheedled out of the best of it either by those of whom they lease their ground or by the merchants to whom they sell." Stansbury helped Richards by arranging for him to sell his cotton to a New York dealer and then to use part of the proceeds to have the AMA purchase supplies in that city and ship them south. She wrote her initial letter on this subject in December and Richards received his first shipment in early February 1870. His order included pork, salt, cheese, coffee, and candy. In March he placed his next request, for rice, salt, molasses, raisins, and "powder and shot." Two months later, he expanded the list, an indication his neighbors appreciated his efforts. Thus the AMA aided in the establishment of a black-owned business, a rare phenomenon in Reconstruction Georgia.[62]

However, very few teachers stepped outside the limits of romantic or moral character reform in their work among the freed people. Their program designed to "elevate" black men and women tells us more about their own way of life and their values and ambivalences than it does about the actual needs of people who remained chained by poverty and discrimination after emancipation. The abolitionists' overwhelming concern with individual morality persisted despite Reconstruction realities. Their belief that "character" was the key to institutional as well as personal change proved inadequate in coping with the massive legal and economic problems that beset the Georgia black population.

Finally, despite their own efforts to influence the freed people on a personal level, the teachers rarely developed close emotional relationships with the "objects of their benevolence." The barriers of race, class, and culture were too high. When the teachers sought companionship, they inevitably turned to one another. The two groups rarely interacted in or outside the classroom and church as "equals." It is perhaps unfair to assign blame for this failure of communication to either party, bound as they were by their own moral imperatives. Certainly, few black adults felt the need or inclination to become friends with a northern white person. Sadly, the result was a lack of basic human understanding between individual members of the two races.

CHAPTER VII

Oases and Outposts: Life in the "Desert South"

In their expectations concerning black personal behavior, the northern aid societies were naive, but not hypocritical. They expected of their teachers the same unreasonably high standards of Victorian morality as they demanded of the freed people. However, in this phase of their professional life, too, the missionaries encountered unanticipated difficulties. The most obvious example was their attempt to recreate traditional patterns of family life in southern mission homes. Each "family" of freedmen's workers was to duplicate relationships characteristic of nuclear households and thus provide members with emotional support and religious inspiration. According to this plan of group living, the family would also serve to discipline its members by discouraging improper behavior. The goal was a "harmony" of purpose and personalities. But in Georgia mission homes the real rarely corresponded with the ideal. "Fathers" often had to struggle to maintain their authority, "mothers" were little more than cooks and maids, and "daughters" refused to conform to the role of obedient children.[1]

Classroom and social work responsibilities consumed a large part of the teachers' time, but living situations and relations with coworkers determined to a large extent whether they considered freedmen's work a glorious adventure or one step on the road to martyrdom. In Georgia mission homes, personal relationships often reached levels of such sheer intensity that they became independent of the larger work and distracted and preoccupied teachers and superintendents alike. Within the context of daily life—getting along with coworkers, superiors, and subordinates—the ideal of missionary self-sacrifice was a fragile one. On the one hand, conflicts based on age, sex, and status often shattered any semblance of goodwill among mission-home inmates. But, on the other, bonds of mutual love and dependence that developed between teachers could prove to be equally disruptive to patterns of "family" living. Ultimately, the teachers attempted to make decisions affecting the quality of their own lives outside the classroom, but they were limited by both the freedmen's aid society bureaucracy and by the southern white population, which was hostile and alien to them.

By the early 1870s, northern teachers assigned to the largest Georgia towns suffered few of the physical privations earlier associated with missionary work in the South. The urban mission homes provided relatively comfortable and secure living quarters. Assisted by a battery of servants, the local superintendent and his matron-wife sought to operate the home efficiently, provide the teachers with nutritious meals, and act as gracious hosts to distinguished New Englanders who visited the freedmen's schools periodically. To both teachers and travelers, the mission home represented a haven —an enclave of Yankee culture, education, and piety nestled deep within "the 'enemies' land.'"

The large Atlanta home functioned as just such an "oasis." The American Missionary Association (AMA) "family" occupied two buildings and made up a small society unto itself. The teachers enjoyed a home library, a large parlor complete with a piano imported from the North, and the genteel company of three superintendents (graduates of Yale and Dartmouth), their teacher-wives, and children. Although the standard fare prepared by the kitchen hardly qualified as sumptuous—university and normal-school boarders also partook of it—it was plentiful and well prepared. A large garden next to the home, cultivated by the mission's "outside man," supplied a cornucopia of fresh vegetables during the summer, and in the winter canned goods that had been prepared by the staff brought a welcome variety to meals.[2]

Life was quite different for those teachers who lived and worked in an "outpost," or rural town. For example, the two AMA teachers in the village of Andersonville led a precarious existence. One of them admitted that only women possessing "a truly devoted Missionary Spirit" could long survive "the horror of Andersonville," where about thirteen thousand soldiers had died within the confines of Confederate stockades during the war. The two women lived "from hand to mouth" in a drafty "old shell of a barn." They did their own housekeeping, and their ancient stove smudged their fingers as well as burned their bread. They felt beleaguered and insecure; harassment by whites in the neighborhood necessitated an escort of musket-bearing freedmen whenever they left their home. Nevertheless, one teacher remained committed to the town and its people until the association abandoned its school there in the mid-1870s.[3]

These two examples highlight some of the differences in life-style between urban and rural teachers of the freedmen in Reconstruction Georgia. But the contrasts between the refined home in Atlanta and the old barn in Andersonville are not as obvious as they might appear on the surface. As a general rule, the larger and more elaborate a mission home, the greater the likelihood that tension and scandal would erupt and make life miserable for the people who lived there. Some teachers actually preferred the primitive but independent existence associated with the outposts, for there they could escape the watchfulness of superintendents and older teachers and run their schools and lives as they pleased, at least within certain limits. Even though "pioneer" teachers faced a multitude of problems never encountered by workers in the towns, a few hardy souls chose to make their own way, even if that choice meant exposing themselves to physical danger. In the end, a trade-off occurred between freedom of action and comfortable physical surroundings. This fact, as much as any other, meant that the life of a teacher was hardly ever dull.

Freedmen's aid societies quickly learned that the quality of housing for their teachers materially affected the educational work in particular localities. Obviously, the better the teachers' diet and health and the lighter their housekeeping burdens, the more time and energy they could devote to the classroom. As an experienced society, the AMA was familiar with the difficulties and rewards of mission-home living (in Wilmington, Charleston, and Nashville, for example) by the time it began its Georgia operations. In the largest towns the association strove for the ideal in missionary accommodations: an efficient teachers' home characterized by a hierarchical family arrangement and an atmosphere of proper piety. Able and eager to dominate black education in the newly opened "field," the AMA assigned a large corps of workers to the most populous areas of the state. Mission homes in Atlanta, Savannah, Augusta, and Macon provided the strength, stability, and continuity necessary for the effort.

The AMA considered itself primarily a missionary society committed to evangelizing both at home and abroad. Georgia teachers, faced with the hostility of southern whites and the cultural peculiarities of the freedmen, had little difficulty perceiving themselves as strangers in an alien land. One teacher noted the lack of "blessings of *civilized Christian* society" outside the Savannah mission home. Another expressed the doubt that any missionary, should he or she travel to "the uttermost parts of the earth," would find a more appropriate field of labor among the heathen of both races. The home thus functioned as a fort in enemy territory, a defensive stronghold in the midst of godlessness, poverty, and "degradation." A member of the Augusta "family" of fourteen remarked that "we have society among ourselves," and she did not feel the loss of social contact "from without."[4]

The home also served to encourage the teachers to renew their own commitment to the freed people through fellowship with their coworkers in a quiet, serious living environment. Daily contact with others devoted to the cause helped each woman derive new inspiration and, it was hoped, a "purer" dedication to her work. Judging from his previous experience in Wilmington, North Carolina, Savannah Superintendent Charles W. Sharp believed that life in a good mission home helped stimulate "zeal and enthusiasm" in each member of the family. Indeed, the early trials of the Savannah AMA staff revealed the problems inherent in boarding with or renting rooms from persons unsympathetic to the work. In the fall of 1865, teachers in that city lodged with (in the words of one woman) "an irritable Irishman who was formerly a captain in the British army and now he wants to be Captain over us." The tyrant objected to the teachers' attempts to educate their black servants, conduct devotional services, or, indeed, make any noise at all. When one of the women began to read aloud in a room adjoining his, "he pounded on the door, and then commenced swearing in a fearful manner and screaming at the top of his voice." Surely the teachers found this a shocking display of temper, and it created an atmosphere that was hardly conducive to Christian benevolence. Freedmen's workers all over the state encountered these and other difficulties when boarding; their most frequent complaints included their inability to instruct blacks in their own quarters, the destructive effects of bad housing upon their health, and the continual threat of rent increases and sudden, arbitrary evictions.[5]

Ever mindful of the need for efficiency in its work, the AMA found the economic argument persuasive in its decision to establish mission homes in large towns whenever possible. Because of inflation and a lack of housing, rents and boarding costs in postwar Georgia were especially high. Superintendents learned it was nearly impossible to acquire lodging for teachers in public or private residences and keep within the weekly four to five dollar limit per person set by AMA headquarters. By way of contrast, about four dollars a week provided teachers with tolerable, if not comfortable, accommodations in houses the association rented on its own or bought outright. AMA bureaucrats figured that boarding costs in "outpost" areas tended to equal or fall slightly below this amount, but the teachers reached relatively few students and had a much lower standard of living. One woman who boarded with a black family on an Albany plantation in 1870 paid only five dollars per month for board, but she taught no more than thirty-four pupils. (She also expressed dissatisfaction with the meals prepared for her by her hosts, and complained that the furniture in her room was "infested with all kinds of vermin.") In the cities, where freedmen filled the classrooms to overflowing, the AMA dollar went further. By the late 1860s, the association had reduced its rural expenses by insisting that the freed people pay the board of white teachers and by sponsoring native black instructors, who worked for lower salaries and could obtain cheaper housing in those areas.[6]

AMA superintendents walked a fine line between keeping the monthly home expenses for rent, staples, groceries, wood, lights, wages, drayage, and furniture as low as possible and making the home pleasant enough to keep teacher morale high. Executive officials acknowledged the difficulty. One field secretary, Erastus M. Cravath, encouraged the Macon superintendent to operate the home as efficiently as possible without injuring the health or comfort of the teachers: "Now you are a *Yankee* and can manage this thing so as not to disturb the sacred life of Lincoln Home." Cravath himself wrote a short treatise defending the expenditure of $41.25 for wood one month at Atlanta. He explained to New York that high prices and the home's sole reliance on fireplaces for heat justified the large sum. The problem frequently prompted a defensiveness on the part of both district secretaries and local superintendents, who feared that home monthly expenses revealed a lack of respect for an appropriately austere missionary life style. In 1869 one official, on a tour of Georgia, assured AMA headquarters that the procurement of a mousetrap for one home did not constitute "extravagance" on his part.[7]

The AMA sought to counteract southern postwar inflation and provide nutritious food for its teachers by sending large quantities of staples from New York to Georgia homes. Items such as crackers, butter, potatoes, lard, condensed milk, dried beef, ham, dried apples, flour, tea, and coffee often cost less in the North, and shipped via steamer provided relatively cheap supplements to the teachers' diets. A circular released by New York in 1870 revealed that superintendents could order cocoa, chocolate, cinnamon, cloves, codfish, farina, ginger, mackerel, molasses, pork, peaches, rice, raisins, to-matoes, tapioca, and yeast powder (among other things) directly from Cincinnati or New York headquarters. Georgia superinten-dents gladly took advantage of this arrangement. In addition, pri-vate individuals often sent barrels of supplies to friends or relatives teaching in the South. As a result, teachers in the larger homes enjoyed well-balanced and tasty diets.[8]

Still, superintendents waged a monthly battle with their account books and frequent, frantic pleas for more money punctuated their correspondence with New York. The Atlanta superintendent tried to conceal his panic in 1866 when he wrote that he owed seven hundred dollars and that the home's financial matters were "just now really embarrassing." His Macon colleague scribbled off a note in April 1867: "Money is a necessity. Please send some—we cannot live by faith!" Just two weeks before Christmas that same year, the AMA official in Augusta had good cause to worry: "Our dinner is pur-chased for today; beyond that we know not. I need $30 immediately." The "sinews of war" often did arrive inconveniently late, but appar-ently no mission home resident ever starved to death. Desperation over money matters led superintendents to borrow from all pos-sible sources, including the Freedman's Savings and Trust Bank, teachers' salaries, and their own pockets. In 1870 Superintendent Edmund Ware dipped into scholarship funds and even used money set aside for the payment of student teachers to keep the Atlanta home going. New York inevitably appreciated this type of Yankee ingenuity.[9]

Within each mission home lived a "family," which ideally con-sisted of a "father"-superintendent, "mother"-matron, and "chil-dren"-teachers. Freedmen, women, and children were hired as ser-vants. Whenever possible, the AMA insisted upon this arrangement under the assumption that the family concept helped to foster a united school staff and stimulate congenial relations among the workers. The teachers themselves recognized the logic of this ap-proach and usually referred to themselves with little self-conscious-ness as members of a particular mission home "family." This ap-proach to missionary life was strengthened by the fact that in many cases members of a real family—spouses, siblings, parents and children—lived together.

Each person's duties and responsibilities within the household depended upon his or her status as a family member, and the larger the home the more elaborate and specialized the hierarchy. For example, in the early 1870s the Atlanta family, responsible for more than 150 normal-school boarders as well as for the maintenance of school buildings and two mission homes, consisted of a minister, two superintendents, a bookkeeper, a maintenance man, a matron, and a dormitory preceptress. Although no other "family" attained this degree of complexity in terms of role assignments, each one had a formal structure to deal with business and social affairs. Still, regardless of the amount of time and energy devoted to defining each person's position within the family, challenges to authority emerged in both subtle and dramatic ways.[10]

Besides serving as school principal, the typical superintendent acted as home business manager, repairman, and spiritual adviser for many as twenty-two family members. He spent much of his time compiling and recording detailed monthly statistics for the New York office, though few of the men could muster any enthusiasm for this tedious chore. The physical condition of the home also demanded the constant attention of each superintendent; he supervised painting, laying of sidewalks, and installation of heating devices as well as routine matters of operation and repair. But most challenging and frustrating was his responsibility to (in the words of one) "manage young ladies so as to keep them comfortably disposed towards one another and himself." Trying to prevent the teachers from overworking, he insisted on short vacations, rest periods, and pleasure excursions when he deemed them necessary. He supervised their diets and arranged their meal schedule, decided whom to admit to the family circle and whom to cast out. When a teacher fell ill, he sometimes substituted for her in school and administered Hosford's Powders to her. And, in the event of ultimate failure, he made arrangements for her burial. He sought to attain a perfect fatherhood—wise, conscientious, solicitous, patient, stern, and loving. Yet he discovered that these tender ministrations sometimes went unappreciated.[11]

As in nuclear families, the mission-home father occasionally found his position challenged, and even usurped, by a woman. But in AMA homes the "daughters" (teachers) more often than the "mother" (matron) showed defiance and resistance. Older female teachers who perceived moral deficiency or a power vacuum at the top of the family hierarchy, especially when a younger man served as superintendent, felt no hesitation in becoming an informal—though no less effective—"father." Julia Shearman spoke for these strong-willed women when she wrote in 1867 of affairs at the Augusta home: "I guess I shall do a little at 'Superintendency' without having the name, for I can't stand by and see things needed and not put a finger in the pie; this would be quite contrary to my nature." In fact, the superintendent derived his power from the consent of the "governed," rather than from a "divine right" or the authority vested in his position. Shearman observed that she and other Augusta teachers would defer to their superintendent as a result of his "moral superiority of character" rather than his formal status or gender. Of her coworkers, she noted, "they cannot be controlled with either man or woman who is lacking in *character*. You must possess the respect of these teachers if you w[oul]d do anything with them." Another expressed a conditional welcome for a new superintendent when she wrote, "If he is an able man and earnest Christian, I shall be very glad to have him in our family." Similarly, a Savannah teacher reported that the official in charge of the mission home there had "won" her "*esteem* and *love*" by his kindness and genial nature. One superintendent, realizing that he lacked the cooperation of his mission-home family, asked New York to relieve him of his duties at the end of the 1868–69 school year; implicit teacher opposition had made it too difficult for him to carry out his responsibilities.[12]

An incident in Augusta during the first year of AMA operation there illustrates the nature of serious revolts against superintendents. Only twenty-three years old, Dewitt C. Jencks had charge of seven teachers in the home. A Freedmen's Bureau official reported in December 1865 that the teachers considered their position "unsufferable" because of Jencks's dictatorial conduct. Two of the women threatened to leave when the young man questioned their missionary fervor after they had purchased some apples for dessert; he considered such delicacies inappropriate for their Spartan diet. He forbade eating between meals and ordered the teachers to consume only what he bought for them. Apparently his insulting manner, as well as the substance of his complaints, offended the teachers, most of whom were older than he. One local AMA official suggested that an older man assume leadership within the house because Jencks "lacked the influence of superior age and experience" and could not effectively issue orders. In June 1866 the AMA revoked his commission and presumably he returned to his native Killingly, Connecticut, and resumed his former job as a bookkeeper. It had proved to be poor training for the position of AMA superintendent. Jencks was replaced by Charles H. Prince, who also lacked professional credentials. He was thirty years old, married, and had served as a captain in the Union army; he had no professional educational experience. The cycle soon started over again, as Julia Shearman's comments in 1867 indicate.[13]

In another case, the Reverend Charles Sharp was dismayed to

learn when he arrived in Savannah in 1869 that Cornelia Drake, a teacher in the city since 1865, had "supreme control of matters" in the mission home and preferred to keep things that way. "Miss Drake likes to rule," observed Mrs. Sharp, and described the problem this way: "She [Drake] is a regular Puritan, rather inclined, I think, to the rigid side of religion. . . . Mr. Sharp being educated at Yale and New York, and not at Princeton, has freer notions of things." Sharp resented the teacher's accusation that his moral leadership in the home was nonexistent. As a result of Drake's persistence (for example, she started an "opposition prayer meeting" in the home), the couple found their position as household heads untenable and left Savannah the following June.[14]

To participants and observers alike, these challenges to superintendents' authority implied a breakdown in roles established by sex. The confusion seemed to stem from the dual nature of the superintendent's job; he served both as "father" and "mother" for the teachers. Most older women supported a superintendent in his duties concerning the physical maintenance of the home and all the paperwork produced by local AMA affairs. But at times they balked when he tried to exert his own brand of "moral influence" within the home. In a practical sense, this included his attempts to define proper missionary behavior in terms of the teachers' diet or their participation in a family prayer meeting. Those men who were young, inexperienced, or weak leaders proved to be particularly vulnerable in this respect.

Ironically, then, teachers who dominated or controlled the social relations within mission homes in effect became "men." Apparently everyone agreed that rebellion against a superintendent provided evidence of the protester's "masculine character." One AMA official explained the difficulty in Augusta, where Caroline Merrick, age forty-one, usurped the power of a young superintendent: "Miss Merrick is . . . really at the head of affairs in Augusta, and is much more of a man than the average!" Julia Shearman, to stress the ineffectuality of her superior's command, observed that she found few "*men*" in the Augusta home or its vicinity. She also expressed the opinion that she was "more of a man" than most freedmen's officials she met in the town. But Merrick, Shearman, and the others were simply carrying to its logical conclusion the injunction to "expand" their own "moral influence" as female missionaries. This self-confident professionalism and passionate commitment to the cause proved to be an explosive combination, and ultimately disrupted relations between the sexes within mission homes just as it had in the schools.[15]

Unlike the superintendent, a matron rarely had to fend off would-be challengers, for her duties proved too arduous and nerveracking for all but a few determined souls. During the school year, she prepared or supervised the preparation of meals, took care of the housecleaning, and tried to "render the family comfortable and happy," at least in physical terms. Her special responsibility was to keep expenses low, and, at the same time, provide a minimum standard of nutrition and variety to meals. In the long run, she felt that she best served "economy" by avoiding waste and keeping the teachers healthy, regardless of the price. One matron declared that *"The best articles are the cheapest"* when forced to justify her expenses to New York. An endless variety of minor irritations compounded the matron's woes. She had to cater to the fastidious tastes of visitors, contend with acute shortages of household necessities such as linens and flatware, and every once in a while wage "an ineffectual war with Ants, Roaches, and Mice." Articles sent from New York might help her cut expenses, but dependence on supplies often proved to be exasperating. One matron wrote AMA headquarters that she had unpacked a box of staples and printed matter only to find that rats had eaten the vegetables and that a mixture of peppercorns and coffee grounds "made the Sermon on the Mount so pungent that we sneezed and wept alternately." It was no wonder that other household members were content to stay out of her way whenever possible.[16]

The problem of an appropriate salary for this "galley slave" prompted some discussion in AMA circles. One superintendent said his wife's duties were very strenuous, but that she derived "sufficient reward" from contributing to the welfare of the family. (However, *she* remained silent on that point, at least in her correspondence to headquarters.) Because couples usually received a joint salary, married women serving as matrons rarely complained about financial compensation. Protests usually emanated from "unattached" matrons who maintained they deserved more than a regular teacher's pay. Field Secretary Edward P. Smith argued with AMA headquarters in 1866 that the position of mother of the family was "one of the most responsible and thankless we have to offer," and should carry with it a commensurate salary—at least five extra dollars a month. He noted that few women were eager to serve as matrons "and when one is found it is wise as well as right to make an inducement for her to accept the position." But financial records indicate the association never adopted a formal policy of paying matrons more than teachers, though it sometimes bowed to pressure from individual women.[17]

The exhausting schedule of the teachers—"the girls"—left them with little time for major household responsibilities. Yet, in the course of daily home life, they performed certain "womanly" functions, and served as seamstresses, nurses, and corresponding secretaries. Of course, a multitude of minor tasks performed within each home received little formal recognition. In 1867 one young superintendent described his satisfaction with mission home living and added, "I feel especially indebted for those little favors of which we men all stand in need at times such as fixing up the buttons, darning the stockings, etc."[18]

Whenever it was financially feasible, each mission home hired servants to assist with cleaning, cooking, and washing. Blacks of both sexes and all ages found employment in the homes. Girls helped women in the laundry and kitchen, men performed maintenance duties, and boys ran errands and did other miscellaneous chores. The AMA paid relatively high wages (i.e., ten dollars a month for cooks and waiters, six dollars for a kitchen helper), and at times provided free clothing and educational instruction to servants. But, despite these benefits—or perhaps, in the case of clothing and food, because of them—the shadow of slavery hung over Georgia mission households. To a black woman scrubbing floors in the Savannah home, the matron's offering of a single piece of bread symbolized her employer's largesse; but, carefully deposited in her apron pocket, it was also the only food her children would eat that day. Despite the flood of correspondence between New York or Cincinnati and Georgia during the first decade after the war, these servants were rarely mentioned by teachers, matrons, or superintendents. The AMA had enlightened attitudes toward race, but it remained a fact of mission home life that black people did the meanest jobs and occupied the lowest position in the household hierarchy; in fact, they were not members of the "family" at all.[19]

The mission home provided comfortable quarters for the teachers, a place where they could relax after a long day in school, read a book from the library, or play the piano. The home and its family arrangement also served broader social functions. Members of each family sought to exercise a certain amount of control or moral suasion over the personal behavior of others in the home; teachers, as well as superintendents and matrons, attempted to curb what they considered the improper activities of their coworkers. As a result, relationships within the home were often charged with resentment on both sides. And yet, though personal differences drove family members apart, their social ostracism within the larger southern society bound them fiercely together. These opposing forces of repulsion and attraction were equally intense. But superintendents perceived any kind of passion—either hatred or unseemly affection—as inappropriate missionary behavior and tried to keep things on an even keel. Paradoxically, those homes best known for their gracious hospitality toward northern guests were also the ones racked by the greatest turmoil.

According to the AMA, its teachers needed a home where they could benefit from moral and spiritual guidance in their work. The superintendent, as paternalistic head of the household, supposedly assumed the lead in fulfilling this responsibility, whether he was an ordained minister or not. In addition, the New York office implicitly encouraged all its teachers to exert a benevolent influence over one another and to offer constructive criticism to those engaging in questionable behavior. For the parent society, the strength of a person's contribution to the spiritual growth of the family provided evidence of his or her devotion to the cause. In practical terms, this meant that members often found it convenient to label as "unchristian" any behavior that upset the household routine or led to personal conflicts. This approach tainted all arguments with the charge of immorality and did little to effect speedy resolutions free from bitterness.[20]

One type of moral censure imposed from within the homes concerned individual teachers' attitudes toward blacks. In this matter, freedmen's aid society workers stressed "prudence and expediency" and condemned actions perceived as either bigoted, on the one hand, or too "familiar," on the other. Members of both the Savannah and Macon households reported that their mission families included young women who failed to treat blacks with proper respect by refusing to associate with them at church or eat at the same table with them in the home. This type of behavior conflicted with the AMA's egalitarian rhetoric, and the three teachers involved were pressured to conform to association standards and to the wishes of the rest of the family.

But teachers also came under fire for relating to freed people in a manner considered socially irresponsible by their coworkers. In 1866 Mary J. Welch of Augusta incurred the disapproval of her AMA family and Freedmen's Bureau Education Superintendent G. L. Eberhart (a frequent visitor to the home) when she indulged in a public display of affection for a pupil. Eberhart dashed off a heated letter to New York on the subject: "For a white Northern lady here to kiss a colored child is very *imprudent* to say the least of it, and, in reply to an insulting remark made by a white person, to say that the negroes are as good as that white person, is *entirely unnecessary.*"

Apparently, appearances were uppermost in the minds of everyone (except Mary Welch). The AMA dismissed her at the end of the year, presumably for creating a public controversy rather than for defying the southern code of race relations.[21]

Scandals producing the loudest and longest reverberations concerned relationships between young female teachers and men living in or outside the home. The association expected its employees to conduct themselves modestly, and even a hint of impropriety could result in the transfer or dismissal of the persons involved. In the most spectacular cases, older women, offended by what they considered shocking or immoral behavior in their younger coworkers, pressed the New York office to take appropriate action. The trials of a twenty-three-year-old teacher from Watertown, Connecticut, provide an illustration. Hattie C. Foote discovered that working in the South did not free her from certain New England moral strictures. During her six-year stay in Georgia beginning in 1865, on at least three occasions she received criticism about her conduct with men. These incidents inspired an extraordinary amount of correspondence among workers in the AMA's northern offices, Augusta, and Macon, and demonstrated the potentially damaging effects of rumor and innuendo on a teacher's reputation as well as her career in freedmen's work.

In the summer of 1866, Field Secretary Samuel Hunt advised the young woman (she was ill) to leave Augusta and return to her parents' home. Basing his charges on reports supplied by an anonymous source, he suggested that her current malady had resulted from "criminal intimacy" with an army surgeon boarding in the mission home. Whether Hunt was referring to pregnancy or venereal disease is unclear. In any case, the physician felt called upon to defend his own honor, denying to Hunt that he was a "Libertine . . . and in other respects, a bad man." Hattie Foote quickly regained her health. At the end of the year she was transferred to Macon where, three years later, an older teacher fueled the fires of another controversy. Mary E. Hart, age thirty-four, complained to New York of Foote's alleged romantic entanglement with Macon Superintendent Frederic Sawtell, age twenty. Three months later, this self-appointed guardian of Macon home morality informed the AMA district secretary that Foote and another teacher had shown indiscretion in socializing with a married army officer. Hart particularly objected to the young women entertaining the soldier on the mission home veranda, at times (she said) until 1:00 A.M.[22]

New York believed the charges serious enough to warrant a major shake-up in Macon affairs. Mary Hart's request for a transfer to

Atlanta was granted. The two younger Macon teachers received orders to return to the North. Foote's coworker, after much soul-searching (and the aid of some of the older teachers) begged forgiveness and admitted her error: "I like gentlemen's society and always did and I suppose always will." She was allowed to stay in the South, but the association transferred her to Savannah. Hattie Foote remained bitterly defiant to the end, convinced that Hart had acted out of jealousy. In October 1870 the AMA revoked her teaching commission.[23]

Other teachers were censured for similarly "unbecoming" conduct. Julia Shearman kept the New York headquarters fully apprised of the riotous situation in Augusta in the spring and summer of 1867, when one woman broke her ankle while horseback-riding with a man and another received "marked and increasing attentions" from a Freedmen's Bureau Hospital physician. (Although married, he soon acquired a divorce so that he and the teacher could wed; still, the happy event did little to mollify Shearman's indignation.) All these daring younger teachers made the mistake of committing their indiscretions within range of Hart and Shearman. "I am more and more persuaded of the importance of *watchfulness* and *purity* and I find something that needs cleansing in almost every place," noted Shearman candidly. Her position of formal powerlessness within the AMA bureaucracy indicates that excessive concern with the lives of other teachers was one way for older women to exercise authority over family members. And yet some teachers continued to take advantage of their new situation and the relative freedom in social relations it provided; they rode with men in open carriages, played cards, attended the theater, and promenaded with army officers, both married and single. The Savannah superintendent could hardly conceal his disgust when he came home at night and found the hat-rack bulging with the hats of gentleman callers without "knowing where the heads were that belonged in them."[24]

If family members believed it was their duty to regulate each others' behavior, they still needed to live with one another and accept the consequences of their own criticism. Short of a transfer or leaving the work altogether, there was nowhere to hide. The correspondence of AMA workers in Georgia reveals a universal obsession with domestic tranquility, or "harmony," within mission homes. Superintendents took it upon themselves to eject from the fold persons who threatened to disturb the delicate balance of interrelationships among young and old, male and female, superior and subordinate. Staffing decisions depended upon personal factors— whether or not a teacher was liked by the others—as well as objective criteria, such as teaching ability. In requesting that New York not assign two particular teachers to Augusta, one superintendent wrote in 1867, "Let us get clear if possible of that *old element of discord*." Another declared bluntly: "I am willing to do anything for harmony's sake."[25]

"Close quarters necessitate much good nature," mused a Georgia worker at one point. Indeed, a frequently uttered complaint concerning living arrangements dealt with the lack of privacy. Most teachers shared a small bedroom with one or two coworkers, and the crowded conditions contributed to tension between roommates—a tension exacerbated by the gossip-mongering that went on in some houses. The problem of keeping such compact little societies at peace with themselves baffled many superintendents. The day-to-day business of just trying to get along with one another, rather than instances of tragedy or adversity, proved to be the greatest trials. The Atlanta experience, in particular, reveals that even a "model" mission home had its problems. The AMA school system in that city boasted the finest facilities and best teaching staff in Georgia, yet a series of personality conflicts and challenges to the superintendent's leadership made life miserable for the renowned Atlanta family.[26]

"Let our Motto be 'Bear and forbear,'" wrote exasperated Superintendent Frederick Ayer to the district secretary during one long, bitter feud that lasted from 1865 to 1867. The charges and countercharges of drunkenness and lying hardly concealed the basic issue: the home matron and orphan asylum matron simply did not like each other. As usual in such conflicts, each person in the home took sides and then wrote long letters to New York detailing various rumors and developments. In 1869 two other controversies erupted. One teacher did her best to obtain the position of Atlanta matron for a dear friend assigned to another city; neither the current matron nor the superintendent appreciated this maneuvering, and the family eventually made life so difficult for the teacher that she left of her own accord. Wrote the superintendent: "her departure gave me a sense of relief I have not had for more than three years." This suggested the tremendous emotional toll these episodes took on everyone.[27]

That same year, Anna Snowden initiated her equal-pay-for-equal-work campaign within the ranks of the AMA. Both she and Amy Williams (who reintroduced the issue three years later) were denounced as "impulsive troublemakers" by two harried Atlanta superintendents. They requested that Snowden be transferred in October 1869; two months later, she saved the AMA some paperwork by leaving the field quite willingly. (Superintendent Ware lived up to his reputation as a resourceful AMA official by reminding the New York office that a Connecticut congregation had donated money to Atlanta in Snowden's name; he suggested that it be collected and sent south immediately.) In 1872 the two men dredged up the time-honored charge of "unchristian behavior" against Amy Williams and, for good measure, also accused her of mercenary motives.[28]

The case of the Reverend George Walker, who arrived in Atlanta in the fall of 1872, reveals that geographical and cultural differences among teachers presented real problems for family "harmony." A self-proclaimed "Oberlinite" and "Westerner," he found that an eastern sentiment held sway over the Atlanta household, which was filled with New England chauvinists who proclaimed Boston as the center of the universe. Objecting to what he termed the authoritarian management of both home and schools in Atlanta, he attributed this severe attitude to the other teachers' upbringing, and reported with amazement that one woman had admitted that her mother had never kissed her as a child. He especially resented the opinion proffered by one of his coworkers: "What ails you is you have never been to New England." Evidently time healed this wound in the family, and by 1873 Walker reported that domestic peace finally prevailed in Atlanta.[29]

Evaluated within the larger context of freedmen's works, these incidents were not of equal significance. The protests of Anna Snowden and Amy Williams centered on the injustice of AMA policies based on sex, and the other disputes originated from personality or cultural differences. But, regardless of their roots, all the episodes had similar implications for family life; the superintendents fussed and fumed over the "troublemakers" and family members lined up on opposing sides, gossiped among themselves, and wrote innumerable letters to society headquarters detailing their respective positions. Undercurrents of frustration and bitterness ran deep beneath the showy exterior of the AMA education complex in Atlanta.

Minimal contact with the surrounding white population only heightened the pressure for conformity within the homes. Because northern teachers rarely enjoyed social intercourse with southern whites, they necessarily depended on the family circle for companionship, and had nowhere else to turn in the face of rejection or unpleasantness. The teachers recognized this relationship between their own ostracism in the South and the quality of life in the homes. One teacher noted, "It is well that we *are happy* in each other for we have not a white friend in the place." But, accustomed to the genteel practice of visiting among friends during the day, they sometimes keenly felt their collective loneliness. And the differences of class, race, and culture between themselves and the freed people meant that interaction with blacks was no substitute for middle-class white society.[30]

On the other hand, lack of all contact with other whites proved to be preferable to rude, informal meetings on the streets. When teachers ventured outside the mission home, they were greeted with cries of "Nigger Teacher." White women screamed profanities, men spat, and children jeered. Teachers all over Georgia—those sponsored by the AMA, MFAS, and AFUC, in large towns or rural areas —all encountered this same rejection, especially in the first years after the war. Their very presence so mortified whites that the northerners learned to accept social proscription as a routine part of freedmen's work. Indeed, at times they prized their isolation, for they appreciated the ability to work without any interference from unsympathetic whites, and cited southern hostility as proof of the righteousness of their cause.[31]

Rejection from without and an esprit de corps within individual mission homes could encourage the formation of close emotional ties among teachers. These newfound friendships spanned generations and regional loyalties, and the end of the school year or reassignment of teachers to other parts of the South often proved traumatic. An Augusta teacher lamented in the late spring of 1868, "Our circle is diminishing—it seems sad bidding Good By to those whom we have become attached and whom we may never meet again." In Columbus, another woman confessed that she and her coworkers had come to depend so heavily on one another that "a separation after an attachment has been formed is a double calamity." Some women adamantly refused to relocate to other areas unless accompanied by a particularly close, tried and true friend: "Miss Engleman and I wish to be together—in fact we cannot consent to be separated," wrote one. Male officials often regarded such requests with amusement at best, contempt and scorn at worst. Writing of these intense relationships among women as they might have described heterosexual lovers, they described friends as "mates" and scoffed at the attempts of some teachers to "win the affections" of others.[32]

Probably as a result of their self-conscious camaraderie, the men in freedmen's work manifested their friendship in a different way. Several had attended college in the North together, and in their letters and conversations they liked to reminisce about "those good old honest talks such as self and college chum used to feast on." Witty correspondence helped to sustain these genial relationships. A prime example was Augusta Superintendent Egbert Bingham's

184 | Soldiers of Light and Love

lengthy admonishment to former classmate Edmund Ware to marry. Recently wed himself, Bingham warned his old friend to take the big step before he became "a sort of excrescence, a superfluity—a good for nothing." In November 1869 Ware followed Bingham's advice and married Jane Twichell, a teacher who lived in the Atlanta home. Their courtship, conducted discreetly in Atlanta and in her hometown of Plantsville, Connecticut, had not been a secret to other family members, and provided quite a contrast to the feuds that were raging in the home at the same time. The pair and thirteen other AMA workers met their future mates in Georgia. Newly wed teachers and superintendents often moved into separate quarters close to the mission home, thus remaining part of the family circle. By the end of 1872, three such couples, still in Georgia, had had their first children.[33]

The marriage of four teachers to officials of either the Freedmen's Bureau or the Freedman's Bank suggests that more than one northerner living in or visiting the South appreciated the hospitality offered by AMA families in Georgia. Judging from the effusive praise of a wide variety of guests from "Yankee land," the mission homes represented tiny enclaves of New England culture and refinement in war-devastated Georgia. "These 'Teachers Homes' are lovely places, Oaces [sic] in the desert south," wrote one northern clergyman of the Savannah household. Another visitor suggested that moving from a southern hotel to a mission home was "like slipping from a confined, oppressive dungeon, into the pure light of heaven." Family members did their best to suppress their own conflicts while entertaining guests on a short-term basis.[34]

Although long-term boarders presented logistical problems (quarters were normally cramped anyway), they at least proved to be financially beneficial, for they paid more than the monthly average board costs per regular family member. On the other hand, the nearly endless procession of visitors stopping for just a few days brought variety and enjoyment to the family's social life, but yielded no such pecuniary advantage. Even though everyone loved the company of distinguished and beloved guests, superintendents forced themselves to compute the price of sociability in dollars and cents at the end of each month. "Our Home has answered in some way the purposes of a Hotel," wrote the Macon official in December 1867. The large numbers of comers and goers caused his Savannah colleague to consider facetiously applying for an innkeeper's license. AMA policy dictated that whenever possible the superintendent should pay the lodging costs of visitors if the home was too full to accommodate them.[35]

Particularly cordial receptions awaited the most frequent and regular of northern guests—those AMA officials, especially the district secretaries, who exercised direct authority over the Georgia operations. Teachers and superintendents alike, frustrated by the inadequacy of written communications to convey a whole range of feelings about the work, appreciated the chance to talk to their superiors face to face. (An anxious Savannah superintendent once compared the visit of Secretary Erastus Cravath to that of a "passing angel.") The mission home also served as a way station for teachers in transit during the fall and spring and as a vacation residence for nearby AMA workers. The Savannah family greeted, entertained, and saw off at the dock teachers en route to Florida, regardless of their sponsoring society. Atlanta and Macon provided temporary lodging for teachers bound for Alabama and southwestern Georgia. Too, teachers living in rural areas enjoyed the chance to visit their coworkers in the towns and spend a few days in the mission home during vacations and weekends. In October 1871 the lone freedmen's teacher in Albany, relaxing in the Macon home, enjoyed the company and the "benefit of Glass windows to Sew by."[36]

Some AMA teachers preferred to live in rural areas, though it is unclear whether this impulse to "rough it" stemmed from a realization of the emotional hazards of mission home living or the desire to embrace adventure and hardship in the name of missionary self-sacrifice. In any case, these women wanted to work and live by themselves, and their sense of duty (or daring) impelled them out of the towns and into isolated regions of the Georgia backcountry. One superintendent, in assigning a teacher to Jonesboro, remarked that she "would go anywhere." A coworker in Savannah reported she had decided to venture out to a small rural school; "The 'Home' presents many attractions and the family are all pleasant and agreeable but still a small voice within says go and I feel that I must heed its call." The pioneer teacher was an anomaly in freedmen's education; she operated outside of the northern bureaucracy on a daily basis, independent of male superintendents and principals. Eventually, she proved too expensive to maintain within an "efficient" educational system.[37]

Teachers assigned to rural areas availed themselves of a variety of living accommodations. Most boarded with private families; some kept house; a few actually lived in their schools; and others stayed in hotels, though this was too expensive for anything but a temporary solution to the housing problem. White women found it difficult to obtain quarters, and local officials often stipulated that sponsoring societies send only black males as instructors. At times, transplanted northern men or women or southerners who had Republican proclivities welcomed the female teachers into their homes, but women who could find lodging only with natives unsympathetic to the cause often discovered themselves in uncomfortable situations. Southern landlords did not hesitate to evict their Yankee boarders if they had any difficulty in paying the rent. Because most AMA teachers depended upon the freed people to pay their board expenses, a permanent home resulted only from a good harvest and fair labor practices. In Georgia, neither of these two factors ever proved to be reliable, and the pioneer teacher's tenure was rarely long or stable.[38]

The AMA and the Freedmen's Bureau insisted that white teachers exhaust all other possibilities before deciding to live with black families. Officials delicately suggested that northern white women might find the arrangement inconvenient. One woman who had taken up residence with a black family in 1868 did report that their cabin was "open, airy, and altogether uncomfortable, their diet is not adapted to my taste." However, it is doubtful whether or not she felt more uncomfortable with her black hosts than teachers staying with native whites who sat down each day to (as one put it) a "nauseating mess" of bacon, collards, and cornbread. In the last analysis, a pleasant boarding arrangement depended more on the location of the home and the host family's economic status than on their race. The teacher who stayed in the home of the surgeon in charge of the Savannah Freedmen's Hospital, a black man, probably had better accommodations than anything other women could hope to find among rural Georgia families, white or black.[39]

Some teachers arranged to keep house on their own, and this situation had both advantages and disadvantages. A housekeeping teacher could cook her own food, entertain black visitors if she wished, and oversee domestic affairs as she liked. But housework consumed much time, and after a long day in the classroom she often had neither the strength nor the inclination to prepare meals or clean. The situation proved more satisfactory for two teachers who could keep each other company and divide the household chores between them. The quality of housekeeping arrangements varied from the large, gracious Wild Horn Plantation near Savannah, occupied by two women in the winter of 1866–67, to the tiny rooms that one teacher partitioned off in her Albany schoolhouse.[40]

Outpost pioneers faced several substantial problems rarely encountered by members of mission home families. Just traveling to and from rural areas in postwar Georgia presented difficulties. Dilapidated stagecoaches, open two-horse buggies, unreliable boats, railroad baggage cars, and carriages pulled by feisty horses or driven by hostile southerners all made travel exasperating and wearisome. En route to their new assignments, many teachers must have anticipated the difficulties in sending and receiving communications with the outside world once they were tucked away in their own "dark corner" of Georgia. And, predictably, few teachers found luxurious accommodations once they arrived. Several reported they lived in "well-ventilated" housing, drafty and damp. Few boarding places were equipped with essential furniture or utensils, and the far-sighted teacher lugged her own bedding, silverware, and dishes into the backcountry. At times, a good imagination proved an asset in making do with a few items. For one teacher in Liberty County, the floor served as a chair and her lap as a table, and a candle in a tin pepper-box made an inexpensive lamp. This woman exhibited the self-sufficiency of many outpost workers when she wrote: "We wash our own windows, do our own cooking, . . . and hold no one responsible."[41]

Tight budgets and the unavailability of certain kinds of food forced most teachers in rural areas to adjust to new diets. Although mission-home inmates feasted on northern-style cooking and a variety of New England delicacies sent south by their society, pioneers complained of "heavy, lardy biscuits," greasy cooking, and scarcities of beef, tea, and coffee. Two teachers, stationed in Thomasville, summed up the biggest differences between southern and northern cuisine when they wrote, "swine flesh in some form is never once absent from the [southern] table, while pies, cake, milk, and preserves are never seen,and butter rarely." (But they hastened to add this disclaimer: "Please do not misunderstand us. The primary desire with reference to our Surroundings is for neither dainties nor elegancies, but strength to perform daily tasks".) Another woman, claiming it was "quite a new experience" to go without breakfast each day, made regular trips to the grocery store in order to supplement her meager diet with a white family in Griffin. In the midst of all these difficulties, gifts of eggs, vegetables, fruit, milk, and berries from the freed people provided occasional relief.[42]

Because no more than three, and usually only one or two, women occupied a rural "garrison" at a time, they had to seek out company on their own. In Brunswick, the lone AMA teacher made the acquaintances of a Freedmen's Bureau agent, a Republican state senator, and a Worcester, Massachusetts, family involved in a local lumbering business. However, few other small towns in Georgia were blessed with such a quota of Union supporters, and outpost teachers frequently expressed a deep sense of personal and social isolation. Explained one woman in 1868: "The White people still let us terribly alone, which I cannot help but feel very much as our Northern circle numbers only three." And another, living by herself at St. Mary's, wrote under the section reserved for "Remarks" on her December 1868 Teacher's Monthly Report: "A little *Northern society needed*." Like their coworkers in the towns, rural teachers rarely considered contact with blacks as "company" or "society," and, in some cases, where the freed people were resistant or hostile to the northern effort, their ostracism was total.[43]

Greater exposure to danger and violence also made outpost living quite different from that in an urban mission home. Isolated female teachers became targets of nighttime harassment and anonymous threats. Methodist male teachers and their families encountered overt hostility and even armed resistance from whites. Met at the Waynesboro railroad depot by an angry crowd, one MFAS missionary clenched an ax handle in his fist and proceeded to march his family through town to the black schoolhouse, where they set up housekeeping temporarily. They and the AMA teachers assigned to Albany had the distinction of living in the two Georgia towns where, according to one northern observer, the whites would "as soon shoot a man as a dog."[44]

And the streets of Atlanta or Savannah rarely afforded such scenes of racial violence as those witnessed by Minnie Hanson in the small town of Newton in December 1871. A forthcoming election prompted an outburst of terrorism as whites whipped and shot freedmen to keep them from voting. Hanson quoted the townspeople as saying that they would "wade knee-deep in blood before Niggers should represent Baker Co." Because the local northern force of occupation had been bribed into inaction, she did her best to deliver election ballots to freedmen in spite of widespread mail fraud. Nevertheless, the Democratic candidates won overwhelming victories in the predominantly black town. The teacher wrote to New York in despair: "In the midst of life we are in death."[45]

Finally, outpost living demanded much of the teachers in terms of administrative responsibility. Most women considered the added duties a measure of their own independence rather than a burden. As the sole freedmen's aid society representatives in the area, female teachers often hired lawyers, negotiated contracts, signed and transferred deeds for houses and schoolhouses, arranged for the auctioning of furniture, paid rent, and found new owners for unused buildings. They made their own decisions regarding social relations with the freed people, at times ignoring the dictates of local Freedmen's Bureau officials. Perhaps most significantly, rural teachers had complete control over their schools. Upon arriving in Madison in the fall of 1867, three AMA teachers learned that the parents of their pupils doubted that young women could ever govern the school. "I hope that before this school year closes, the people will see their mistake," wrote one of them, and she expressed no apprehension over teaching without the benefit of a superintendent's fatherly advice.[46]

Except for one in Augusta, closed by the AMA in 1870, the mission homes were permanent institutions in Georgia during the decade after the war. Superintendents worried constantly where the next dollar was to come from; nevertheless, large households provided stability to freedmen's work in the larger towns. In contrast, outpost work assumed a highly temporary character. The existence of a rural school often depended on the resourcefulness of one teacher and the economic well-being of the black community; a poor crop could force her back into the city. Methodist missionaries sometimes turned to farming to provide for themselves and their families, but AMA teachers—single women—relied more directly on the support of freed people. Predictably, the northern societies gradually phased out these pioneers, for they reached few students and were difficult to monitor within the context of a centralized educational bureaucracy.

Each teacher's southern experience was shaped by the quality of her living conditions and relationships with other freedmen's workers, as well as by her performance in the classroom. But it is difficult to generalize about the connection between a woman's boarding arrangements and her attitude toward the work in general. Certainly, most appreciated the amenities afforded by life in a large mission home, but they had to pay a price for the companionship and physical comfort. Regardless of their commitment to freedmen's education, some teachers and superintendents succumbed to the pressures inherent in a situation where so many people lived so closely together under less than ideal circumstances. Personal animosities, jealousy, and disputes over policy all made inroads into the missionary ideal of brotherly and sisterly love. The strict hierarchy of roles within the largest households further eroded any semblance of tranquillity, for strong-minded persons of both sexes vied for positions of real, if not official, power. Like blood relatives in a traditional nuclear arrangement, the teachers found it nerveracking to live in a big family plagued by constant financial worries and the overt disapproval of its closest neighbors. In the end, some women preferred the primitive life of an outpost pioneer.

But, for most teachers, regardless of how or where they lived, disappointment, frustration, and happiness all mingled together in this great adventure. Whether they stayed in well-staffed mission homes or in leaky rural schools, the women discovered challenges never encountered at home in the North. Many took advantage of this opportunity to test the limits of their own physical and emotional endurance. The benevolence of a sponsoring society and the paternalism of a superintendent sheltered each teacher only so far; beyond that point lay a wide range of possibilities for the most daring to explore.

CHAPTER VIII
Epilogue

By 1870 the northern freedmen's aid societies had begun to retrench in Georgia. The demise of the Freedmen's Bureau, coupled with declining contributions in the North, made cutbacks and the consolidation of operations necessary. Some groups, such as the American Freedmen's Union Commission (AFUC), ceased to exist altogether. Those that continued to sponsor black schools in the South began to channel the bulk of their financial resources and personnel into normal schools and colleges. This was especially true of the American Missionary Association (AMA), which remained the most active northern society in Georgia throughout the late nineteenth century. During the 1870s, the association pared its common-school efforts to three cities—Macon, Savannah, and Atlanta—and began to concentrate on prestigious Atlanta University and a handful of secondary schools.

This change in priorities on the part of the AMA coincided with the first successful attempt by Georgia whites to establish a statewide system of public education. The association hoped to take advantage of state and local education funds to insure a smooth transition between the private and public support of black elementary schooling. The process of transferral was erratic, for local conditions rather than statutory provisions determined whether or not reluctant white administrators would assume financial responsibility for black education. Moreover, the northern teachers who participated in the negotiation process at times had to contend with another group unsympathetic to their efforts: black leaders who were determined to replace the white interlopers with native Georgians of their own race. This impulse occasionally led to an alliance between members of the black community and white officials whose first priority was the removal of all Yankees from the field. It was no wonder that the few AMA workers still at their posts in the mid-1870s felt beleaguered and unappreciated.

Soon after the end of the Civil War, a few Georgia towns and counties began to allocate local tax moneys for schooling purposes. The likelihood that blacks would derive any assistance from these public education funds (though they of course contributed to them) usually depended upon two factors: local officials' willingness to aid black schools, and the political strength of the black population in the area. The second factor often influenced the first. Thus from the small town of Valdosta one AMA teacher reported in 1870, "Our Public School officers are willing to lend us *no* Assistance. They are not in favor of the 'Nigger' being educated. And consequently throw every obstacle in our way to prevent our progress." On the other hand, northern teachers stationed in Augusta received some financial support from Richmond County as early as 1868, probably as a result of the large number of Republicans in that city (white and black) and the presence of the Freedmen's Bureau superintendent of education. But, although the public school superintendent agreed to cooperate with northern officials, the volatile political situation in the county together with a depleted civil treasury meant that public aid to black education was sporadic at best. AMA teachers rarely saw their paychecks until the end of the school year (even then they considered themselves lucky), and they received less than their counterparts who taught white children. This pattern of discrimination and unreliability of funding recurred throughout the state at the local level.[1]

The Georgia General Assembly passed a law in October 1870 that provided for a state superintendent of education (former Freedmen's Bureau officer John R. Lewis was the first appointee), one school district in each county, and "separate and equal facilities" for members of both races (but the legislature did not specify that funds should be allocated on the basis of race). However, this statute made no provisions for the levying of local taxes to pay teachers' salaries, and consequently no state-supported public schools existed in Georgia in 1870 or in 1871. The following year, the state's "redeemed" (Democratic) legislature relieved Lewis of his responsibilities and rectified the salary oversight. It also stipulated that county officials should distribute school funds according to color and that the schools should be segregated. This marked the beginning of Georgia's state public education system. AMA officials quickly launched a concerted campaign to pry from the clenched fists of Democrats as much money as possible for black education. Again, their success varied according to local politics, personalities, and prejudices.[2]

The AMA schoolteachers as a group understood the financial and ideological imperatives involved in this transition phase, but most agreed with Sarah Stansbury when she wrote of the white school officials in Cuthbert, "I am chary of these Southerners." Field secretaries were bombarded with pleas to proceed cautiously before making any compromises with whites in return for school aid. Commented Superintendent Niles in 1874, "I don't believe the time has yet come when the interests of the colored people would be safe in the hands of the white people of Savannah." He reminded Field Secretary Michael E. Strieby that the public board of education in that city supported one white teacher (of black children) whose brother had just received recognition for his essay attempting "to prove that the blacks were descended from the 'Rematangs.'" Other teachers cringed at the prospect of relinquishing their pupils to "unreconstructed" white women and former slaveholders and Confederate military officials—in other words, to their "enemies." "To leave the work to the public is to deprive the children of anything like an education," wrote one AMA representative in Macon. He reported that public officials preferred to hire "exconfederate soldiers' wives" over black candidates and that black children in public schools were not allowed to learn penmanship or anything beyond fractions in arithmetic. Another teacher in the same town wrote plaintively to her superior in the North, "I hope you will not give [the school] up to them."³

But, in at least some cases, it was not a matter of northern freedmen's aid societies abandoning black people to the mercy of southern white supremacist school officials. Many teachers were disturbed by what they perceived to be the unseemly haste with which black parents withdrew their children from northern-sponsored (tuition) schools and enrolled them in public (free) ones. Although the issue was always complicated by the race of the rival teachers involved, it appears that at times financial considerations were significant in shaping the preferences of blacks. Or at least that is what they told their white benefactors.

Teachers who watched wholesale defections from their classes reacted with dismay, and, in some cases, anger. A few in rural areas, fearing that incompetent whites or blacks would become teachers, worked against efforts to establish public schools. Apparently just the rumor of "free schools" was enough to provoke an exodus among the children. From Albany came a familiar lament: "The expectation of having free schools is the cause [of declining attendance]," wrote Mary P. Stewart in January 1871. Macon's Lizzie Parsons echoed: "Owing to the colored people looking for the promised free school it was impossible to get much of a school or collect much money."

Superintendents reported from other parts of the state that even patrons withdrew their children from AMA schools at the mention of a free alternative.[4]

Despite the misgivings of their workers in the field, northern officials continued to press hard for Georgia public education funds, usually the first step in the transfer of all association operations to local authorities. As a matter of policy, the AMA outlined several terms that each county or municipal school board had to meet before it would approve the transaction. The association reserved the right to choose at least some of the teachers hired by the public system, and to use classroom facilities for religious purposes in the evenings and on Sunday. It tried to insist that its own teachers receive the same compensation as instructors of white children. In return, it allowed the city to use its buildings free of charge for the school year.

Regardless of the terms of individual leases, white school officials were definitely bent on making the whole transition as difficult as possible for the northerners. Local school committees often insisted on subjecting association teaching "candidates" to a public examination. Although almost all of them passed, they felt humiliated in the process. Six Atlanta teachers angrily confronted the Reverend C. W. Francis in 1872 and explained they "did not propose to be turned over like the furniture of the building to the control of the city." An Atlanta instructor summed up the feelings of her coworkers when she declared that the public examination required of her "hurt my pride a good deal. For a Southern Superintendent to complain of the literary qualifications of Northern teachers is quite too bad . . . it touches my patriotism as well as my pride."[5]

Local boards almost always discriminated against northerners and blacks in salaries. They failed to pay on time, and often "forgot" about any compensation at all (or pleaded financial "embarrassment") for months on end. AMA teachers were excluded from staff meetings, and ordered to move out of association mission homes if they expected to receive public support. Black schools were opened later than white schools and closed earlier; in some cities, they were conducted only during the hottest months of the year in order to discourage attendance. Despite contract stipulations to the contrary, public administrators allowed AMA buildings to fall into disrepair. Most leases had to be renegotiated at the beginning of the new school year, and each time the AMA felt pressed to defend itself against the attempts by local boards to force new concessions.

The issue of teacher hiring—how many and what kind—was the focus of most disputes between AMA and public officials. Although large numbers of children in the cities were turned away for lack of teachers and space, the whites consistently refused to increase support for black schools. A teacher in Augusta reported in 1878 that at least three hundred of the one thousand black children of school age in that city were in effect denied an education because of the board's intransigence. The situation was even worse in Savannah; the city schools there accommodated no more than two hundred children, though two thousand were eligible to attend. Predictably, white officials tried to be as selective as possible when they had a chance to hire teachers for these schools. Favoring Confederate sympathizers, they only grudgingly employed native blacks from the area or (worse yet, in their minds), blacks associated with the AMA, or white northern teachers. Public officials sometimes acquiesced to black demands for black teachers (again, the political climate of the area was a determining factor), but most balked at hiring graduates of Atlanta University. By and large, of course, they filled openings with native whites (often women).[6]

It soon became obvious to the association that southerners had decided to provide a minimum amount of support for black education in order to eliminate white northerners from the whole enterprise as soon as possible. In other words, "the better class" of whites agreed that "the race must be educated or lost," but that the Yankee teachers and their outrageous notions of "social equality" must be banished from the state one way or another. White fears of "social equality" between the races pervaded discussions of black elementary education in the 1870s. AMA teachers in the field, for example, dreaded the passage of the Civil Rights Bill in 1875 because they feared that the possibility of federally enforced school integration would jeopardize all state aid to black education (that provision was eliminated from the final version). White school committee members recoiled at reports of AMA black and white teachers boarding together and of white instructors and black students dining together at Atlanta University.[7]

Indeed, the Atlanta dining hall assumed heightened symbolic importance among southerners and northerners alike during this period. The Reverend Frank Haley, still at work in Atlanta in 1874, recognized that attacks on the AMA were "based solely on the fact that our workers recognize respectable colored men and women *socially*. We open our parlors to them; we invite them to our tables; we eat with them in our own homes." Although Haley overestimated the AMA's egalitarian impulses outside Atlanta (the Savannah and Macon staffs were divided over the issue of whites and blacks boarding together in the mid-1870s), it appears that native Georgians universally perceived AMA workers as purveyors of the insidious doctrine of racial integration. The teachers were, in the words of one unreconstructed rebel, "the Skum of the earth."[8]

Continued black ambivalence toward the northerners (especially in the larger towns) threw the teachers off balance during their delicate negotiations with white officials. From the bewildered Savannah superintendent came a comment on black community support for the public school system: "It is a little amazing to have comparisons made between *our* schools and the *free* schools to our disadvantage." The AMA official in Atlanta reported in 1876 that blacks wanted "colored teachers substituted for white" and that many black leaders "actively hostile" to the AMA were ready to support the public system in hopes of hiring more black teachers. Indeed, it was not unusual, especially in towns characterized by a large percentage of black voters, for white southerners and black leaders to strike some sort of bargain in terms of teacher selection. In Savannah, the AMA's Robert F. Markham noted that James Porter, the prominent black activist, had been hired as a teacher by the city board because, according to a white school official, Porter was "an influential man . . . [and] the Board wanted to have men that had an influence with the colored people." Porter, incidentally, was characteristic of post-Redemption black leaders who possessed a keen sense of political opportunism; early in the 1870s he had received a commission from the AMA to serve as a city missionary. By the time Markham was denouncing him in 1877, he had allied himself with the Democratic party.[9]

Obviously the whites' primary objective was to get rid of the Yankees and perhaps even curry favor with local black voters. The main issue was the race (and nativity) of teachers in black schools. Blacks pushed for their own neighbors, and white school officials were willing to compromise on the matter if such an agreement would hasten the departure of the hated northerners. But AMA representatives also tried to exploit the potential of blacks as a political force. For example, Atlanta University officials cautioned white state legislators against discontinuing the annual appropriation of $8,000 to the school in 1875: "The point that we have pressed most is that the colored people are satisfied with the present arrangement and would be likely to make trouble if it should be discontinued."[10]

Thus the city's political climate could have a direct bearing on official white support for black education. Macon provides an example of a town where the black electorate was too weak and disorganized at first to win even informal recognition of the schooling needs of its children. Black leaders, who vacillated in their attitude toward the

AMA there, hoped for teachers of their own race but were convinced they had no leverage with white public school officials. The situation was complicated by the fact that the AMA superintendent in the 1870s, William A. L. Campbell (a black clergyman from the North), usually sided with community members on the issue of teacher selection. Furthermore, he agreed with prominent ministers in the town that the association should sell its buildings directly to their own education society rather than work through the white school committee. Whites in Macon openly scorned all efforts at black education. According to one teacher, public opinion was decidedly "against white people paying . . . hard earned money to educate a rack [i.e., the blacks] to rule them, whose proper sphere is manual labor." Set afire by an incendiary, the AMA's Lewis High School and chapel burned to the ground in 1875 while white firemen looked on.[11]

By the end of the decade, matters were still unresolved in the last three AMA strongholds in Georgia. The white school board in Macon finally agreed to allow the association to choose four white and two black teachers for the public schools "with the promise that the two colored be 'natives of the South and now residents of this state.'" After a period of tortuous negotiations and unsatisfactory contracts with Savannah authorities, the AMA in 1878 decided to reclaim Beach Institute (a secondary school) from the public system. Soon after the Savannah superintendent made his intentions known on this matter, an arsonist destroyed the school. Nevertheless, the AMA managed to wrench the fire insurance money from the school board (no easy task) and construct another building, over which it kept control. That same year, the Storrs School in Atlanta reverted to the association when a dispute arose between the society and the city board over teacher-hiring practices. An AMA official charged that "a majority of the School Board . . . [want] to get rid of northern teachers. There is a determination in certain quarters to drive us all from the state. . . . They may succeed but not until we have accomplished our work. When we are gone, our work will remain." The AMA retained the college as a bulwark, and it remained committed to private elementary education for blacks in Atlanta.[12]

And what about the teachers? Twenty years after the war's end, eleven of the original AMA workers who had begun teaching in Georgia during the 1865–70 period were still laboring there in the vineyards of the Lord. Their devotion to the black people of Georgia was long-lasting (indeed, for most of these persons, lifelong), though their optimism and evangelical fervor had worn a bit thin. For example, a series of controversies within the AMA community in the 1870s revealed that times had indeed changed since the self-sacrificing sixties. Some teachers, required to turn over all or most of their salaries from public sources to their sponsors, tried to keep the money; they maintained they had earned it and deserved to keep it. Amy Williams' coworkers in Atlanta reacted angrily when they learned that she had made a discreet arrangement with New York headquarters to hold on to a sizable chunk of her salary while the others continued to subsist on fifteen dollars a month. Similarly, relative newcomers to the work sometimes sounded more like Gilded Age businesswomen than Civil War missionaries. One Macon teacher who negotiated with her superior in the North for a salary of $400 annually in 1876 coolly informed him that she had other offers in New England if he was not willing to comply with her request.[13]

Still, most teachers must have stayed on because of some higher commitment; their circle of friends had shrunk and life could not have been too pleasant for the determined few who remained. Old problems persisted: the blacks' poverty, intemperance, rowdy church services, and "misguided" notions of religious and educational self-sufficiency. Native whites continued to express their outrage toward the northerners and all they represented. Representatives of the AMA, the Methodist Freedmen's Aid Society (MFAS), and the American Baptist Home Missionary Society (ABHMS) withdrew further into their enclaves of Yankee piety—secondary schools in Atlanta, Athens, Macon, McIntosh County, Savannah, Albany, LaGrange, Waynesboro, and Rome—away from hostile blacks and whites alike. Thus they were able to concentrate their efforts on a small, select group of young black people who would someday become ministers and teachers. Yet, as James McPherson and Raymond Wolters have shown, eventually even these schools came under attack from within as black teachers and students began to press their demands for more control over administration and curriculum. By the third decade of the twentieth century, southern blacks had offered dramatic—and in some cases successful—challenges to northern paternalism in higher education.[14]

Despite the demise of Yankee elementary schools, black children in Georgia still had access to the rudiments of a primary education. Indeed, the inauguration of the state school system dramatically affected attendance rates among blacks as well as whites. The northern teachers had reached only 5 percent of the school-aged population in any one year between 1865 and 1870. In 1871 a little more than one-fifth of all white children attended public classes at some time during the year, though this figure tells us little about the duration or quality of their schooling. Schools throughout the state received public support for the first time in 1873, but most could afford to stay open for only three months. About a third of all white and 13 percent of all black children went to public schools that year. Attendance figures for both races climbed steadily during the decade; after 1875 the black rate was consistently two-thirds that of the white. In 1880 some 63 percent of all white children were listed on the public rolls, and 43 percent of black children. White rates continued to increase slowly in the 1880s, while the figure for blacks leveled off at 40 percent (Appendix J).[15]

Clearly, state aid to black education—no matter how miniscule and unreliable—often enabled larger numbers of children to attend school than would have been able to do so otherwise. Outside financial support increased enrollments in two ways: first, by paying teachers' salaries so that pupils could attend free of charge; and, second, by allowing communities to expand their facilities and accommodate more pupils. Yet this kind of growth was limited in terms of the total amount of school money available from the state and the funds allocated (always on a discriminatory basis) to black and white schools at the county level. In fact, a chronic shortage of funds for education meant that even public schools often were forced to charge tuition fees, and an insufficient number of seats in classrooms also kept black attendance rates artificially low.

By the end of the century, as Louis Harlan has shown, Georgia's separate and unequal school systems had become institutionalized. In 1896 black children represented almost half of the state's school-aged population. Yet, as a result of the discretion exercised by local authorities in distributing the state school fund, the black "system" had only half the number of teachers as its white counterpart, and those teachers were paid only a third as much as whites. Schools in districts independent of the state (four urban counties and the largest cities) fared better than others because their local boards had the right to raise money directly for educational purposes. But, inasmuch as the black population was overwhelmingly rural, few black children benefited from this urban-rural dichotomy. In 1915 the statistics spoke for themselves: despite a public school "awakening" in Georgia, the black pupil "received one-sixth as much as the white child; one twenty-fifth of the amount for buildings and one-fifteenth of the repairs on them, one-twelfth of the supplies, one thirtieth of the equipment, and none of the transportation, though his schools were 50 percent more widely scattered." Left to their own devices, Georgia whites were determined to thwart the black desire for education. And yet this inferior, segregated public school system, combined with black efforts at self-help and initial assistance from northern freedmen's aid societies, produced impressive results; fifty years after the end of the war, almost 70 percent of Georgia's black people were literate.[16]

After the Democrats took over the state government in 1871, blacks found it increasingly difficult to challenge the system of white hegemony, even in areas where they represented a majority of the eligible voters. Indeed, after a brief period of intense "competition" between the races during Reconstruction, black people descended gradually to a nadir of complete disfranchisement. But, in some areas, political struggles continued well into the 1880s. During the last quarter of the nineteenth century, it became clear that black schooling per se served as an ineffective force for social change; increases in school attendance and literacy rates held little promise that black people would be able to achieve economic or political rights in the near future. Therefore, the significance of black education lay not in its potential for integrating blacks into the larger white society (at least not directly, and not for many years), but in its short- and long-term influences on black individuals and communities.[17]

Patterns of economic discrimination initiated during the late 1860s and early 1870s continued. In 1880 blacks owned less than 2 percent of Georgia's total acreage. Proportionately, black farm workers throughout the Deep South planted about half as much crop land as whites and were more dependent on cotton for their livelihood. Only 7 percent of black household heads owned their own farms. About one out of three black workers was a tenant, either a sharecropper or renter. Southern financial institutions ensnared blacks in a vicious cycle of economic dependence and debt that in many cases amounted to peonage. Traditional assumptions about market economics simply did not apply in the South, where whites refused to patronize skilled black artisans (regardless of the prices they charged) and landowners refused to sell property to blacks, even if they could afford to pay.[18]

The election of 1880 marked the last statewide contest for eighty years in which more than 50 percent of Georgia's blacks cast ballots. J. Morgan Kousser has illustrated the effectiveness of the cumulative poll tax in restricting the black electorate. This process began in the 1870s and culminated in the total elimination of blacks as a political force around the turn of the century. The Georgia constitution of 1868 established a one dollar poll tax, but Republicans ignored the provision in an attempt to bolster the voting strength of poor white and black farmers, their supposed allies. In 1871 the Democratic party (now in control of the state's election machinery) began

to enforce the law, and six years later a state constitutional convention made the tax cumulative to insure that "the Georgia GOP would
never rise again." The "Georgia Plan" of black disfranchisement, as
it came to be known, soon proved its worth; the Republicans could
not muster enough voting power to conduct a statewide campaign
after 1876. According to Kousser, the significantly lower voter turn-
out in Georgia compared to other southern states in the 1880s reveals
"the centrality of the poll tax in Georgia's late nineteenth-century
politics."[19]

Beneath these statewide statistics lay a story of continued struggle
on the part of blacks to exercise their political rights. This struggle
was manifested in several ways. One was the tendency for white
school officials to make concessions to blacks in the area of teacher-
hiring. Election fraud and intimidation indicated that black people
had not been completely cowed by Democratic attempts to discourage them from going to the polls. In Macon the whites made no
pretenses during the election of 1874; black voters were "driven
away [from the polls] by brickbats and were obliged to retreat entirely when the shooting began" (several lay dead after this melee).[20]

White politicians had to take black voters in the Savannah area
seriously, and in 1876 Democrats could be seen "patting the colored
man on the back" to win votes. Although six thousand blacks (as
opposed to four thousand whites) were eligible to participate in that
year's January election, a third of them were disqualified because
they had not registered to vote the year before. An AMA superintendent in the town noted that whites recognized the potential
power of the blacks in Chatham County and reacted accordingly.
His prediction that the state legislature would not hesitate to pass
laws to restrict the electorate proved to be accurate, as evidenced by
the 1877 constitutional convention. Some blacks like James Porter
recognized their helpless position and switched their support to the
Democratic party in an attempt to win patronage and other favors.
(Thus it is difficult to calculate the extent of the black vote exclusively on the basis of the number of Republican ballots cast in
any one election.) Northern society officials tended to view such
political maneuverings as further proof that black people had "not
intelligence [*sic*] to manage their affairs."[21]

Within this context of systematic economic and political exploita-
tion, formal education proved ineffective as a means of upward social mobility. As Roger Ransom and Richard Sutch have pointed
out, "Most blacks who sought an education hoped that literacy
and elementary education would make them better farmers or farm
managers or open the possibility of becoming independent land-

owners or artisans. But such individuals were frequently disappointed, not because education was worthless for these pursuits, but rather because blacks were never allowed to pursue these occupations." In effect, discrimination often destroyed black incentive to acquire new skills, except to the extent they could meet a demand for certain services within the confines of their own communities.[22]

In October 1877 an AMA teacher visited Dalton, a small town in the northwestern corner of the state, to encourage the black people there to send their children to school (whether she meant the local elementary school or an AMA-sponsored secondary institution is unclear). She wrote of their response:

> Some are very anxious to have their children educated, but again the greater number think they must make farmers of their sons and daughters before they educate them. Many very often say to me, when I tell them they can be better workers with an education, "O, no they will think themselves above working when they get a little learning and leave us, and our farms." And thus some of the country people are really afraid to send their children to school.

Surely her words convey the poignancy of the dilemma faced by blacks in the South. Reading and writing were prized skills, but many realized that a true widening of intellectual horizons would not result in a higher standard of living for them as farm laborers. Young people who had acquired an education might find it increasingly difficult to acquiesce in the humiliation of their own people in rural society, and leave the community to seek work and a better life elsewhere. Perhaps this is what the parents in Dalton feared most—the loss of their children.[23]

This is not to suggest that parents were necessarily justified in believing that their children were better off without schooling, according to the premise that ignorance is bliss. Literacy immeasurably enriched the lives of individuals, and in the long run contributed to the political awareness of the Afro-American community. But most persons born in the nineteenth century never lived to see the day when the resultant racial self-consciousness had an impact on southern society as a whole. Not until the mid-twentieth century civil-rights movement drew on broad-based support from literate black people as well as religious and educational leaders did the effects of formal education dramatically affect the group status of blacks. That upheaval confirmed the lesson of freedom for black people, the lesson that the northern teachers never really learned: collective economic and political power, rather than individual character reform, was the most effective weapon in the war against oppression.

Patterns in Georgia freedmen's education were duplicated in other states. Indeed, black people all over the South demonstrated their commitment to schooling in remarkable, and highly similar, ways. Scholars who have focused on individual states during the Civil War and the Reconstruction era, as well as Leon F. Litwack in his general study of blacks during these periods, outline essentially the same themes. The former slaves celebrated their freedom by going to school. Children and adults, male and female, attended classes whenever possible, despite the explicit opposition of southern whites and the fundamental conflict between economic advancement and formal education. They demonstrated their hunger for knowledge by walking long distances to school, by seeking out teachers on their own, and by making personal sacrifices so that other members of their families could unlock the secrets of the written word. Blacks in all of the southern states raised money for their neighborhood schools, and encouraged their literate brothers and sisters to assume responsibility for teaching in them. Relatively prosperous, cohesive communities strove for an educational self-sufficiency with a determination that matched their quest for religious autonomy.[24]

Sponsored by a variety of freedmen's aid societies, northern volunteers did their best to provide necessary skills and services to the incipient black education movement, but they were unequal to the demands made upon them. In no state did the teachers reach more than 15 percent of the black population, and few pupils were able to attend school with any degree of regularity. Together, the societies and the Freedmen's Bureau cooperated to establish state systems of education, which concentrated on urban areas to maximize their efficiency. Gradually, as private and federal resources dwindled, the societies and bureau began to focus on a few select institutions of higher learning. But the first common schools sponsored by native blacks, northern whites, and the federal government provided a framework for black public education in the post-Redemption period.

Historians have discovered in several states a direct correlation between white antagonism to black schooling and the intensity of political activities during Radical Reconstruction. Some have argued that whites initiated the most violent attacks against black schools and teachers in 1867–68 in direct response to the federal program of military occupation. This again signifies the political implications of black education. From all areas of the South came reports that the "better class" of whites attempted to turn the issue to their own advantage; their first priority was to rid themselves of the Yankee teachers and thus eliminate a major source of tension between the races. Black people, through their control of that prized commodity, labor, were able to win minimal concessions in the area of elementary education. But little was granted them freely. For example, even Radical Republicans shied away from the issue of public education, and, though most Radical constitutional conventions of the 1860s provided for statewide systems of tax-supported education, the freed people received little benefit from the paperwork. When Democratic politicians recaptured state governments, they often left intact these statutory provisions, but in the process systematized discriminatory funding policies in an effort to stunt black education at the common-school level.

Thus the case of Georgia represents but a variation on a theme. Northern teachers began work in the state at a relatively late date (1865). The AMA dominated the scene, and provided a certain amount of strength and continuity to the northern presence. (States heavily reliant on the AFUC experienced a void of sorts when that society disbanded.) The Republican party in Georgia produced precious little in the way of support for black education, or even civil rights; the issue of integrated schools was not even debated at the state level, as it was in some other areas of the South. This was at least partly because the most prominent black leaders in the state (unlike those in Virginia for example) felt no inclination to press for mixed schools; their strong sense of racial identity precluded a serious effort in that direction, which would have been, in any case, doomed from the start.

Because of the strength of conservative forces (Georgia was "redeemed" fairly early by the Democrats—in 1871, before seven other states), supporters of black education had to engage in trench warfare and hand-to-hand combat in towns and rural areas. Indeed, many of the achievements in the field were the result of strong personalities (black and white) or favorable local conditions rather than of concerted support provided by the highest echelons of state government. But, although black elementary school attendance rates lagged behind those in other cotton states through the 1870s, Georgia was well on its way to becoming a center of black higher education in the South, primarily because northern societies had shown an early interest in the postwar boom town of Atlanta.

Events in Georgia offer some insights into the difficult problem of racial segregation in the Reconstruction era. The issue was a two-edged sword wielded by both whites and blacks. Integrated schools were never a viable option in the state after the war, and the position of the northern teachers on the matter is almost irrelevant. The idea of black and white pupils sitting beside each other in school so offended native whites that they would have sacrificed their own children's education as a sign of outrage. Thus, even if the state legislature had established "integrated" schools (by law), "mixed classes" still would never have materialized simply because whites would not have patronized them. At the same time, the freed people did not see integrated classrooms as a goal during this period; on the contrary, many did not even want sympathetic northern white teachers if they could help it. This, of course, is not to suggest that Georgia blacks were apathetic about their rights, or that they accepted southern oppression. Leaders throughout the state made desperate pleas for equal voting rights and equal access to public transportation and accommodations. Because they valued the school as a community institution, they believed it must remain separate from the larger white society. There is no reason to assume that black parents considered it important for their own children to go to school with those of poor whites or their former owners. They did, however, argue strenuously—and again, unsuccessfully—for a fair division of state school funds.

For these reasons, it is unfair to charge, as some scholars have, that the northern teachers capitulated to southern racial mores by not working more actively for integrated schools. The reformers' priorities were shaped as much by black preferences as by white. However, the northern societies' lack of support for black independent educational efforts deserves careful attention. Today the rationale behind the freed people's "racial exclusivity" in their schools as well as their churches can be seen in sharp detail, primarily because of our better understanding of the underlying dynamics of Afro-American culture. Forces were at work in Reconstruction Georgia that the teachers perceived only dimly, if at all. The notion of cultural relativism was alien to them. They believed that, without the benefit of a rigorous Yankee-style education, black teachers would only perpetuate in their pupils the evils of slavery. The reformers possessed very definite ideas about personal morality, and they quickly condemned people with different standards as sinful. It is true that the system of slavery produced a degree of social pathology among its victims; perhaps the recent literature goes too far in mitigating the effects of bondage on black people. But the teachers focused only on this "degradation" and ignored the wellspring of faith and community that provided blacks with a means to endure the most extreme forms of oppression. After the war, Afro-American traditions still proved to be viable; although the slave system had disappeared, the caste system had not.

Modern "affirmative action" programs to correct past abuses in minority employment practices call for the suspension of formal culture-bound qualifications in certain hiring situations. Freedmen's aid societies might have put similar policies to good use. But the teachers seemed almost perverse in their attempts to thwart efforts at black self-help in education, from denying literate blacks teaching commissions to subverting the Savannah Education Association. Thus the benefits of affirmative action were beyond the purview of the northern societies. Similarly, the civil-rights movement in this country has pointed up the power of boycotts, civil disobedience, and other forms of collective action to effect social change. The "ethos of mutuality" among freed people was a potentially significant force.

And, in the last few years, the federal government has taken a more positive stance in the area of civil rights, especially integration and voting. But the preconditions for meaningful changes that went beyond the Emancipation Proclamation were absent in mid-nineteenth century America. Blacks were poverty-stricken and illiterate. The Republican party operated under assumptions of racial superiority, which eliminated the possibility of effective social and economic welfare programs. Within thirty-five years after the end of the war, southern whites (with the complicity of northern groups and institutions) were able to recreate the economic, political, and social barriers that had existed between the races under slavery. Such was the nature of "reconstruction."

All this is to say that relatively modern ideas and concepts—school desegregation, affirmative action, agitation for civil rights—might enhance understanding of the limitations of the nineteenth-century northern approach to black "uplift," but they do not provide a basis for evaluating the reformers' intentions. The problem hinges on the "idealism" of the young women and men who went south after the Civil War. Their vision of social change was at once their strength and their tragic flaw. The most sensitive chroniclers of the northern effort in the South have argued quite understandably that the teachers' vision of an egalitarian society was dramatically at odds with prevailing notions of black inferiority. The analogy between the teachers of the 1860s and the young people who joined the Peace Corps and southern freedom marches just a hundred years later has a great deal of validity. The factors of race and class often hindered the growth of emotional bonds between southern blacks and well-educated, middle-class white women and men, and the economic program of the teachers and later civil-rights activists was fuzzy and perhaps even nonexistent. Still, both groups of whites were guided by humane and honest impulses, born of compassion as much as privilege. And, given the enormity of the task, they were intensely "idealistic."

On the other hand, idealism implies a visionary or imaginary quality—something existing "only in the mind." The northern teachers of the Georgia freed people were never able to break out of a certain mode of thinking, even when confronted with an overwhelming amount of evidence that directly contradicted many of their assumptions. They persisted in their emphasis on moral character reform throughout the period, sometimes to the point of pathos. Thus a veteran AMA worker in Atlanta could note the widespread poverty of the black people and comment, "If the colored people will learn to be careful and provident, all will be well; they will learn in time" (this is 1876).[25] The teachers' ideological stubbornness is noteworthy in light of the flexibility they demonstrated in other areas of their work: their ability to conduct classes under primitive conditions and their willingness to break out of formal roles within the bureaucracy to challenge their superiors. Nevertheless, the world in which black character reform would lead to a more just society existed only in the minds of the teachers themselves.

Finally, the story of the Georgia freedmen's teachers helps to illuminate the complexity of "woman's sphere" in early Victorian New England. Despite their confinement within an increasingly constricted realm of domesticity, middle-class women found opportunities for public action and group influence. They banded together in an effort to assert their own "moral superiority" over men; women's religious crusades—missionary and reform work—led to a heightened consciousness of their "shared and special destiny" based on gender.[26] Although it is difficult to label this reform impulse as "feminist," it did represent an explicit challenge to the repressive ideology of "sentimental womanhood." The teachers, in particular, exploited their societies' call for self-sacrifice. They stayed within the bounds of female "nurture" in their roles as schoolteachers and social workers, but within those limits they ignored male-imposed bureaucratic strictures that they feared would lessen their "usefulness." Their experiences within society mission homes suggest, however, that differences of age, culture, race, and personality could sometimes fray the bonds of sisterhood.

The teachers have left an ambiguous legacy. As individuals, they turned their backs on racial prejudice and cast off the cloak of female domesticity to don the armor of freedmen's work. Highly committed to this effort, they often suffered many physical aggravations while achieving personal fulfillment. They offer a sharp contrast to persons throughout American history who have been content only to write or speak about the need for social justice. Yet their determination as well as their convictions of right and wrong were not enough to overcome postwar southern realities. In the long run, they were only foot soldiers plodding doggedly along, shortsighted yet heroic in their own way, as they fought the war against racism. But, on a more personal level, they also did battle with conventional notions about what a woman should do and be. Leaving the homes of their fathers, they searched for ways to use their talents in a higher spiritual realm. Perhaps on a modest scale the triumph was theirs after all.

Appendixes

Appendix A. Societies Sponsoring Teachers in Georgia

Table A.1. Number of Teachers Sponsored by Northern Freedmen's Aid Societies in Georgia, 1865–1873 (N =367)

Society	Number of Teachers Sponsored	Percentage of Total
American Missionary Association/ Western Freedmen's Aid Commission	290	79
Freedmen's Aid Society of the Methodist Episcopal Church	31	8.5
American Freedmen's Union Commission, New England branch	30	8
American Freedmen's Union Commission, New York branch	4	1
American Baptist Home Missionary Society/National Theological Institute	11	3
New York Yearly Meeting of Friends	1	.3

SOURCE: Compiled from annual lists of freedmen's teachers published in *American Missionary, American Freedman,* and *Freedmen's Record; Annual Reports* of the Freedmen's Aid Society of the Methodist Episcopal Church; and data in Henry L. Morehouse, "Historical Sketch of the American Baptist Home Missionary Society for Fifty Years," in *Baptist Home Missions in North America . . .* (New York: Baptist Home Mission Rooms, 1883), pp. 291–619.

Appendix B. Biographical Data on Northern Freedmen's Aid Society Teachers in Georgia, 1865–1873

Table B.1. Teachers' Sex (N =368)

Sex	Number of Teachers	Percentage of Total
Female	289	78.5
Male	79	21.5

SOURCE (all Appendix B tables): compiled from *American Missionary*, *American Freedman*, and *Freedmen's Record*; *Annual Reports* of the Freedmen's Aid Society of the Methodist Episcopal Church; Federal Manuscript Census for the years 1860 and 1870; collection of family genealogies at the American Antiquarian Society, Worcester, Massachusetts; and Archives of the American Missionary Association, Amistad Research Center, New Orleans, Louisiana.

Table B.2. Teacher's Race (N =363)

Race	Number of Teachers	Percentage of Total
White	344	94.8
Black	18	5.0
Native American (Indian)	1	.2

Table B.3. Teachers' Race, By Sex (N =363)

	Female		Male	
	Number	Percentage	Number	Percentage
White	279	81	65	19
Black	7	39	11	61
Native American (Indian)	1	100	0	0

Table B.4. First Year in the South for Georgia Teachers (N=368)

Year	Number of Teachers	Year	Number of Teachers
1862	1	1868	66
1863	10	1869	29
1864	23	1870	10
1865	67	1871	11
1866	74	1872	7
1867	70		

Table B.5. Teachers' Age, First Year in Georgia and First Year in the South

Age	First Year in Georgia (N=158)		First Year in South (N=149)	
	Number	Percentage	Number	Percentage
17–21	12	7.6	15	10
22–26	43	27	42	28
27–31	43	27	37	25
32–36	22	14	22	15
37–41	18	11.4	19	13
42–46	9	5.7	7	5
47–51	3	2	3	2
52–56	4	2.5	3	2
57–61	1	.6	0	0
62–66	2	1	1	.6
67–71	1	.6	0	0

NOTE: First year in Georgia, average 31.4, median 29; first year in South, average 30.4, median 28.

Table B.6. Teachers' Age, By Sex (N = 149)

| Age | Female | | Male | | Total |
	Number	Percent	Number	Percent	
0–17	1	50	1	50	2
18–25	39	87	6	13	45
26–30	31	79.5	8	20.5	39
31–40	35	78	10	22	45
41–49	10	83	2	17	12
50–up	2	33	4	67	6

Table B.7. Highest Level of Teachers' Education (N = 82)

Type of Institution	Number of Teachers	Percentage of Total
College/theological seminary	38	46
Female seminary/academy	26	32
Normal school	14	17
High school	3	4
Common school	1	1

Table B.8. Highest Level of Teachers' Education, By Sex (N = 82)

| Type of Institution | Female | | Male | |
	Number	Percentage	Number	Percentage
College/theological seminary	6	16	32	84
Female seminary/academy	24	92	2	8
Normal school	13	93	1	7

Table B.8. (Continued)

Type of	Female		Male	
Institution	Number	Percentage	Number	Percentage
High school	2	67	1	33
Common school	0	0	1	100

Table B.9. Teachers' Marital Status (N = 355)

Status	Number of Teachers	Percentage of Total
Married	65	18
Single	261	73.5
Widowed	13	4
Divorced	0	0
Married in Georgia	16	4.5

Table B.10. Teachers' Marital Status during Their First Year in the South, By Age (N =146)

Status	Age						Total
	0–18	19–25	26–30	31–40	41–50	51–up	Number
Married							
Percentage	0	0	28	48	8	16	
Number	0	0	7	12	2	4	25
Single							
Percentage	1.79	34.82	24.11	29.46	8.04	1.79	
Number	2	39	27	33	9	2	112
Widowed							
Percentage	0	0	100	0	0	0	
Number	0	0	1	0	0	0	1
Married in Georgia							
Percentage	0	62.50	37.50	0	0	0	
Number	0	5	3	0	0	0	8

Table B.11. Teachers' Previous Occupations (N = 121)

Occupation	Number	Percentage
Attorney	1	.8
Physician	1	.8
Clergyman	30	25.0
School Principal	2	2.0
Teacher	75	61.5
Reporter, journalist	1	.8
Nurse	2	2.0
Merchant	1	.8
Manufacturer	1	.8
Farmer	1	.8
Bookkeeper	1	.8
Minor government official	1	.8
Seamstress	2	2.0
Milliner	1	.8
Mechanic	1	.8

Table B.12. Teachers' Denominational Affiliations (N = 179)

Denomination	Number	Percentage
African Methodist Episcopal	5	3
Baptist	18	10
Congregational	111	62
Dutch Reformed	1	.6
Episcopalian	1	.6
Free Will Baptist	2	1
Methodist	30	17
Presbyterian	4	2
Quaker	3	1.7
Swedenborgian	3	1.7
Unitarian	1	.6

Table B.13. Teachers' Home States (N = 347)

Region and State	Number	Percentage
NEW ENGLAND		
Connecticut	47	13.5
Maine	13	3.8
Massachusetts	102	29.0
New Hampshire	12	3.5
Rhode Island	5	1.5
Vermont	17	5.0
Subtotal	196	56.3
MID-ATLANTIC		
New Jersey	7	2.0
New York	52	15.0
Pennsylvania	6	1.7
Washington, D.C.	2	.6
Tennessee	1	.3
Virginia	1	.3
Subtotal	69	19.9
MIDWEST		
Indiana	5	1.5
Kentucky	1	.3
Michigan	13	3.8
Ohio	43	12.5
Illinois	5	1.5
Iowa	4	1.0
Kansas	1	.3
Minnesota	6	1.7
Wisconsin	1	.3
Subtotal	79	22.9
FOREIGN		
England	1	.3
Nova Scotia	1	.3
Subtotal	2	.6

Table B.14. Teachers' State of Birth (N = 116)

Region and State	Number	Percentage
NEW ENGLAND		
Connecticut	21	18.0
Maine	6	5.0
Massachusetts	38	32.8
New Hampshire	5	4.3
Rhode Island	3	2.6
Vermont	7	6.0
Subtotal	80	68.7
MID-ATLANTIC		
New Jersey	3	2.6
New York	12	10.3
Pennsylvania	1	.9
Subtotal	16	13.8
SOUTH		
Virginia	2	1.8
Georgia	1	.9
Alabama	1	.9
Louisiana	1	.9
Subtotal	5	4.6
MIDWEST		
Indiana	1	.9
Michigan	2	1.8
Ohio	9	7.7
Illinois	1	.9
Wisconsin	1	.9
Subtotal	14	12.2
FOREIGN		
Nova Scotia	1	.9

Table B.15. State of Birth of Teachers' Parents

Region and State	Father (N = 75)		Mother (N = 52)	
	Number	Percentage	Number	Percentage
NEW ENGLAND				
Connecticut	20	26.7	15	28.8
Maine	4	5.3	3	5.8
Massachusetts	22	29.3	15	28.8
New Hampshire	5	6.7	5	9.6
Rhode Island	3	4.0	0	0
Vermont	7	9.3	7	13.5
Subtotal	61	81.3	45	86.5
MID-ATLANTIC				
New Jersey	3	4.0	0	0
New York	6	8.0	4	7.7
Pennsylvania	1	1.3	0	0
Delaware	0	0	1	1.9
Subtotal	10	13.3	5	9.6
SOUTH				
Virginia	1	1.3	2	3.8
MIDWEST				
Ohio	2	2.7	0	0
FOREIGN				
Nova Scotia	1	1.3	0	0

Table B.16. Size of Teachers' Hometown (N = 313)

Town Size, 1860	Number of Teachers	Percentage of Total Number of Teachers
Under 1,000	38	12.1
1,000–2,500	85	27.2
2,501–5,000	58	18.5
5,001–10,000	37	11.8
10,001–20,000	29	9.3
Over 20,000	66	21.1

Table B.17. Occupation of Teachers' Fathers (N = 88)

Class and Occupation	Number	Percentage
PROFESSIONAL		
Attorney	2	2.3
Physician	1	1.1
Clergyman	17	19.3
High government official	1	1.1
Professor	2	2.3
Subtotal	23	26.1
SEMIPROFESSIONAL, MERCHANTS, AND MANUFACTURERS		
Teacher	1	1.1
Merchant (unspecified)	3	3.4
Storekeeper	2	2.3
Real estate agent	1	1.1
Freighter	1	1.1
Grocer	1	1.1
Banker	2	2.3
Manufacturer		
Clothing	1	1.1
Metal Products	1	1.1
Other	1	1.1
Subtotal	14	15.7
FARMER	27	30.7
CLERICAL		
Minor government official	1	1.1
SKILLED TRADESMEN AND WORKERS		
Shoemaker	2	2.3
Tailor	1	1.1
Coachmaker	1	1.1
Boxmaker	3	3.4
Blacksmith	3	3.4
Tinsmith	2	2.3
Carpenter	4	4.5
Brickmaker	2	2.3
Railroad engineer	1	1.1
Butcher	2	2.3
Subtotal	21	23.8

Table B.17. (Continued)

Class and Occupation	Number	Percentage
SEMISKILLED AND SERVICE WORKERS Moulder	1	1.1
UNSKILLED WORKERS Drover	1	1.1

Table B.18. Status of Teachers' Parents during Teachers' First Year in the South (N = 80)

Status	Number of Teachers	Percentage
Both parents dead	25	31.2
Father dead, mother living	21	26.3
Mother dead, father living	7	8.7
Both parents living	27	33.8

Table B.19. Total Number of Children in Teachers' Families (N = 108)

Number of Children	Number of Teachers	Percentage
1	2	1.8
2	14	12.8
3	16	14.7
4	15	13.8
5	12	11.0
6	16	14.7
7	12	11.0
8	8	7.3
9	9	8.3
10	1	.9
11	1	.9
12	1	.9
13	0	0

Table B.19. (Continued)

Number of Children	Number of Teachers	Percentage
14	0	0
15	1	.9

NOTE: Average is 5.3 children.

Table B.20. Teachers' Sibling Rank (N = 102)

Sibling Rank	Number of Teachers	Percentage
1	31	30.1
2	18	17.5
3	17	16.5
4	14	13.6
5	8	7.8
6	4	3.9
7	3	2.9
8	3	2.9
9	3	2.9
10	0	0
11	1	1.0

NOTE: Average is 3.2 sibling rank.

Table B.21. Teachers' Family Members in Georgia: Siblings Teaching (N =362)

Number of Siblings Teaching	Number of Teachers	Percentage
0	333	92.0
1	26	7.2
2	3	.8

Table B.22. Teachers' Family Members in Georgia: Parents Teaching (N =362)

Number of Parents Teaching	Number of Teachers	Percentage
0	352	97.2
1	8	2.2
2	2	.6

Table B.23. Teachers' Family Members in Georgia: Children Teaching (N = 359)

Number of Children Teaching	Number of Teachers	Percentage
0	348	97.0
1	10	2.8
2	1	.3

Table B.24. Teachers' Marital Status and Status of Spouses (N =355)

Marital and Spouse Status	Number of Teachers	Percentage
Spouse accompanied teacher	59	16.6
Spouse remained in the North	6	1.7
Teacher was single	261	73.5
Teacher was widowed	13	3.7
Teacher married in Georgia	16	4.5

Appendix C. Nature and Length of Service in the South and Georgia of Northern Freedmen's Aid Society Teachers

Table C.1. Total Number of States in Which Georgia Teachers Served, 1865–1873 (N = 338)

Number of States	Number of Teachers	Percentage
1	175	51.8
2	107	31.7
3	39	11.5
4	11	3.2
5	6	1.8

SOURCE (all Appendix C tables): Compiled from annual lists of freedmen's teachers published in *American Missionary*, *American Freedman*, *Freedmen's Record*, and *Annual Reports* of the Freedmen's Aid Society of the Methodist Episcopal Church; and data in Henry L. Morehouse, "Historical Sketch of the American Baptist Home Missionary Society for Fifty Years," in *Baptist Home Missions in North America . . .* (New York: Baptist Home Mission Rooms, 1883), pp. 291–619.

Table C.2. Total Number of Years Georgia Teachers Served in the South, 1862–ca. 1915 (N = 330)

Number of Years	Number of Teachers	Percentage
1	111	33.1
2–3	107	32.4
4–5	50	14.9
6–7	23	6.9
8–9	6	1.8
10–15	17	5.1
16–20	7	2.1
21–30	6	1.8
31–40	1	.3
41–50	2	.6

Table C.3. Total Number of Years Teachers Spent in
Georgia, 1865–1873 (N = 367)

Number of Years	Number of Teachers	Percentage
1	225	61.3
2	71	19.3
3	21	5.7
4	22	6.0
5	16	4.4
6	8	2.2
7	2	.5
8	2	.5

NOTE: Average, 1.8 years; median, 1.

Appendix D. Teachers' Positions within Freedmen's Societies

Table D.1. Teachers' Society Positions, by Sex, 1865–1873 (N =368)

Position	Female Number	Female Percentage	Male Number	Male Percentage
Teacher	279	85.6	47	14.4
Missionary	5	100.0	0	0
Minister	0	0	2	100.0
Superintendent, principal	0	0	31	100.0
Matron	4	100.0	0	0

SOURCE: Compiled from data in *American Missionary, American Freedman, Freedmen's Record; Annual Reports* of the Freedmen's Aid Society of the Methodist Episcopal Church; and Archives of the American Missionary Association, Amistad Research Center, New Orleans, Louisiana.

Appendix E. The Scope of Freedmen's Education in the South and in Georgia

Table E.1. Freedmen's Education in the South, 1865–1870

Year	Number of Teachers	Number of Schools	Number of Pupils
1865–66	1,405	964	90,778
1866–67	2,087	1,382	111,442
1867–68	2,202	1,875	100,487
1868–69	1,961	1,961	96,332
1869–70	3,633	2,677	149,589

SOURCE (all Appendix E tables): Compiled from annual statistical reports published in *Semi-Annual Reports* of the United States Freedmen's Bureau Superintendent of Education; and from data in *American Missionary*, *Freedmen's Record*, and *American Freedman*.

Table E.2. Freedmen's Education in Georgia, 1865–1870

School Year (Oct.–May)	Number of Teachers	Number of Schools	Number of Pupils
Northern Freedmen's Aid Societies			
1865–66	48	n.a.	n.a.
1866–67	95	84	6,034
1867–68	119	n.a.	n.a.
1868–69	139	84	n.a.
1869–70	97	49	n.a.
Freedmen's Bureau/Black Independent Efforts			
1865–66	72	n.a.	n.a.
1866–67	160	148	6,138
1867–68	101	n.a.	n.a.
1868–69	113	148	n.a.
1869–70	142	163	n.a.

Table E.2. (Continued)

School Year (Oct.–May)	Number of Teachers	Number of Schools	Number of Pupils
	Totals		
1865–66	120	79	7,792
1866–67	255	232	12,172
1867–68	220	156	10,544
1868–69	252	232	13,263
1869–70	239	212	11,206

Appendix F. "Suggestions to Local Superintendents in the Middle West Department"[1]

1. Each Local Supt will receive directly from this office funds for the general expenses of the work under his charge.

2. Each remittance of money should be immediately acknowledged by a stamped receipt.

3. At the close of each month a duplicate receipt prepared on the blanks furnished should be sent embracing all the remittances of the month.

4. Each Supt should forward at the close of each month his account showing somewhat in detail the expenses attending the work under his charge.

5. These accounts should be written on regular *"Bill Paper"* *foolscap size* and *signed officially.*

6. The accounts should be kept in a permanent form for examination and future reference.

7. As a rule, Bills should be required where money is expended, and these properly receipted should be filed as vouchers.

8. The salaries of commissioned persons should in no case enter into the general account, but a bill should be prepared monthly or quarterly, and sent to this office to be approved and forwarded to W. E. Whiting Asst. Treas. to be paid.

9. Money from tuition, sale of books, etc. should be entered in the monthly account with specifications as to its source.

10. Transportation of teachers from their homes to their fields of labor will be paid by the Asst. Comm. of the Freedmen's Bureau for the state in which the teachers are laboring on paper certificates

[1] E. M. Cravath to Frederick Ayer, Cincinnati, Ohio, 9 Oct. 1866, Ayer Papers.

and each Local Supt is authorized to sign as Agt of the AMA the certificates of the teachers respecting transportation.

11. The transportation thus collected will be paid directly to the teacher and the teacher instructed to enter no account with the AMA for transportation. Other expenses of travel can be included in the bill with the salary.

12. Each Supt is requested to send near the close of the month, an estimate of the amount of funds that the work under his charge will require from this office for the next month.

13. Duplicate reports will be required of each teacher at the close of every month, one to be sent to the Rev. Samuel Hunt, 53 John St., New York, the other to this office.

14. Local Supts should see that each box of clothing or supplies received from the North is properly acknowledged by a letter addressed to the donors.

E. M. Cravath
89 West 6th St., Cin., Ohio
per L.A.C.
Cincinnati, Ohio, Oct. 9th 1866

Appendix G. Examples of Textbooks Used in Northern-Sponsored Georgia Freedmen's Schools, 1865–1873

READERS

Sanders: Charles W. Sanders, *The School Reader . . .* , published in New York during the 1840s, 50s, and 60s; plus editions of *The New School Reader* (First through Fourth Readers).

McGuffey's Reader: Any one of several editions published in Cincinnati during the 1840s and 50s, such as William H. McGuffey, *McGuffey's Eclectic First Reader*.

Sheldon's: Possibly one of the editions of Russell J. Webb's *Webb's Normal Reader*, published by Sheldon & Co. in New York during the 1850s and early 1860s.

National Series: Richard Greene Parker and James Madison Watson, *The National* (First through Fifth?) *Reader* (sometimes referred to as "Parker and Watson"), published by A. S. Barnes & Co., New York, in the last half of the 1860s. Most widely used series.

Webster's: Any one of several Noah Webster Readers published in the late eighteenth and early nineteenth centuries, such as *An American Selection of Lessons in Reading and Spelling*.

SPELLERS

Sanders: *Sanders' Spelling Book*, published in the 1840s, 50s, and 60s by Charles W. Sanders.

National: J. Madison Watson, *National Elementary Speller*, published at New York in 1866 by A. S. Barnes.

GEOGRAPHIES

Guyot: Arnold Henry Guyot, *Physical Geography*, New York, Armstrong, 1866; or Arnold Henry Guyot and Mary Howe Smith, *Common School Geography*, New York, Charles Scribner & Co., 1866.

Mitchell: S. Augustus Mitchell, *A System of Modern Geography*, Philadelphia, several editions; or *Mitchell's Primary Geography*, published in the late 1840s, 50s, and 60s.

Cornell: S. S. Cornell, *Cornell's Grammar-School Geography*, Appleton & Co., New York, 1870; or *Cornell's Physical Geography*, New York, D. Appleton & Co., 1870.

Monteith: Most widely used geography series.

GRAMMARS

Quackenbos (Quackenbush or Quackenboro)

Clark

ARITHMETICS

Quackenbush

Robinson's Practical and Written

Davis (Davies?) Primary

Filter's Primary

Appendix H. Texts of Letters Sent from the Ku Klux Klan to Representatives of Freedmen's Aid Societies in Georgia

The *Freedmen's Record* reprinted the following letter, which was sent in 1868 to Harrison Leland, who was assigned to Jonesboro and sponsored by the New England Branch of the American Freedmen's Union Commission. The *Record* noted that it "shows that the spirit of secession is not quite extinct. Our types cannot reproduce the charming symbols which accompany this note, but the orthography is given verbatim."[1]

[1] *FR* 5 (May 1868):80.

Ku Klux Klan Headquarters
A———B———You are dern aberlition puppy and scoundrel if
We hear of your name in the papers again we will burn your
hellish house over your head cut your entrals out.

The KKs are on your track and you will be in hell in four
days if you dont mind yourself. Mind that you dont go the same
way that G.W.A. [G. W. Ashburn, prominent Republican who
had recently been assassinated in Columbus] went some night.
Yours in hell
KKK

Addressed to the Rev. H. W. Pierson, representative of the American
Missionary Association in Macon, February 1869 (a skull and cross-
bones served as a letterhead):[2]

Dr. Pierson (so called)

The citizens of this community are aware of a few facts relative to yourself, which I will proceed to designate. In the first
place, they know you to be a wandering *vagrant, carpet-bagger*
without visible means of support, and living at present on the
earnings of those who are endeavoring to make an honest living
by teaching. You have also proved to be a *scoundrel* of the deep-
est dye, by maliciously interfering in matters which do not in
the least concern you to the detriment of some of our citizens.

This therefore is to warn you to *leave* this country forth-
with, twenty four (24) hours from the above date is the time
allowed you to leave.

If after the said time your devilish countenance is seen at *this
place or vicinity your worthless life will pay the forfeit.* Congressional Reconstruction, the military, nor anything else
under heaven, will prevent summary justice being meted out
to such an incarnate fiend as yourself.
By order of committee

[2] Macon, 12 Feb. 1869, AMA Archives.

Appendix I. Illiteracy among Blacks in Georgia

Table I.1. Black Illiteracy Rate in Georgia, 1860–1880

Year	Percentage of Black Adults	Percentage of Blacks, Aged 10–20
1860	95–97	95–97
1870	94.1	n.a.
1880	84.3	77.3

Source: Compiled from data in *Eighth Census* of the United States (1860); and Charles Warren and J. L. M. Curry, "Illiteracy in the U.S. with Appendix on National Aid to Education," Department of Education Circular (Washington: Government Printing Office, 1884).

Appendix J. School Attendance of Georgia Blacks

Table J.1. Black School Attendance in Georgia, 1870–1880

Year	Number of Black Schools	Number of Black Pupils (aged 5–9)	Percent Attendance
1870	233	11,150	5
1871	n.a.	n.a.	n.a.
1872	n.a.	n.a.	n.a.
1873	n.a.	n.a.	n.a.
1874	669	37,267	n.a.
1875	879	55,268	n.a.
1876	1,075	48,643	n.a.
1877	1,134	62,330	34
1878	1,436	72,655	36
1879	1,436	79,435	40
1880	1,688	86,623	40

Source: Compiled from data in *Annual Reports* of the U.S. Commissioner of Education, 1870–1880 (Washington: Government Printing Office); U.S. Bureau of Refugees, Freedmen, and Abandoned Lands, *Tenth Semi-Annual Report on Schools for Freedmen*, by J. W. Alvord (Washington: Government Printing Office, 1870); *First Annual Report of the State School Commissioner of the State of Georgia* (Atlanta: Public Printer, 1871); H. Barnard, "History of Schools for the Colored Population," *Special Report*, U.S. Commissioner of Education (Washington: Government Printing Office, 1871), pp. 339–42; *Ninth* and *Tenth Census* of the United States (1870 and 1880); and *American Missionary* (1870–80).

Notes

Abbreviations to the Notes

AF	*American Freedman*, organ of the Washington, D.C., Branch of the American Freedmen's Union Commission (AFUC)
AM	*American Missionary*, magazine of the American Missionary Association (AMA)
AMA Archives	American Missionary Association Archives, Amistad Research Center, New Orleans, Louisiana
Ayer Papers	Frederick Ayer Papers, Negro Collection, Atlanta University Center Trevor Arnett Library, Atlanta, Georgia
BRFAL	Records of the United State Bureau of Refugees, Freedmen, and Abandoned Lands, Record Group 105, National Archives, Washington, D.C.
Chase Papers	Chase Family Papers, American Antiquarian Society, Worcester, Massachusetts
Douglass Papers	Esther W. Douglass Papers, Rackham Library, University of Michigan, Ann Arbor, Michigan
FASME Archives	Archives of the Freedmen's Aid Society of the Methodist Episcopal Church, Interdenominational Theological Center, Atlanta, Georgia
FOR, BRFAL	Field Office Records of the Georgia Freedmen's Bureau Superintendent of Education, Records of the United States Bureau of Refugees, Freedmen, and Abandoned Lands, National Archives, Record Group 105, Washington, D.C.
FR	*Freedmen's Record*, magazine of the New England Freedmen's Aid Society (later New England branch of the American Freedmen's Union Commission)
GSE, LS and LR, BRFAL	Georgia Freedmen's Bureau Superintendent of Education, Letters Sent and Letters Received, Records of the United States Bureau of Refugees, Freedmen, and Abandoned Lands, Record Group 105, National Archives, Washington, D.C.
NF	*National Freedman*, organ of the New York branch of the American Freedmen's Union Commission
Rockwell Scrapbook	John A. Rockwell and Martha D. Ayres Scrapbook, Amistad Research Center, New Orleans, Lousiana
SMR	Superintendent's Monthly Report (AMA Archives, Ayer Papers and BRFAL)

TMR Teacher's Monthly Report (AMA Archives and BRFAL)
Ware Papers Edmund Asa Ware Papers, Negro Collection, Atlanta
University Center Trevor Arnett Library, Atlanta, Georgia

Chapter I

1. Joe Gray Taylor (*Louisiana Reconstructed*, p. 455), Vernon Lane Wharton (*The Negro in Mississippi*, p. 246), and Alan Conway (*The Reconstruction of Georgia*, p. 94) suggest the blacks' interest in schooling was somewhat naive.

2. Ronald G. Walters, *The Antislavery Appeal*, p. 86; James M. McPherson, *The Struggle for Equality* and *The Abolitionist Legacy*.

3. For discussions of the Republican world view, see Eric Foner, *Free Soil, Free Labor, Free Men*, and Alan Dawley, *Class and Community*, pp. 97–104.

4. W. E. B. Du Bois, *The Souls of Black Folk*, pp. 100, 25. Henry L. Swint (*The Northern Teacher in the South*) argues that the teachers were tools of the Republican party and only served to foment conflict between the races in the South.

5. W. J. Cash, *The Mind of the South*, pp. 140–41. In a similar vein, E. Merton Coulter contends that the teachers were "pious young females of the Puritan persuasion [who] . . . innocently awakened in the African heart longings for what could not be" (*College Life in the Old South*, p. 334).

6. McPherson, *Struggle for Equality* and *Abolitionist Legacy*, pp. 143–202.

7. Sandra E. Small, "The Yankee Schoolmarm in Freedmen's Schools," p. 402.

8. For examples of the recent work of historians favorable to the teachers, see Peter Kolchin, *First Freedom*, pp. 80–84; Joel Williamson, *After Slavery*, pp. 212–217; Taylor, *Louisiana Reconstructed*, p. 456; Joe M. Richardson, *The Negro in the Reconstruction of Florida*, pp. 97–106.

9. McPherson, *Abolitionist Legacy*, pp. 165–66.

10. Edward Magdol, *A Right to the Land*, p. 11.

11. Eugene D. Genovese, *Roll, Jordan, Roll*, p. 294; John W. Blassingame, *The Slave Community*, pp. 160–62, 188, 204, 215. Leon F. Litwack discusses this theme as it relates to black education and religion after the war in *Been in the Storm So Long*, pp. 450–501.

12. Nathaniel P. Rogers, quoted in Walters, *Antislavery Appeal*, p. 105.

13. Tilton, quoted in McPherson, *Abolitionist Legacy*, pp. 68–69; Gerda Lerner, *The Grimké Sisters from South Carolina*, pp. 162, 368; Eleanor Flexner, *Century of Struggle*, pp. 47, 142–55; Blanche G. Hersh, *The Slavery of Sex*.

14. Michael P. Johnson, *Toward a Patriarchal Republic*, pp. xxii–xxiii.

15. Willie Lee Rose, *Rehearsal for Reconstruction*; Louis S. Gerteis, *From Contraband to Freedman*; Taylor, *Louisiana Reconstructed*, pp. 455–56; Litwack, *Been in the Storm So Long*, pp. 375–77.

16. Relevant secondary works dealing with the debate over southern school segregation and white-sponsored black education include Henry Allen Bullock, *A History of Negro Education in the South*; Louis R. Harlan, *Separate and Unequal*; McPherson, *Abolitionist Legacy*; Donald Spivey, *Schooling for the New Slavery*; William Preston Vaughn, *Schools for All*; Raymond Wolters, *The New Negro on Campus*; and Carter Godwin Woodson, *The Mis-Education of the Negro*.

Chapter II

1. *AM* 9 (Sept. 1865):180; James M. McPherson, *The Struggle for Equality*, pp. 3, 170–72, 387, and *The Abolitionist Legacy*, pp. 3–10.
2. Ronald G. Walters, *The Antislavery Appeal*, p. 60.
3. McPherson, *Abolitionist Legacy*, pp. 143–45; Julius H. Parmelee, "Freedmen's Aid Societies, 1861–1871," pp. 268–95.
4. *AM* 9 (Nov. 1865):255; *AM* 12 (Mar. 1868):59; McPherson, *Struggle for Equality*, pp. 401–2. For very favorable historical accounts of the AMA, see Augustus F. Beard, *A Crusade of Brotherhood*; Fred Brownlee, *New Day Ascending*; and Clifton Herman Johnson, "The American Missionary Association." Other relevant works include Richard B. Drake, "The American Missionary Association and the Southern Negro," and Bertram Wyatt-Brown, *Lewis Tappan and the Evangelical War against Slavery*, pp. 287–309.
5. Johnson, "American Missionary Association." See the AMA's statement of evangelical principles printed inside the front cover of most issues of the *American Missionary* published during the Civil War era.
6. Gregory H. Singleton, "Protestant Voluntary Organizations and the Shaping of Victorian America," pp. 549–60.
7. Walters, *Antislavery Appeal*, p. 40.
8. Aileen S. Kraditor, *Means and Ends in American Abolitionism*, p. 22; Singleton, "Protestant Voluntary Organizations," p. 550.
9. Kraditor, *Means and Ends*, pp. 79, 241, 252; Wyatt-Brown, *Lewis Tappan*, pp. 292–93; Singleton, "Protestant Voluntary Organizations," pp.550–52; Charles I. Foster, *An Errand of Mercy*. Singleton's article contains an extensive bibliography on the secondary literature of antebellum evangelical reform.
10. McPherson, Kraditor, and Lewis Perry *(Radical Abolitionism)* stress the differences among "radical" Garrisonians, "conservative" evangelicals, and political abolitionists within the antislavery movement. McPherson, *Abolitionist Legacy*, pp. 3–5, and *Struggle for Equality*, pp. 2, 170–72, 387. In the discussion that follows, the term "abolitionist" applies to evangelicals who were radical in their critique of slavery but conservative in their support of established religious denominations in the North.
11. Perry, *Radical Abolitionism*, pp. xi, 9, 47–49, 53; Walters, *Antislavery Appeal*, pp. 54–61.
12. *AM* 5 (June 1861):129; Perry, *Radical Abolitionism*, p. 48; Walters, *Antislavery Appeal*, pp. 57–58; McPherson, *Abolitionist Legacy*, pp. 60–69, and *Struggle for Equality*, pp. 134–53.
13. *AM* 8 (Aug. 1864):194; Perry, *Radical Abolitionism*, pp. xiii, 270; Kraditor, *Means and Ends*, pp. 237–40.
14. *AM* 9 (Feb. 1865):28–29; Wyatt-Brown, *Lewis Tappan*, p. 299; McPherson, *Abolitionist Legacy*, p. 5, and *Struggle for Equality*, pp. 221–37; *AM* 6 (May 1862):106–7; George Fredrickson, *The Black Image in the White Mind*, pp. 130–64; Eric Foner, *Free Soil, Free Labor, Free Men*, pp. 295–300.
15. Perry, *Radical Abolitionism*, p. 68; Kraditor, *Means and Ends*, p. 17; Walters, *Antislavery Appeal*, pp. 45–47; Wyatt-Brown, *Lewis Tappan*, pp. 312–13, 317; William G. McLoughlin, *The Meaning of Henry Ward Beecher*, pp. 190–201, 210.
16. *AM* 5 (Oct. 1861):227; Perry, *Radical Abolitionism*, pp. 232–39, 251, 269–70; Kraditor, *Means and Ends*, p. 103.
17. *AM* 12 (June 1868):130.
18. *AM* 6 (Jan. 1862):10; *AM* 8 (Oct. 1864):242; *FR* 1 (Oct. 1865):157; *NF* 2

(Aug. 1866):211; statement by the Reverend J. W. Parker on the official letterhead of the ABHMS, AMA Archives.

19. *AM* 12 (May 1869):98; *AM* 5 (Oct. 1861):227; Singleton, "Protestant Voluntary Organizations," p. 553; Johnson, "American Missionary Association," p. 574.

20. *AM* 12 (Dec. 1868):275; *AM* 11 (Apr. 1867):82; *AM* 9 (Apr. 1865):82; *AM* 9 (May 1865):103–4; Ronald G. Walters, *American Reformers*, pp. 214–15; Singleton, "Protestant Voluntary Organizations," p. 550. Walters suggests that antebellum reformers were both "backward-looking" and "forward-looking"; Singleton terms them "conservative" as well as "progressive." Perry argues that by 1800 sin had become "equivalent to social disorder" in the minds of American Protestants (*Radical Abolitionism*, p. 39).

21. *AM* 9 (Nov. 1865):251.

22. Daniel Walker Howe, "American Victorianism as a Culture," pp. 507–32.

23. Carl F. Kaestle, "Social Change, Discipline, and the Common School in Early Nineteenth-Century America," p. 7; Michael B. Katz, "Origins of the Institutional State," pp. 6–23; Stanley K. Schultz, *The Culture Factory*; David B. Tyack, *The One Best System*; Carl F. Kaestle, *Evolution of an Urban School System*.

24. *Fourth Annual Report of the Freedmen's Aid Society of the Methodist Episcopal Church*, p. 4; McPherson, *Abolitionist Legacy*, pp. 53–55, 151, 188–93.

25. McPherson, *Abolitionist Legacy*, pp. 56–57, 71–72, 184, and *Struggle for Equality*, pp. 246–49; Wyatt-Brown, *Lewis Tappan*, pp. 294–97; *AM* 5 (Oct. 1861):222; Johnson, "American Missionary Association," pp. 309–55; *AM* 9 (Feb. 1865):28–29.

26. *AM* 6 (June 1862):131; *AM* 6 (Feb. 1862):29; *AM* 7 (Aug. 1863):179; *AM* 9 (Jan. 1865):12; *AM* 9 (Feb. 1865):29; McPherson, *Struggle for Equality*, pp. 10–24, 60, 71–117, 222.

27. McPherson, *Struggle for Equality*, pp. 257–59, 335–50; Otto H. Olsen, "Setting the Record Straight on the Reconstruction South," p. 334; Donald G. Nieman, "Andrew Johnson, the Freedmen's Bureau, and the Problem of Equal Rights, 1865–1866," pp. 399–420; Leon F. Litwack, *Been in the Storm So Long*, pp. 386, 408–19; William S. McFeely, *Yankee Stepfather*.

28. *AM* 9 (Jan. 1865):15.

29. *AM* 12 (Sept. 1868):207; McPherson, *Struggle for Equality*, pp. 178, 190, 393; *AM* 7 (Oct. 1863):224–25; *AM* 9 (July 1865):146–47; *AM* 11 (Sept. 1867):193. In his unpublished Ph.D. dissertation, "Reading, 'Riting, and Reconstruction," Robert C. Morris argues that the reform impulse for freedmen's education was politically and socially conservative.

30. George P. Rawick, ed., *The American Slave* (Georgia Narratives), vol. 13, sec. 4, p. 348. See also Litwack, *Been in the Storm So Long*, pp. 380, 403.

31. G. L. Eberhart to Samuel Hunt, Augusta, 23 May 1866; G. L. Eberhart to Samuel Hunt, Augusta, 4 June 1866; J. E. Bryant to Sec., Augusta, 12 June 1866; Mary J. Welch to Samuel Hunt, Augusta, 26 Feb. 1866; Gen. Davis Tillson to George Whipple, Augusta, 4 July 1866, AMA Archives. Letters cited from this and all other MS collections originated in Georgia unless otherwise indicated. Also, unless otherwise specified, all correspondence subsequently cited is from the AMA Archives.

32. *AM* 10 (June 1866):134–35; Mary J. Welch to Samuel Hunt, Augusta, 1 May 1866.

33. *AM* 9 (May 1865):103–4; Robert F. Markham to Michael E. Strieby, Savannah, 15 Mar. 1877.

34. McPherson, *Abolitionist Legacy*, pp. 53–56.

35. 1870 United States Federal MS Population Census, Sunderland, Franklin

County, Mass., p. 20; 1860 MS Federal Census, Sunderland, Franklin County, Mass., p. 47; 1860 MS Federal Census, Deerfield, Franklin County, Mass., p. 42.

36. Jennie F. Stowell to S. Jocelyn, S. Deerfield, Mass., 10 May 1864; William Henry Harrison Stowell, *Stowell Genealogy*, p. 388; Cyrus H. Stowell to E. P. Smith, S. Deerfield, Mass., 16 Dec. 1867; Jennie F. Stowell to E. P. Smith, S. Deerfield, Mass., 24 Sept. 1869.

37. John Montague Smith, *History of the Town of Sunderland, Massachusetts*, p. 425; Sarah Hunt to Samuel Hunt, Sunderland, Mass., 25 Sept. 1865; Sarah Hunt to E. P. Smith, Sunderland, Mass., 3 Sept. 1869.

38. O. W. Dimick to John Ogden, Macon, 7 Mar. 1866.

39. McPherson, *Abolitionist Legacy*, pp. 155, 167–68, 177, 181, 269, Appendix A.

40. *FR* 5 (May 1866):86; *AM* 9 (Feb. 1865):35; *AM* 8 (Jan. 1864): 11.

41. *AM* 9 (Apr. 1865):90.

42. *FR* 2 (Sept. 1866):161.

43. *FR* 1 (Sept. 1865):139; *AM* 10 (July 1866):152–53; N. J. Burton to AMA, Hartford, Conn., 15 Nov. 1867. The AMA's printed application form is included in the AMA Archives; see Vermont #HI-1716, AMA to Lydia E. White, New York City, 9 Jan. 1864.

44. American Missionary Association, "Woman's Work for the Lowly as Illustrated in the Work of the American Missionary Association Among the Freedmen."

45. *AM* 10 (July 1866):151–52.

46. FR 4 (Sept. 1868):122; *FR* 2 (Nov. 1865):182; Jane McNeil to George Whipple, Amherst, Mass., 20 Aug. 1868; Emily F. Campbell to William E. Whiting, Boston, Mass., 3 Sept. 1872; Ayer Obituary (handwritten), Atlanta, ca. 1 Jan. 1868, AMA Archives; Mary Conkling to E. P. Smith, Augusta, 11 May 1867; Mary Conkling to E. P. Smith, Augusta, 29 Jan. 1867; Sarah Chase to Mr. May, Columbus, 1 Nov. 1866, Chase Papers; Sarah Chase to Mrs. May, Columbus, 5 Feb. 1866, in Henry L. Swint, ed., *Dear Ones at Home*, p. 194.

47. J. K. Warner to William E. Whiting, Augusta, 4 Dec. 1867; H. H. Grosvenor to William E. Whiting, Macon, 23 May 1868; O. W. Dimick to E. A. Ware, Oak Hill, Mass., 14 Sept. 1868, Ware Papers.

48. C. L. Woodworth to Samuel Hunt, Amherst, Mass., 29 Aug. 1865; C. L. Woodworth to E. P. Smith, Boston, Mass., 15 Nov. 1867.

49. For discussions of this ideal and of the virtue of self-sacrifice in particular, see Ann Douglas, *The Feminization of American Culture*, pp. 44–47; Nancy F. Cott, *The Bonds of Womanhood*, pp. 75–79, 145–46, 155; Barbara Welter, "The Cult of True Womanhood, 1820–1860," pp. 155–74.

In the 1850s Beecher wrote, "The most elevated and ecstatic happiness is combined with the keenest suffering, and suffering is the chief cause of the happiness thus secured." By her own admission, female self-sacrifice represented the *"grand law"* of her social system, which was designed to stimulate the moral regeneration of the nation. Kathryn K. Sklar, *Catharine Beecher*, pp. 251, 253. For fuller treatment of the ideology of domesticity and the importance of self-denial, see pp. xiv, 85–86, 164, 172, 186, 244–57.

50. R. S. Billings to E. P. Smith, Shelburne, Mass., 25 Oct. 1867; Ann D. Gordon and Mari Jo Buhle, "Sex and Class in Colonial and Nineteenth-Century America," pp. 284–87. Female missionary work in general during this period is discussed in Cott, *Bonds of Womanhood*, pp. 134–35, and Douglas, *Feminization*, pp. 106–7. The argument in the text of the present volume concerning the motivation of female freedmen's teachers closely parallels Jane Addams's analysis of the middle-class origins of the reform impulse. Jane Addams, *Twenty Years at Hull-House*, pp. 113–28.

51. Emily F. Campbell to George Whipple, Clinton, Mass., 4 July 1864.
52. Annie Allender to George Whipple, New London, Conn., 1 Aug. 1864; Clara C. Chappel to "Dear Friends," Savannah, 23 May 1870.
53. William C. Capron to Michael E. Strieby, Uxbridge, Mass., 26 Sept. 1864.
54. Caroline Damon to George Whipple, Holden, Mass., 16 Nov. 1865; R. F. Laurence to AMA, New London, Conn., 4 Oct. 1865; Harriet M. Haskell to George Whipple, Clinton, Mass., 5 July 1864; Clara Rossiter to AMA, Pittsfield, Mass., 4 Sept. 1865; Susan R. Child to E. P. Smith, Boston, Mass., 14 Sept. 1870.
55. May E. Hilliard to George Whipple, Northfield, Mass., 26 July 1864; Harvey J. Graff, "Patterns of Dependency and Child Development in the Mid-Nineteenth Century City," pp. 134, 139–40; Carroll Smith-Rosenberg, "The Female World of Love and Ritual," pp. 16–18; Joseph F. Kett, "Growing Up in Rural New England, 1800–1840," pp. 8–10, 13–14.
56. Eliza H. Twitchell to E. P. Smith, Chelsea, Mass., 8 Oct. 1868; Ella Roper to E. P. Smith, Templeton, Mass., 19 July 1870; Phebe McKean to Michael E. Strieby, Andover, Mass., 10 Dec. 1864.
57. Jane McNeil to AMA, Charlotte, Vt., 14 Aug. 1869.
58. Annie M. Bartemus to E. P. Smith, Groton Junction, Mass., 9 Oct. 1867. See the article by Smith-Rosenberg, "The Female World of Love and Ritual." On the ability of female friendships to compensate for the emotional segregation of men and women, she says, "the supposedly repressive and destructive Victorian sexual ethos may have been more flexible and responsive to the needs of particular individuals than those of the mid-twentieth century" (p. 29). In a similar vein, Sklar writes that "Female friendship was the nineteenth-century antidote to the wounds inflicted by the inequities of gender" (*Catharine Beecher*, p. 195).
59. Sallie Curtis to E. P. Smith, Augusta, 29 Jan. 1867.
60. Richard M. Bernard and Maris A. Vinovskis, "The Female School Teacher in Antebellum Massachusetts," pp. 332–45.
61. Julia Shearman to E. P. Smith, Augusta, 13 Oct. 1867; Minnie Hanson to AMA, Newton, Mass., 1 Feb. 1871; Mary Pomeroy to E. M. Cravath, Atlanta, 3 June 1871; Ann Douglas Wood, "The 'Fashionable Diseases,'" pp. 25–52; Catharine Beecher, "Statistics of Female Health," pp. 165–78.
62. Lucy Case to E. M. Cravath, Atlanta, 11 Nov. 1871; Carrie Ritter to W. E. Whiting, Augusta, 12 July 1869; Josie Barbour to E. A. Ware, Madison, 10 Feb. 1869, Ware Papers; Fidelia Morgan to "Dear Friends," Augusta, 12 Dec. 1866; Fidelia Morgan to E. P. Smith, Greenfield, Mass., 12 Aug. 1867.
63. Hannah C. Bullard to Samuel Hunt, Boston, Mass., 13 Sept. 1865.
64. Sarah M. Proctor to E. P. Smith, Macon, 15 Jan. 1869; Harriet F. Tradewell to E. M. Cravath, Lowndes County, 10 Mar. 1873.
65. Carrie Morse to E. P. Smith, Athens, 1 Feb. 1869.

Chapter III

1. A black newspaper editor in Georgia called on his readers to strive for "soul liberty" in spite of continued oppression from whites after emancipation. "Hints for the Times: 'Soul Liberty,'" *Freemen's Standard* 7 (Mar. 1868):1.
2. Hattie Foote to Samuel Hunt, Augusta, 2 July 1866.
3. Michael P. Johnson, *Toward a Patriarchal Republic*, p. xxiii; Ralph Betts Flanders, *Plantation Slavery in Georgia*; T. Conn Bryan, *Confederate Georgia*, p. 118. The state's cotton crop sold for $25 million in 1860. Other major agricultural products

included corn (almost $25 million worth produced in 1860) and slaughtered livestock ($11 million).

4. Johnson, *Patriarchal Republic*, pp. 128, 144, 167.

5. Clarence Lee Mohr, "Georgia Blacks During Secession and Civil War, 1859–1865," pp. 5–6, 68.

6. Bryan, *Confederate Georgia*; Mohr, "Georgia Blacks," pp. 209–10.

7. Alan Conway, *The Reconstruction of Georgia*, pp. 42–52, 175–77; Elizabeth Studley Nathans, *Losing the Peace*, pp. 144–46, 204, 222.

8. Nathans, *Losing the Peace*, pp. 41–42, 88–89; J. E. Bryant, "The Georgia Educational Movement," Augusta, ca. 31 Jan. 1867, AMA Archives.

9. Conway, *Reconstruction*, pp. 166–69, 229; John M. Matthews, "Negro Republicans in the Reconstruction of Georgia," pp. 151–52, 159; Nathans, *Losing the Peace*, pp. 68, 90–97, 121–23. As C. Vann Woodward argues, most Radical Republicans in Congress also were more interested in obtaining black political support than in advancing the civil-rights cause (*American Counterpoint*, pp. 163–83).

10. Matthews, "Negro Republicans," pp. 146–49; Nathans, *Losing the Peace*, pp. 19–21, 24–27, 57–58. Constitutions of the GEA and "subordinate associations" are in Folder 20-B-1-C, Ware Papers. For GEA guidelines for running a local education association meeting, see William L. Clark to "President," Bainbridge, 25 Feb. 1869, FOR (series 786, vol. 184, pp. 34–35), BRFAL. Issues of the *Loyal Georgian* and the AMA Archives contain a great deal of information on the GEA, Bryant, and Bryant's relation to northern freedmen's aid societies.

11. George R. Bentley, *A History of the Freedmen's Bureau*, pp. 68–71, 112, 129, 164, 185, 215; Conway, *Reconstruction*, pp. 244, 75–99; Nathans, *Losing the Peace*, p. 19; James M. McPherson, *The Struggle for Equality*, pp. 257–59; Matthews, "Negro Republicans," p. 147; Sarah Chase to Mrs. May, Columbus, 9 March 1866, in Henry L. Swint, ed., *Dear Ones at Home*, p. 199. See also Donald G. Nieman, "Andrew Johnson, the Freedmen's Bureau, and the Problem of Equal Rights, 1865–1866"; Louis S. Gerteis, *From Contraband to Freedman*, pp. 185–88; Daniel A. Novak, *The Wheel of Servitude*, pp. 15–16, 26–28. Novak argues that, during Reconstruction, "the situation of the black agricultural laborer in Georgia was almost a classic definition of peonage" (p. 28).

12. Bentley, *Freedmen's Bureau*, pp. 84, 157, 209; Roger L. Ransom and Richard Sutch, *One Kind of Freedom*, pp. 56–61; Conway, *Reconstruction*, pp. 75–99; Sidney Andrews, *The South Since the War*, p. 322; Lyman Abbott, "The Results of Emancipation in the United States of America," pp. 25–26; Leon F. Litwack, *Been in the Storm So Long*, pp. 336–449.

13. Charles Stearns, *The Black Man of the South, and the Rebels*, pp. 107–9, 524–27; Susan P. Harrold to E. P. Smith, Darien, 12 Apr. 1869; Mrs. Mary Jones to Charles C. Jones, Jr., Montevideo, 28 May 1866, in Robert Manson Myers, ed., *The Children of Pride*, pp. 1340–41; John Richard Dennett, *The South As It Is*, pp. 276–77; William S. McFeely, *Yankee Stepfather*, p. 311.

14. Ransom and Sutch, *One Kind of Freedom*, pp. 12–13, 81, 85–86; Conway, *Reconstruction*, p. 106.

15. Frances B. Leigh, *Ten Years on a Georgia Plantation Since the War*, pp. 55–56; Conway, *Reconstruction*, pp. 55–59, 117, 131; Ransom and Sutch, *One Kind of Freedom*, pp. 56–61, 65–67; Leon F. Litwack, "Free at Last," pp. 161–62.

16. Ransom and Sutch, *One Kind of Freedom*, pp. 64–72; Conway, *Reconstruction*, pp. 89, 115–17, 227. For a summary of recent interpretations of the decline in cotton production in the postbellum South, see Peter Temin, "The Post-Bellum Recovery of the South and the Cost of the Civil War," pp. 898–907.

17. Ransom and Sutch, *One Kind of Freedom*, pp. 88, 94–97.

18. Ibid., p. 105; Nathans, *Losing the Peace*, p. 225.

19. Ransom and Sutch, *One Kind of Freedom*, pp. 5–6, 55. In his article "The Anatomy of Fear," Dan T. Carter argues persuasively that white panic over rumored insurrections in 1865 amounted to "a secular ritual—an elaborate psychodrama—which temporarily resolved the tensions of a perilously unstable society" (p. 351). This theme is developed on a southern-wide level in Litwack, *Been in the Storm So Long*.

20. Clarence Lee Mohr, "Before Sherman," p. 23; Anthony Wilson to E. P. Smith, Elliots Bluff, 3 Aug. 1870.

21. George P. Rawick, ed., *The American Slave* (Georgia Narratives), vol. 13, sec. 4, pp. 189, 317–18; sec. 2, 274; Flanders, *Plantation Slavery*, p. 25; Ransom and Sutch, *One Kind of Freedom*, p. 17.

22. Richard R. Wright, "Brief Historical Sketch of Negro Education in Georgia," pp. 18–20; Rawick, ed., *American Slave*, vol. 13, sec. 3, p. 212.

23. Rawick, ed., *American Slave*, vol. 12, sec. 1, pp. 5, 10, 180, 219, 234, 257, 270, 323; sec. 2, pp. 5, 33–34, 131, 226, 283, 189, 304; sec. 3, p. 270; sec. 4, pp. 236, 318.

24. Mohr, "Georgia Blacks," pp. 209–10; Litwack, "Free at Last," pp. 131–71; Mohr, "Before Sherman." See also Bryan, *Confederate Georgia*, pp. 123–28.

25. Mohr, "Before Sherman," p. 17, and "Georgia Blacks," p. 52; Rawick, ed., *American Slave*, vol. 12, sec. 1, p. 257. See also Susie King Taylor, *Reminiscences of My Life in Camp*.

26. Edward Magdol, *A Right to the Land*, pp. 11, 49–50, 80, 160–70; John W. Blassingame, "Before the Ghetto," pp. 474, 466; Matthews, "Negro Republicans," pp. 152–53; Litwack, *Been in the Storm So Long*, pp. 502–56.

27. Samson Gardner, Warrenton, Oct. 1867, TMR, BRFAL. See also F. A. Sawtell to E. P. Smith, Macon, 6 Jan. 1870; W. A. Golding to E. M. Cravath, Golden Grove, 6 Jan. 1873; *AF*, 2 (Sept. 1866):86. An article entitled "Meeting of an Educational Association Among the Freedmen" (*AM* 13 [Feb. 1869]:29–30) includes a detailed account of "the endeavors of our colored friends, in a certain locality in Georgia, to manage their own affairs."

28. "The Georgia Educational Association" (minutes of Oct. 1867 meeting), p. 26, Ware Papers; Freedmen's Bureau, Fourth and Eighth *Semi-Annual Report on Schools for the Freedmen*; Sarah Stansbury to E. P. Smith, Cuthbert, 14 Sept. 1869; Lucy Case to E. P. Smith, Albany, 5 Feb. 1869; Ransom and Sutch, *One Kind of Freedom*, p. 28.

29. *AM* 10 (Feb. 1866):33; Marion Sellmer to G. L. Eberhart, Woodville Plantation, 12 Feb. 1867.

30. Ellen E. Adlington to E. P. Smith, Berne, 28 Feb. 1868; *FR* 5 (June 1865):91; Mary Colburn to E. P. Smith, Savannah, 31 Jan. 1867; Laura Parmelee to E. P. Smith, Andersonville, 25 Dec. 1868.

31. This summary of biographical data is based on a random sample taken from the Federal MS Population Census for forty-five Georgia counties in 1870, including four coastal counties, nine in the wire-grass region, twenty in the Black Belt, and nine in the northwestern part of the state. The results of this modest study were disappointingly meager. Only forty black teachers were located, about seven for every one hundred white teachers in those counties. The attendance of black children in several districts that listed no blacks as teachers indicates that the census was not an accurate source of information on this subject.

There are several possible explanations for what was obviously an underenumeration of black schoolteachers in Georgia in 1870. First, in some areas the census was taken in June, a month when many schools were not in session and teachers were probably working in the fields. Second, clergymen who taught in the local school might have listed their occupation only as "preacher." Third, some teachers might have been reluctant to admit to a white census-taker that they taught school; in 1870 the Georgia Ku Klux Klan was on the rampage and black schools and teachers were among its favorite targets.

32. J. W. Brooks, Bibb County, n.d., TMR, BRFAL; J. J. Gideons, Decatur County, Sept. 1869, TMR, BRFAL.

33. R. M. Mitchell, Macon, Apr. 1869, TMR, BRFAL.

34. Harrison Watkins to E. M. Cravath, Byron, 9 Oct. 1874; Anthony Wilson to E. P. Smith, Woodbine, 30 Sept. 1870.

35. Rawick, ed., *American Slave*, vol. 13, sec. 3, p. 312.

36. Abbie Case to Samuel Hunt, Savannah, 22 Apr. 1866. For examples of northern teachers' complaints about rival schools taught by native black men and women, see Sarah Stansbury to E. P. Smith, Cuthbert, 6, 20 Feb., 1 Apr. 1871; Minnie C. Owen to E. P. Smith, Darien, 28 Oct. 1869; Frank Haley to E. P. Smith, Macon, 1 Dec. 1867; Anna Ludlow to E. M. Cravath, Savannah, 22 Apr. 1872; E. A. Ware to E. P. Smith, Atlanta, 8 May 1867; John A. Bassett to J. R. Lewis, Augusta, 18 June 1869, GSE, LR, BRFAL.

37. Eugene D. Genovese, *Roll, Jordan, Roll*, pp. 153–54; Mohr, "Before Sherman," pp. 13–14; Mrs. Mary Jones, Journal, Montevideo, Dec.-Jan. 1864–65, in Myers, ed., *Children of Pride*, pp. 1248, 1236–38; Gerteis, *From Contraband to Freedman*, p. 6; Rawick, *American Slave*, vol. 12, sec. 1, p. 262.

38. Robert F. Markham to Michael E. Strieby, Savannah, 9 Oct. 1877; *AM* 15 (Feb. 1871):44; Daniel Walker Howe, "American Victorianism as a Culture," pp. 507–32; Daniel T. Rodgers, *The Work Ethic in Industrial America, 1850–1920*.

39. This discussion is based on John W. Blassingame, *The Slave Community*; Genovese, *Roll, Jordan, Roll*; Lawrence W. Levine, *Black Culture and Black Consciousness*; Herbert G. Gutman, *The Black Family in Slavery and Freedom, 1750–1925*; and Litwack, *Been in the Storm So Long*.

40. Magdol, *Right to the Land*, pp. 4–11.

41. William Steward to E. P. Smith, Americus, 24 June 1869; Hezekiah Brown to George Whipple, Savannah, 10 Aug. 1869; Hezekiah Brown to E. P. Smith, Savannah, 30 Apr. 1869; William Steward to E. P. Smith, Americus, 21 May 1869.

42. Floyd Snelson to M. E. Strieby, McIntosh County, 18 July 1874, 4 Dec. 1875. See also Tunis G. Campbell, "Sufferings of the Rev. T. G. Campbell and His Family in Georgia."

43. E. A. Ware to Fannie Randall, Atlanta, 24 Sept. 1867, GSE, LS, BRFAL; E. A. Ware to E. P. Smith, Atlanta, 20 Aug. 1867, GSE, LS, BRFAL; J. R. Lewis to Fannie A. Maxwell, Augusta, 6 Aug. 1867, GSE, LS, BRFAL; E. A. Ware to M. W. Early, Atlanta, 26 Aug. 1867, GSE, LS, BRFAL.

44. *FR* 1 (Sept. 1865):139; G. L. Eberhart to Ira Pettibone, Augusta, 19 Oct. 1866; Ira Pettibone, Savannah, Nov. 1866, SMR.

45. M. E. Sands to E. M. Cravath, Macon, 10 June 1872. A black man reported to the AMA's William L. Clark in September 1873 that the freed people of Thomasville had met to discuss educational matters "and when the question arose who we should have to teach, the people agreed almost to a man that we should have northern teachers." H. B. Doudell to W. L. Clark, Thomasville, 25 Sept. 1873.

46. Blassingame, "Before the Ghetto," pp. 463–73. Northern journalist Whitelaw Reid saw "well-dressed blacks" in "large and well-furnished houses" in Savannah in the spring of 1865. Reid, *After the War*, p. 147.

47. Blassingame, "Before the Ghetto," pp. 463, 468, 473.

48. Ibid., pp. 476–78; Magdol, *Right to the Land*, pp. 104–6, 126; Nathans, *Losing the Peace*, p. 29; Matthews, "Negro Republicans," pp. 156–57; Litwack, *Been in the Storm So Long*, pp. 450–52, 463–64, 502, 546–47.

49. Campbell, "Sufferings," p. 3.

50. Blassingame, "Before the Ghetto," pp. 471, 479. For a discussion of the somewhat different situation in Atlanta, which did not have a viable antebellum black community, see Howard N. Rabinowitz, "From Reconstruction to Redemption in the Urban South," pp. 169–94.

51. Wright, "Brief Historical Sketch," pp. 16–22; *AM* 9 (Feb. 1865):41; Blassingame, "Before the Ghetto," p. 471. *NF* 1 (Apr. 1865):98 contains capsule biographies of twenty Savannah churchmen who met with Sherman in January 1865 to discuss their education program.

52. *FR* 1 (May 1865):72; *AM* 9 (Nov. 1865):256–58; W. T. Richardson to AMA, Savannah, 2 Jan. 1865; S. W. Magill to AMA, Savannah, 16 Feb. 1865.

53. S. W. Magill to AMA, Savannah, 28 Jan., 3, 16 Feb. 1865.

54. S. W. Magill to AMA, Savannah, 6 Feb. 1865; S. W. Magill to Rufus Saxton, Savannah, 3 Apr. 1865; *FR* 1 (June 1865):92.

55. S. W. Magill to AMA, Savannah, 26 Feb., 5 Apr. 1865; S. W. Magill to Rufus Saxton, Savannah, 3 Apr. 1865.

56. S. W. Magill to AMA, Savannah, June 1865; E. A. Cooley to Samuel Hunt, Savannah, 17 Oct. 1865.

57. *AM* 9 (Nov. 1865):256–58; E. A. Cooley to Samuel Hunt, Savannah, 22 Nov., 2, 20 Dec. 1865, 2 Jan., 3 Feb. 1866.

58. E. A. Cooley to Samuel Hunt, Savannah, 9 Apr. 1866.

59. Ira Pettibone, Savannah, Nov. 1866, SMR; A. N. Niles to E. M. Cravath, Savannah, 26 Oct. 1870. In the mid-1870s, AMA officials in Savannah were still complaining about the "Spirit of opposition" among blacks to association efforts in that city. A. Rowe to E. M. Cravath, Savannah, 28 May 1875.

Ironically, Blassingame states of the SEA, "Because of the expense, the educational campaign would probably have failed or been sharply curtailed if sympathetic Northern whites had not supported it" ("Before the Ghetto," p. 471). See Jacqueline Jones, "The 'Great Opportunity,'" pp. 99–105, for more extensive documentation of the SEA's history.

60. James Snowden to E. P. Smith, McIntosh County, 15 Mar. 1869. As Genovese argues, the slave church in America had never been a "revolutionary" force; for this reason, whites were probably not overtly suspicious of black religious activities after the war. *Roll, Jordan, Roll*, pp. 279, 283.

61. See the article by Vernon Burton, "Race and Reconstruction," pp. 31–56, on the "fierce competition between blacks and whites for political and economic power" (p. 31) in Edgefield County, South Carolina. Ransom and Sutch, *One Kind of Freedom*, pp. 186, 197.

62. John H. Caldwell, *Reminiscences of the Reconstruction of Church and State in Georgia*, pp. 9–11, 14–21; J. H. Caldwell to J. F. Chalfant, LaGrange, 20, 27 Aug., 1, 8 Oct. 1866, 4 Mar., 3 Sept. 1867, FASME Archives; Nathans, *Losing the Peace*, pp. 128–30, 169–70.

63. H. A. N. Hart to E. P. Smith, McIntosh Station, 23 Feb., 18 Apr., 16 May 1870. Hart never received any financial support from the AMA, though she applied for it. See also A. E. Alden to P. M. Bartlett, Athens, 27 July 1874.

64. J. W. Yarborough to J. F. Chalfant, Oxford, 24 May 1866, FASME Archives; Hattie Emerson to E. P. Smith, St. Mary's, 5 June 1868.

65. Quoted in Rufus B. Spain, *At Ease in Zion*, p. 59; Conway, *Reconstruction*, p. 86.

66. *NF* 2 (Apr. 1866):117. AMA Superintendent E. A. Ware noted in 1868 that whites did not bother to distinguish among the various northern groups at work in Georgia: "It is enough for them to know that they are Yankee teachers." E. A. Ware to E. P. Smith, Savannah, 24 Nov. 1868. See also Ransom and Sutch, *One Kind of Freedom*, p. 26.

67. James L. Roark, *Masters Without Slaves*, pp. 120–31, 131–41, 159, 153, 158, 166, 205–6; Conway, *Reconstruction*, pp. 111–15. One plantation mistress in Augusta noted of her black workers immediately after the war, "they work or not just as it best suits their convenience and pleasure." Mrs. Eva B. Jones to Mrs. Mary Jones, Augusta, 27 June 1865, in Myers, ed., *Children of Pride*, p. 1276. See also Carter, "Anatomy of Fear," pp. 355, 359–60; Ransom and Sutch, *One Kind of Freedom*, p. 46; Litwack, *Been in the Storm So Long*, pp. 336–86.

68. P. A. Lawson to O. H. Howard, Griffin, 4 Jan. 1870, GSE, LR, BRFAL. Both Conway (*Reconstruction*, pp. 227, 89) and Ransom and Sutch (*One Kind of Freedom*, p. 94) describe the sharecropping system as a "compromise" between white landowners and black workers during this period.

69. Douglas Risley to E. P. Smith, Brunswick, 5 Oct. 1868; C. W. Parker to J. F. Chalfant, Griffin, 14 Nov. 1866, FASME Archives; Frederick Ayer to Samuel Hunt, Atlanta, 31 Mar. 1866; Ellen E. Adlington to E. P. Smith, Berne, 20 May 1868. See also William P. Vaughn, *Schools for All*, pp. 20–21; Julius H. Parmelee, "Freedmen's Aid Societies, 1861–1871," pp. 268–95. Parmelee states that in 1867 only 1,348 out of 111,000 pupils in Freedmen's Bureau schools throughout the South were white.

70. These actual episodes are recorded in the AMA, FASME, and BRFAL Archives, 1865–73.

71. John H. Caldwell to J. F. Chalfant, LaGrange, 10 Sept. 1866, FASME Archives; J. T. Trowbridge, *The South*, pp. 463–500. Allen W. Trelease documents the growth of the Georgia Klan in his book *White Terror*, pp. 19, 27, 73–79, 117, 235–39, 326–38. For contemporary accounts, see John Calvin Reed, "What I Know of the KKK"; Stearns, *Black Man of the South*, pp. 416, 418, 425; *AM*, 15 (Mar., Apr., June 1871):60–61, 84–85, 132–33; R. H. Gladding to E. P. Smith, Greensborough, 13, 24 Nov. 1869; *The Condition of Affairs in Georgia*.

72. *AM* 10 (Dec. 1866):272–73; Sarah Champney to E. P. Smith, Cuthbert, 1 Dec. 1868.

73. A. N. Niles to E. M. Cravath, Savannah, 12 Oct. 1872.

74. Carrie Morse to E. P. Smith, Athens, 14 Dec. 1868, AMA Archives; Trelease, *White Terror*, p. 240; Stearns, *Black Man of the South*, pp. 156–57.

75. L. J. Kelly to E. P. Smith, Athens, 25 Jan. 1868.

Chapter IV

1. William L. Clark to E. P. Smith, Bainbridge, 26 Oct. 1868.

2. Alan Conway, *The Reconstruction of Georgia*, pp. 75–99; George R. Bentley, *A History of the Freedmen's Bureau*, pp. 169–83.

3. Georgia Freedmen's Bureau Superintendent Edmund A. Ware complained about "a little piece of 'red tape' here in the office" in his letter to Harrison Leland, Atlanta, 27 Jan. 1868, GSE, LS, BRFAL.

4. Dorothy Orr, *A History of Education in Georgia*; Martin V. Calvin, "Recent Progress of Public Education in the South," pp. 5–7; *AM* 13 (Nov. 1869):241–43; Conway, *Reconstruction in Georgia*, p. 84; John M. Matthews, "Negro Republicans in

the Reconstruction of Georgia," pp. 146–49; J. E. Bryant to E. P. Smith, Augusta, 9 July 1867; E. A. Ware to E. P. Smith, Atlanta, 8 May 1867; Elizabeth Studley Nathans, *Losing the Peace*, pp. 25–27, 43, 57–58, 69, 88–89, 132, 138, 197.

5. James M. McPherson, *The Abolitionist Legacy*, p. 15; Conway, *Reconstruction of Georgia*, p. 229; Matthews, "Negro Republicans," p. 159; Nathans, *Losing the Peace*, pp. 68, 90–91.

6. Carl F. Kaestle, *Evolution of an Urban School System*, pp. 159–84; Stanley K. Schultz, *The Culture Factory*, pp. 3–131; Michael B. Katz, *Class, Bureaucracy and Schools*, pp. 56–104; David B. Tyack, *The One Best System*, pp. 28–77; Jonathan Messerli, *Horace Mann*, p. 442.

7. E. M. Cravath to Hiram Eddy, Nashville, Tenn., 6 Jan. 1866, Rockwell Scrapbook; *AM* 10 (Oct. 1866):225. This article contains extracts from a report prepared by the AFUC's special committee on education and religion.

In his history of the AMA, Augustus F. Beard noted, "Thorough organization and concentration became missionary wisdom" (*A Crusade of Brotherhood*, p. 145).

8. E. B. Bingham to J. R. Lewis, Augusta, 1 Feb. 1869, FOR (series 772, vol. 154, p. 19), BRFAL; J. S. Banfield to G. L. Eberhart, Columbus, 10 Jan. 1867; Gregory H. Singleton, "Protestant Voluntary Organizations and the Shaping of Victorian America," pp. 355–57.

9. E. M. Cravath to John A. Rockwell, Nashville, 29 May 1866, Rockwell Scrapbook.

10. *FR* 1 (Aug. 1865):129; Conway, *Reconstruction of Georgia*, p. 89.

11. Penciled note of E. P. Smith, Georgia, Feb. 1868, AMA Archives.

12. *FR* 2 (June 1866):112–13; Nathans, *Losing the Peace*, pp. 22–23.

13. O. O. Howard to J. R. Lewis, Washington, D.C., 14 Aug. 1869, GSE, LR, BRFAL. The statistics were compiled from Teacher's and Superintendent's Monthly Reports, 1865–1870, contained in BRFAL and AMA Archives. See also Conway, *Reconstruction of Georgia*, p. 90; Bentley, *Freedmen's Bureau*, p. 183.

14. *FR* 1 (Aug. 1865):130; Circular (untitled) prepared by Stuart Eldridge, Acting Asst. Adj. Gen., to G. L. Eberhart, Washington, D.C., 29 Oct. 1866, GSE, LR, BRFAL; G. L. Eberhart to Frederick Ayer, Savannah, 15 Feb. 1867, GSE, LS, BRFAL.

15. Records of the South Carolina Freedmen's Bureau Superintendent of Education, Box 26, TMR, BRFAL. Eberhart's letter to Captain W. W. Deane, 1 Dec. 1865, is mistakenly filed in this box. G. L. Eberhart to Samuel Hunt, Augusta, 2, 3, 20 Dec. 1865; Bentley, *Freedmen's Bureau*, pp. 173–74.

16. For more information on the Peabody Fund, see Richard R. Wright, "Brief Historical Sketch of Negro Education in Georgia," pp. 27–28; William P. Vaughn, "Partners in Segregation," pp. 260–75; Richard B. Drake, "The American Missionary Association and the Southern Negro," pp. 186–212; James D. Anderson, "Education for Servitude," pp. 6–13; *AM* 16 (Aug. 1872):183–84; E. A. Ware to E. P. Smith, Atlanta, 22 Sept. 1869; J. R. Lewis to E. P. Smith, Atlanta, 23 Nov. 1869; William L. Clark to E. P. Smith, Thomasville, 27 Sept. 1869.

17. E. P. Smith to George Whipple, Augusta, 26 Sept. 1866; E. P. Smith to E. A. Ware, New York City, 21 Oct. 1867, Ware Papers; O. W. Dimick to E. P. Smith, Savannah, 25 Sept., 9 Oct. 1867; E. P. Smith to E. A. Ware, New York City, 5 Nov. 1868, Ware Papers; E. A. Ware to E. M. Cravath, Atlanta, 9 June 1871; G. L. Eberhart to E. P. Smith, Savannah, 5 Dec. 1867; J. R. Lewis to E. E. Rogers, Atlanta, 4 Nov. 1869.

The following correspondence pertains to the controversy surrounding the construction of the Savannah teachers' home: O. W. Dimick to E. P. Smith, Savannah, 25 Sept. and 9 Oct. 1867.

18. Freedmen's Bureau, *Eighth Semi-Annual Report on Schools for the Freedmen*,

p. 4; Charles Prince to E. P. Smith, Augusta, 10 Jan. 1867; Harriet N. Phillips to E. P. Smith, Atlanta, 8 Apr. 1867; John Rockwell to W. E. Whiting, 23 Sept. 1867.

19. William L. Clark to Levi Burkett, Bainbridge, 16 Feb. 1869, FOR (series 786, vol. 184, pp. 16–17), BRFAL; G. L. Eberhart to John Rockwell, Augusta, 18 Oct. 1866, Rockwell Scrapbook; William L. Clark to Maria Quarles, Bainbridge, FOR (series 787, vol. 181, p. 105), BRFAL; Douglas Risley to E. P. Smith, Brunswick, 11 Jan. 1868; Harriet Billings to E. P. Smith, Madison, 8 Feb. 1869.

20. See, for example, Rebecca Craighead to Samuel Hunt, Atlanta, 30 Apr. 1866.

21. On the role of the society's chief policymakers, see Beard, *Crusade of Brotherhood*, pp. 129–34, 205–12, 267–68, 316; Drake, "The American Missionary Association and the Southern Negro," pp. 76–112; McPherson, *Abolitionist Legacy*, pp. 153–54; Henry L. Morehouse, "Historical Sketch of the American Baptist Home Missionary Society for Fifty Years," pp. 366, 434–35; *FR* 1 (Jan. 1865): 16.

22. E. M. Cravath to D. E. Emerson, Atlanta, 21 June 1873; E. M. Cravath to Frederick Ayer, Cincinnati, Ohio, 9 Oct. 1866, Ayer Papers; E. P. Smith to John Rockwell, Charleston, S.C., 11 Oct. 1866, Rockwell Scrapbook; E. M. Cravath to John Rockwell, Nashville, Tenn., 7 June 1866, Rockwell Scrapbook; E. M. Cravath to John Rockwell, Atlanta, 26, 27 Mar. 1866, Rockwell Scrapbook.

23. William A. Campbell, ed., "A Freedmen's Bureau Diary by George Wagner"; Douglas Risley to E. P. Smith, Brunswick, 11 Feb. 1868; William F. Eaton to AMA, St. Simons Island, 26 May 1865; William L. Clark to Joseph Butler, Camilla, FOR (series 786, vol. 184, pp. 92–93), BRFAL; John H. Caldwell to E. A. Ware, La Grange, 5 Oct. 1867, GSE, LR, BRFAL.

24. *AM* 9 (June 1865):134; *AM* 10 (Dec. 1866):266.

25. *AF* 1 (July 1866):62.

26. *AM* 16 (Apr. 1872):87–90; E. M. Cravath to D. E. Emerson, Savannah, 17 Mar. 1873; E. A. Ware to E. M. Cravath, Atlanta, 14 May 1872; *NF* 1 (Oct. 1865):293; *NF* 1 (July 1865): 228; *FR* 3 (Jan. 1867):3.

27. George Whipple to Hiram Eddy, New York City, 16 Jan. 1866, Rockwell Scrapbook; S. F. Goodell to E. P. Smith, 23 Nov. 1867.

28. S. S. Ashley to M. E. Strieby, Atlanta, 8 Dec. 1876; McPherson, *Abolitionist Legacy*, pp. 58–59.

29. Mary N. Withington to G. D. Pike, Atlanta, 2 Apr. 1869; M. E. Hart to S. Jocelyn, Macon, 2 Mar. 1869. See also Frederick Ayer to E. P. Smith, Atlanta, 29 Aug. 1867; S. W. Magill to Secretaries of the AMA, Savannah, June 1865; Mary Battey to E. P. Smith, Andersonville, 11 Dec. 1866; Julia Shearman to E. P. Smith, Augusta, 12 Apr. 1867.

30. E. M. Cravath to Frederick Ayer, Cincinnati, Ohio, 2 Mar. 1867, Ayer Papers.

31. *AF* 1 (July 1866):62.

32. John Eaton, *Grant, Lincoln, and the Freedmen*, p. 195; E. A. Ware to E. P. Smith, Atlanta, 17 March, 5 May 1869.

33. J. P. Newman to Supt. of Education, Washington, D.C., Apr. 1869, GSE, LR, BRFAL; J. R. Lewis to O. O. Howard, Atlanta, 19 May 1869, GSE, LS, BRFAL; Bentley, *Freedmen's Bureau*, p. 171. For evidence of preferential treatment for the AMA, see J. R. Lewis to E. P. Smith, Atlanta, 9 Nov. 1869; E. B. Bingham to E. P. Smith, Augusta, 17 Apr. 1869; E. A. Ware to E. P. Smith, Atlanta, 15 Apr. 1869; *AM* 14 (July 1870):155; Bentley, *Freedmen's Bureau*, p. 175.

34. E. E. Rogers to E. M. Cravath, Macon, 11 Sept. 1872. The AMA did not use typewriters until 1876. Fred Brownlee, *New Day Ascending*, pp. 264–65.

35. Abbie Case to Samuel Hunt, Savannah, 27 July 1866; C. W. Sharp to E. P. Smith, Savannah, 11 Jan. 1869.

36. For recent discussions of the feminization of teaching and its relation to

common-school reform in the nineteenth century, see Richard M. Bernard and Maris A. Vinovskis, "The Female School Teacher in Antebellum Massachusetts," pp. 332–45; Ann Douglas, *The Feminization of American Culture*, pp. 76, 166–67; Nancy F. Cott, *The Bonds of Womanhood*, pp. 121–22; Kathryn K. Sklar, *Catharine Beecher*, pp. 136, 173; Michael B. Katz, *The Irony of Early School Reform*, pp. 56–58, 193, 224; Lois Banner, "Women's History," p. 156.

37. The New England branch of the AFUC made all salaries equal (theoretically) in the last year of its existence. See *FR* 1 (Mar. 1865):47; *FR* 1 (Nov. 1865):182; *FR* 4 (Jan. 1868):5.

38. Cott, *Bonds of Womanhood*, pp. 140–41.

39. Anna O. Snowden to E. P. Smith, Atlanta, 22 Dec. 1869; Amy Williams to E. M. Cravath, Atlanta, 29 July 1872.

40. C. W. Francis to E. P. Smith, Atlanta, 27, 28 Oct., 31 Dec. 1869; E. A. Ware to E. P. Smith, Atlanta, 3 Aug. 1869; Amy Williams to E. M. Cravath, Atlanta, 15 Feb. 1875; McPherson, *Abolitionist Legacy*, p. 171.

41. Julia Shearman to E. P. Smith, Augusta, 24, 28 Jan., 14 Mar., 12 Apr., 26 July 1867; TMR, Nov. 1867, AMA Archives.

42. E. T. Ayer to George Whipple, Atlanta, 4 Aug. 1867. Sarah Burt referred to herself and her coworkers as the "children" of Field Secretary E. P. Smith in her letter to him from Augusta, 10 Nov. 1867.

43. Mary Hart to G. D. Pike, Macon, 25 Nov. 1870; Anna Ludlow to E. M. Cravath, Savannah, 27 Dec. 1873; Teachers' Petition to E. P. Smith, Savannah, 18 Jan. 1869, AMA Archives; Ira Pettibone to E. P. Smith, Savannah, Dec. 1866; Julia Shearman to W. E. Whiting, Augusta, 6 Feb. 1867.

44. Freedmen's Bureau, *Fourth Semi-Annual Report on Schools for the Freedmen*, p. 92; *AF* 2 (May 1867):210; *AM* 13 (Feb. 1869):34; Ralph Ernest Morrow, *Northern Methodism and Reconstruction*, p. 161; McPherson, *Abolitionist Legacy*, p. 144; E. A. Ware to E. P. Smith, Atlanta, 25 Apr. 1869.

45. Martin Abbott, *The Freedmen's Bureau in South Carolina, 1865–1872*, pp. 133–34.

Chapter V

1. A number of recent works on the nature and purposes of common-school reform provide an overview of northern public education in the mid-nineteenth century. Case studies include Carl F. Kaestle, *Evolution of an Urban School System*; Stanley K. Schultz, *The Culture Factory*; Selwyn K. Troen, *The Public and the Schools*; and Michael B. Katz, *The Irony of Early School Reform*. See also Michael B. Katz, *Class, Bureaucracy and Schools*; David B. Tyack, *The One Best System*; Merle Curti, *The Social Ideas of American Educators*; Joseph F. Kett, *Rites of Passage*, pp. 112–13; and Carl F. Kaestle, "Social Change, Discipline, and the Common School in Early Nineteenth-Century America." For a discussion of freedmen's education in particular, see James M. McPherson, *The Abolitionist Legacy*, pp. 71–72, 188–89, 200. McPherson (pp. 163–64, 184) discusses the "Puritan" values of the northern teachers.

2. Lewis Perry, *Radical Abolitionism*, p. 40; Gilbert Osofsky, "Cardboard Yankee," p. 605; McPherson, *Abolitionist Legacy*, p. 200.

3. Daniel T. Rodgers, *The Work Ethic in Industrial America, 1850–1920*, pp. 14, 34–35. According to Rodgers, "The work ethic and war zeal joined" in the "Reconstruction vision" (p. 32). See also Herbert G. Gutman, "The Reality of the Rags to Riches 'Myth'"; Alan Dawley, *Class and Community*, pp. 35–40, 121, 169–70; Stephan Thernstrom, *The Other Bostonians*, pp. 232–61.

4. McPherson, *Abolitionist Legacy*, p. 184; Roger L. Ransom and Richard Sutch, *One Kind of Freedom*, p. 8.

5. E. A. Cooley to Samuel Hunt, Savannah, 22 Nov. 1865.

6. Mary Withington to George Whipple, Augusta, 15 Feb. 1868; John Bassett to E. P. Smith, Augusta, 18 Jan. 1869.

7. "Joy in Service: My Life Story," Douglass Papers. Esther Douglass kept a diary while she was teaching in Ogeechee and the South Carolina Sea Islands. "Joy in Service" is a handwritten account of her experiences and includes portions of the diary.

8. *AM* 9 (July 1865):159; Mary Colburn to Samuel Hunt, Savannah, 31 May 1865.

9. *AM* 12 (June 1868):122; E. P. Smith to John A. Rockwell, Charleston, S.C., 11 Oct. 1866, Rockwell Scrapbook.

10. This analysis is based primarily on Arthur O. Norton, ed., *The First State Normal School in America*, pp. 85–86, 91–92, 100, 107–117, 138, 153, 155, 190–200, 214; N. A. Calkins, "Objective Teaching," pp. 126–31; Amory D. Mayo, "Methods of Moral Instruction in Common Schools," pp. 14–21; and Katz, *Irony of Early School Reform*, pp. 126, 151.

11. *AM* 11 (Mar. 1867):58; Timothy Lyman to Samuel Hunt, Savannah, 1 Aug. 1865; John Rockwell to Samuel Hunt, Macon, 1 June 1866.

12. *AM* 9 (Jan. 1865):16; E. A. Ware to T. G. Maughon, Atlanta, 11 Sept. 1867, GSE, LS, BRFAL; *FR* 2 (Dec. 1866):213; O. W. Dimick to E. P. Smith, Savannah, 1 Nov. 1867; Jennie Stevenson to "Brother Ware," Nashville, Tenn., 24 Sept. 1868, Ware Papers.

13. Ruth M. Elson, *Guardians of Tradition*, pp. 65–185, 282–99; William L. Clark to E. P. Smith, Bainbridge, 21 Dec. 1868; Douglas Risley to E. P. Smith, Brunswick, 31 Dec. 1868; Sarah Jenness to W. E. Whiting, Savannah, 8 Nov. 1865; *AM* 11 (Sept. 1867):209–10. Some teachers used a special plan of study called the "Guyot Method" in the teaching of geography. See C. W. Sharp to E. A. Ware, 21 Jan. 1869, Ware Papers; *AM* 12 (Nov. 1868):245.

14. Harriet Billings to E. P. Smith, Madison, 8 Feb. 1869; Marcella Farwell to E. M. Cravath, Atlanta, 18 Dec. 1871; Susan P. Harrold to E. P. Smith, Darien, 12 Apr. 1869.

15. Julia Shearman to E. P. Smith, Augusta, 7 Feb. 1867. On the use of black assistants in the classroom, see Carrie S. Dickson to E. P. Smith, Cuthbert, 17 Aug. 1869; L. J. Kelley to E. P. Smith, Athens, 6 Jan. 1868; Clara Janes to E. P. Smith, Brunswick, 1 Feb. 1870.

16. *FR* 5 (June 1869):20; M. Louise Pettibone to Samuel Hunt, Savannah, 30 Dec. 1865; Mary Battey to E. P. Smith, Andersonville, 11 Dec. 1866; Susan P. Harrold to E. P. Smith, Darien, 12 Apr. 1869.

17. A. Rowe to E. M. Cravath, Savannah, 19 Apr. 1875; Hattie Foote to Samuel Hunt, Augusta, 2 Feb. 1866; George Walker to E. M. Cravath, Atlanta, 3 May 1873.

18. *AM* 9 (Aug. 1865):176; *AM* 9 (July 1865):159. *NF* 2 (Feb. 1866):43; McPherson, *Abolitionist Legacy*, pp. 60–61, 168–69.

19. *AM* 11 (Apr. 1867):89.

20. Sarah Jenness to W. E. Whiting, Savannah, 8 Nov. 1865; *AM* 13 (Apr. 1869):73; *AM* 12 (July 1868):145–46; *Freemen's Standard* 1 (Feb. 1868):3; E. A. Cooley to Samuel Hunt, Savannah, 22 Nov., 20 Dec. 1865.

21. *AM* 11 (Feb. 1867):28; Frederick Ayer to W. E. Whiting, Atlanta, 16 Jan. 1866; Sophia Russell to E. P. Smith, Brunswick, 1 Mar. 1868; Ellen E. Adlington to E. P. Smith, Berne, 18 Nov. 1868; M. Calhoun to Mrs. McMahon, Putney and Flagg Plantation, 20 Apr. 1869; *AM* 12 (June 1868):127.

22. Harriet Billings to E. P. Smith, Madison, 2, 27 Dec. 1868.

23. William P. Russell to M. E. Strieby, Augusta, 6 May 1866.

24. Esther W. Douglass to Samuel Hunt, Savannah, 27 Dec. 1865; Frances Littlefield to Samuel Hunt, Ogeechee District, 30 Dec. 1865. See also Sandra E. Small, "The Yankee Schoolmarm in Freedmen's Schools," p. 393.

25. Susan P. Harrold to E. P. Smith, Darien, 12 Apr. 1869.

26. Lucy Case to E. P. Smith, Macon, 10 Aug. 1869; *AF* 1 (Nov. 1866):119. The AFUC adopted as one of its "Principles of Operation" the requirement that the Bible be used in all its schools, which were "none the less Christian because unecclesiastical." The stated purpose of the group was to "render the subjects of our education better fitted to be not only citizens of the Republic, but children of our Father who is in heaven."

27. *AM* 15 (June 1871):136–37. McPherson suggests that the teachers were "aware of the danger of becoming surrogate masters." *Abolitionist Legacy*, pp. 186–87.

28. Julia Marshall to Samuel Hunt, Savannah, 1 May 1866; Sarah Champney to E. P. Smith, Albany, 31 Jan. 1870; *AM* 12 (Aug. 1868):174. On the importance of punctuality to the common-school reformers, see Kaestle, "Change, Discipline, and the Common School," p. 3.

29. O. W. Dimick to E. P. Smith, Savannah, 19 Nov. 1867; Maria L. Root to E. P. Smith, Andersonville, 1 Nov. 1869. In the 1930s, a Georgia black man recalled that under slavery, "Mistess done larned the cook to count the clock, but none of the rest of our niggers could count the clock." George P. Rawick, ed., *The American Slave* (Georgia Narratives), vol. 12, sec. 1, p. 97. See also Eugene D. Genovese, *Roll, Jordan, Roll*, pp. 285–94.

30. *AM* 10 (Mar. 1866):63.

31. Mayo, "Methods of Moral Instruction," p. 14; E. A. Ware to T. G. Maughon, Atlanta, 11 Sept. 1867, GSE, LS, BRFAL; *FR* 2 (Dec. 1866):213.

32. Rose Kinney to Samuel Hunt, Atlanta, 1 May 1866; E. B. Bingham to Lucian Hayden, Augusta, 1 Feb. 1869, FOR (series 772, vol. 154, p. 22), BRFAL.

33. A. N. Niles to G. D. Pike, Savannah, 12 Dec. 1870; E. A. Ware to E. M. Cravath, Atlanta, 2 Aug. 1872; A. N. Niles to E. M. Cravath, Savannah, 8 May, 31 Oct., 13 Nov. 1871; C. W. Sharp to E. P. Smith, Savannah, 6 May 1869.

34. Carol Billman, "McGuffey's Readers and Alger's Fiction," pp. 615–16; Elson, *Guardians of Tradition*. In *The Freedmen's Book*, Child states that these stories "prove the power of character can overcome all external disadvantages, even that most crushing of all disadvantages, Slavery" (p. 269). Robert C. Morris analyzes the curriculum of freedmen's schools in his Ph.D. thesis, "Reading, 'Riting, and Reconstruction."

35. *AM* 11 (Sept. 1867):212–13. See also "Undated Teaching Fragment," prepared by Lucy and Sarah Chase, in Henry L. Swint, ed., *Dear Ones at Home*, p. 253.

36. *AM* 13 (June 1869):134.

37. A. N. Niles to E. M. Cravath, Savannah, 8 May 1871.

38. "Joy in Service," p. 15, Douglass Papers.

39. N. D. Brooks to E. M. Cravath, Athens, 28 Mar. 1871; Susan Hosmer to Samuel Hunt, Augusta, 30 Sept. 1866; Lizzie Parsons to E. P. Smith, Savannah, 19 Feb. 1870; Abbie Johnson to E. M. Cravath, Savannah, 12 May 1871; Hattie Foote to Samuel Hunt, Savannah, 24 June 1870; Ira Pettibone to E. P. Smith, Savannah, 25 Feb. 1867.

40. E. A. Cooley to Samuel Hunt, Savannah, 11 May 1866. For examples of rival black schools started over the summer, see Frank Haley to E. P. Smith, Macon, 1 Dec. 1867; Anna Ludlow to E. M. Cravath, Savannah, 22 Apr. 1872; C. R. Bent to E. P. Smith, Savannah, 20 Feb. 1870.

41. Laura Parmelee to E. M. Cravath, Andersonville, 27 Jan. 1872.

42. Lizzie Parsons, Bainbridge, Dec. 1870, TMR, AMA Archives; Carrie Morse to E. P. Smith, Athens, 14 Dec. 1868.

43. Annie Stevens to E. P. Smith, Frederica, 1 Feb. 1869; Mary Colburn to Samuel Hunt, Savannah, 30 Jan. 1866; Lucy Kinney to Samuel Hunt, Atlanta, 27 Jan. 1866; James Hagerman to E. P. Smith, Altama, 1 May 1868; *FR* 2 (July 1866):133; J. B. Foster, Rome, Nov. 1868, TMR, BRFAL.

44. Laura Parmelee, Andersonville, Dec. 1869, TMR, BRFAL; Laura Parmelee to E. P. Smith, Andersonville, 24 Dec. 1869.

45. Harriet Ashley to E. M. Cravath, Covington, 10 Sept. 1870.

46. Jennie Barnum to Samuel Hunt, Atlanta, 27 Jan. 1866.

47. Anthony Wilson to E. M. Cravath, Woodbine, 7 Mar. 1871; Esther W. Douglass to Samuel Hunt, Apr. 1866.

48. Abbie W. Johnson to E. M. Cravath, Savannah, 28 Nov. 1870.

49. Cornelia Drake to E. P. Smith, Athens, 17 Jan. 1870; Annie Stevens to E. P. Smith, Frederica, 5 Sept. 1869. According to Stephan Thernstrom, during this period Irish workers in Newburyport, Massachusetts, often saved enough money to buy a house at the expense of their children's education (*Poverty and Progress*, pp. 117–20, 155). This indicates that schooling and a family's economic advancement were often incompatible goals for working-class northerners as well as southern blacks.

50. Eliza T. Ayer to Samuel Hunt, Atlanta, 30 Apr. 1866.

51. Petition on behalf of "B. C. Jencks" [*sic*], from his students to AMA, Augusta, 19 June 1866, AMA Archives; *AM* 12 (Oct. 1868):221; Ellen E. Adlington to E. P. Smith, Berne, 31 Mar. 1868; Floyd Snelson to Mary Battey Smith, Andersonville, 16 May, 24 June 1869.

52. Hiram Eddy to M. E. Strieby, Macon, 18 Jan. 1866; *AM* 10 (Apr. 1866):80–81; Floyd Snelson to E. P. Smith, Andersonville, 15 June 1868. See also McPherson, *Abolitionist Legacy*, p. 170.

53. Myron W. Adams, *A History of Atlanta University*; McPherson, *Abolitionist Legacy*, pp. 166–67, 191–99, 213, 221, 239, 295, 315; *AM* 14 (July 1870):152–53. These three paragraphs are based on material in the Ware Papers and the AMA Archives.

54. *AM* 16 (Aug. 1872):178–79.

55. "Report of Visitors Appointed by Gov. Bullock . . . ," Atlanta, 26, 27 June 1871, Ware Papers. The August 1871 issue of the *American Missionary* contained the following articles: "Report of Board of Visitors. Atlanta University" (pp. 183–85); "The Atlanta Examination" (pp. 181–82); "From the New Era, June 29 . . . " (p. 183); and "Our College Record, Atlanta University" (p. 182).

56. *AM* 15 (Aug. 1871):181–83. A subsequent Committee of State Board of Visitors, in its report on Atlanta University in July 1876, noted that "The pupils, as a rule, have evidently been attentive and docile in responding to the teachers' instructions." Its members were "impressed with the quiet and general deference of their deportment, but offered the following criticisms: It occurred . . . often that recitations, especially in the higher classes, were taught, or at least permitted to be rendered by the students too much by rote; that not enough effort was made to develop independent thought and personal enterprise in the work." Article, Atlanta *Daily Times*, 21 July 1876, AMA Archives. This comment reveals that exhibitions for visitors were often staged performances; it is not necessarily an accurate indication of the instruction offered at the school. The criticism, of course, was a bit ironic, coming as it did from three white Georgia Democrats.

57. McPherson, *Abolitionist Legacy*, p. 160.

58. Carter G. Woodson, *The Mis-Education of the Negro*, pp. 6–7, 33.

59. For analyses favoring the first view, see James M. McPherson, *The Struggle for Equality* and *Abolitionist Legacy*; William Preston Vaughn, *Schools for All*; and Henry Allen Bullock, *A History of Negro Education in the South*. For works presenting a negative analysis of white-sponsored black education, see James D. Anderson, "Education for Servitude"; Donald Spivey, *Schooling for the New Slavery*; and Morris, "Reading, 'Riting, and Reconstruction."

60. Kaestle discusses the need for discipline in classrooms with large numbers of children ("Social Change, Discipline, and the Common School," p. 7). See also Rodgers, *Work Ethic*, p. 33; McPherson, *Abolitionist Legacy*, p. 72.

Chapter VI

1. Abbie Howe to E. P. Smith, Bell, 31 Mar. 1868; Ronald G. Walters, *The Antislavery Appeal*, pp. 67–68.

2. C. W. Francis to E. P. Smith, Atlanta, 31 Dec. 1869; *AM* 12 (Oct. 1868):218; *AM* 13 (Nov. 1869):254; *NF* 1 (July 1865):230–31; Cornelia Drake to George Whipple, Savannah, 27 Jan. 1868; Walters, *Antislavery Appeal*, pp. 54–56, 70–87; James M. McPherson, *The Abolitionist Legacy*, pp. 184, 188–89.

3. Mary Withington to E. P. Smith, Augusta, 30 May 1868; Walters, *Antislavery Appeal*, pp. 63–66; McPherson, *Abolitionist Legacy*, p. 67. Wrote one teacher: "here are rational, moral, and immortal beings, created in God's image, and destined for good or evil." Sarah Andrews to E. P. Smith, 5 Feb. 1868.

4. McPherson, *Abolitionist Legacy*, pp. 68–69, and *The Struggle for Equality*, p. 143; Walters, *Antislavery Appeal*, pp. 56–60.

5. Eugene D. Genovese, *Roll, Jordan, Roll*, pp. 240–41, 232–55; Lawrence W. Levine, *Black Culture and Black Consciousness*, pp. 136–89.

6. Ellen E. Adlington to E. P. Smith, Berne, 31 March 1868; Genovese, *Roll, Jordan, Roll*, pp. 599–612; Levine, *Black Culture*, p. 142.

7. Sophia Russell to E. P. Smith, Brunswick, 12 Nov. 1867; "Joy in Service: My Life Story," p. 13, Douglass Papers; Ellen E. Adlington to E. P. Smith, Berne, 8 Oct. 1869.

8. Laura Parmelee to E. M. Cravath, Andersonville, ca. May 1873.

9. Rose Kinney to George Whipple, Atlanta, 20 Feb. 1866. Levine (*Black Culture*, pp. 190–227) includes a discussion of Afro-American songs. On African retentions and the Gullah dialect in the Sea Islands, see Clarence L. Mohr, "Georgia Blacks During Secession and Civil War, 1859–1865," pp. 11–13; and Works Project Administration, Georgia Writers Project, Savannah Unit, *Drums and Shadows*. See also Sandra E. Small, "The Yankee Schoolmarm in Freedmen's Schools," pp. 390–91.

10. Carl R. Osthaus, *Freedmen, Philanthropy, and Fraud*, pp. 99, 125; R. F. Markham to M. E. Strieby, Savannah, 7 Dec. 1875.

11. Levine, *Black Culture*, p. 152; *AM* 16 (Oct. 1872):218; *AM* 10 (Mar. 1866):55; *AM* 11 (July 1867):161; McPherson, *Abolitionist Legacy*, pp. 53–58; Malvina Higgins to E. P. Smith, Augusta, 25 Dec. 1867.

12. E. P. Smith to John Rockwell, New York City, 13 Dec. 1866, Rockwell Scrapbook; *AF* 1 (Aug. 1866):73; W. P. Russell to Samuel Hunt, Savannah, 22 May 1866. See also Small, "The Yankee Schoolmarm," pp. 399–400.

13. Harriet Gaylord to W. E. Whiting, Savannah, 28 Nov. 1865; E. A. Ware to E. P. Smith, Atlanta, 28 Feb. 1867.

14. Cornelia Drake to George Whipple, Savannah, 27 Jan., 27 Feb. 1868.

15. Abbie W. Johnson to E. M. Cravath, Savannah, 28 Dec. 1870, 25 Jan., 24 Apr., 1 May 1871. See also Ayer Account Book, Ayer Papers; Hardy Mobley to Ira Pettibone, Savannah, 2 Jan. 1867.

16. Rebecca Craighead to Samuel Hunt, Atlanta, 15 Jan. 1866; Mary Chase to E. M. Cravath, Atlanta, 27 Nov. 1871.

17. List of goods distributed by Rebecca Craighead and Harriet Phillips, Atlanta, Feb. 1866, AMA Archives; Sarah Chase to Mrs. May, Columbus, Georgia, 5 Feb., 9 March, 21 May 1866, in Henry L. Swint, ed., *Dear Ones at Home*, pp. 194–95, 199–200, 203–5.

18. *AM* 15 (Mar. 1871):51–52.

19. *AM* 11 (Mar. 1867):54.

20. H. E. Gaylord to Mrs. Dickinson, Grove Hill Plantation, 12 Feb. 1866.

21. The three teachers were Harriet Phillips, Rebecca Craighead, and Mary S. Battey. Mary E. Hart to E. P. Smith, Macon, 2 Mar. 1869; Cornelia Drake to E. P. Smith, Savannah, 4 June 1867; Mrs. William T. Conkling to E. P. Smith, Augusta, 4 Nov. 1867; see Linus P. Brockett, *Woman's Work in the Civil War*.

22. Martha D. Ayres to E. P. Smith, Macon, 22 Oct. 1866.

23. On the role of the slave mistress in antebellum Georgia, see Ralph Betts Flanders, *Plantation Slavery in Georgia*, p. 164; Frances Anne Kemble, *Journal of a Residence on a Georgian Plantation in 1838–39*, pp. 67, 98, 130, 154, 254–58; Ronald Killion and Charles Waller, eds., *Slavery Time When I Was Chillun Down on Marster's Plantation*, pp. 52, 84–85; James I. Robertson, Jr., ed., "The Diary of Dolly Lunt Burge Robertson," Part 3, p. 444. Compare the following accounts provided by Kemble to statements made by the northern teachers after the war: Kemble, *Journal*, pp. 49, 50, 66, 91, 94, 96, 127, 169, 174; *AM* 10 (Mar. 1866):55; and 1866 Fragment, Douglass Papers. See also Genovese, *Roll, Jordan, Roll*, pp. 81–83.

24. Circular (untitled), Oct. 1867, New York City, Ware Papers.

25. Hardy Mobley to Ira Pettibone, Savannah, 2 Jan. 1867; Herbert G. Gutman, *The Black Family in Slavery and Freedom, 1750–1925*. See also William Harris, "Work and the Family in Black Atlanta, 1880," pp. 322, 324.

26. Amelia E. Johnson to E. P. Smith, Andersonville, 1 Dec. 1868; Abbie W. Johnson to E. P. Smith, Savannah, 25 Dec. 1869; *AM* 11 (Mar. 1867):58–60; Cornelia Drake to George Whipple, Savannah, 1 June 1866; McPherson, *Abolitionist Legacy*, pp. 194–95; Walters, *Antislavery Appeal*, pp. 91–110; Daniel Walker Howe, "American Victorianism as a Culture," pp. 529–30; Joseph F. Kett, *Rites of Passage*, pp. 114–16; Bernard W. Wishy, *The Child and the Republic*, pp. 16, 57.

27. *AM* 13 (Feb.–Mar. 1869):35, 59–60.

28. Cornelia Drake to E. P. Smith, Savannah, 4 June 1867: H. E. Gaylord to Samuel Hunt, Savannah, 29 Sept., 28 Nov., 1 Dec. 1865; Carrie Morse to E. P. Smith, Athens, 1 Feb. 1869.

29. Ellen E. Adlington to E. P. Smith, St. Mary's, 11 June 1868.

30. Lucy Case to E. A. Ware, Albany, 20 Apr. 1869, Ware Papers; Sarah Stansbury to John Ogden, Cuthbert, 15 Apr. 1868; Sarah Stansbury to E. A. Ware, Cuthbert, 26 Apr. 1869, Ware Papers. See also McPherson, *Abolitionist Legacy*, p. 194.

31. Cornelia Drake to George Whipple, Savannah, 27 Jan., 27 Feb. 1868.

32. See the correspondence of Rose Kinney and Frederick Ayer to Samuel Hunt, Atlanta, June-Aug. 1866; *AM* 11 (Feb. 1867):29; Frederick Ayer, Atlanta, Jan. 1867, SMR, Ayer Papers. On the asylum reform movement during the nineteenth century, see David J. Rothman, *The Discovery of the Asylum*.

33. Rebecca Craighead to E. P. Smith, Atlanta, 25 Apr., 5 May 1867. It is unclear what happened to these children. The 1870 Federal Population Census for Adrian, Michigan, lists just one Georgia-born black child living in a white household. The AMA had closed the asylum in the late 1860s.

34. E. A. Ware to E. P. Smith, Atlanta, 27 Jan. 1869; *FR* 5 (Aug. 1869):30.

35. For discussions of slave religion and its significance, see Genovese, *Roll,*

Jordan, Roll, pp. 159–284; Levine, *Black Culture*, pp. 3–80; and John W. Blassingame, *The Slave Community*, pp. 60–75. See also Leon F. Litwack, *Been in the Storm So Long*, pp. 450–71.

36. Eliza Ayer to Samuel Hunt, Atlanta, 3 Feb. 1866; Malvina Higgins to E. P. Smith, Augusta, 25 Dec. 1867; *AM* 10 (May 1866):115. Some teachers compared black people they met in Georgia with characters from the Stowe novel. For example, in May 1868 Ellen Adlington described one of her favorite pupils as "a real little Topsy"; "her wicked looking eyes are full of mischief and she is always full of Jim Crow, monkey shines to make the other children laugh." Ellen E. Adlington to E. P. Smith, Berne, 20 May 1868. See also McPherson, *Abolitionist Legacy*, pp. 151–52.

37. Genovese, *Roll, Jordan, Roll*, pp. 267–68; Ellen E. Adlington to E. P. Smith, Berne, 31 Mar. 1868; John A. Bassett to E. P. Smith, Augusta, 23 Dec. 1868; Ellen E. Adlington to E. P. Smith, Berne, 8 Oct. 1869. For a description of a "shout" on Pine Bluff Plantation, see Spencer Bidwell King, Jr., ed., *The War-Time Journal of a Georgia Girl 1864–65* (Eliza Frances Andrews), pp. 89–90.

38 *AM* 14 (Sept. 1870):193–95.

39. C. W. Sharp to E. A. Ware, Binghamton, N.Y., 9 Aug. 1869, Ware Papers; *AM* 11 (Dec. 1867):277; Fifth *Annual Report* of the MFAS, pp. 11–12. See also *FR* 4 (Nov. 1868):173; *AM* 15 (Feb. 1871):42; *AM* 13 (Sept. 1869):205–6.

40. John Murphy to J. F. Chalfant, Jonesboro, 3 Aug. 1866; FASME Archives. On the efforts of northern Methodists to establish churches in the South during this period, see Henry Morrison Johnson, "The Methodist Episcopal Church and the Education of Southern Negroes, 1862–1900"; and Ralph Ernest Morrow, *Northern Methodism and Reconstruction*.

41. Johnson, "Methodist Episcopal Church," p. 202.

42. *AM* 11 (Sept. 1867):203. Data on church membership were compiled from forms entitled "For 'Annual Report,' American Missionary Association," 30 Sept. 1873, AMA Archives. Congregational churches established in Georgia, along with their founding dates and membership, as of 1873, included: Andersonville (1868–34 members); Atlanta (1869–129); Savannah (1868–97); Byron (1873–14); Ogeechee (1872–34); Canal (1871–14); Belmont (1873–18); and Macon (1868–89).

43. *AM* 12 (Nov. 1868):244; E. A. Ware to E. M. Cravath, Atlanta, 29 Dec. 1871; *AM* 12 (Apr. 1868):80–81.

44. *AM* 16 (July 1872):145; *AM* 15 (Mar. 1871):52–53.

45. *AM* 11 (Sept. 1867):197–98; *AM* 16 (Oct. 1872):220; R. F. Markham to M. E. Strieby, Savannah, 27 Feb. 1877. See also Kett, *Rites of Passage*, pp. 117–21; Anne Mary Boylan, "The Nursery of the Church."

46. A. N. Niles to E. M. Cravath, Savannah, 12 Dec 1873; Frank Haley to E. M. Cravath, Macon, 15 June 1874.

47. J. W. Alvord, "Letters from the South Relating to the Condition of Freedmen," pp. 9–10; Abbie Howe to E. P. Smith, Bell, 3 Mar. 1868; A. N. Niles to E. M. Cravath, Savannah, 9 Dec. 1873. See also Walters, *Antislavery Appeal*, pp. 70–87. It was not uncommon for slaves to celebrate holidays and other special occasions by drinking. George P. Rawick, ed., *The American Slave* (Georgia Narratives), vol. 13, sec. 3, pp. 49, 99, 255; sec. 4, 81.

48. Sophia Russell to E. P. Smith, Brunswick, 1 Mar. 1868; Abbie W. Johnson to E. P. Smith, Andersonville, 1 Dec. 1868.

49. The Band of Hope publications included "Band of Hope Melodies: Adapted to Hope, Cadet, and Other Temperance Meetings" and "The Band of Hope Rituals, To Which is Prefaced a Form of Constitution and Rules for the Use of Bands of Hope."

50. Sarah Stansbury to E. M. Cravath, Cuthbert, 3 May 1871.

51. John Bassett to E. P. Smith, Augusta, 23 Dec. 1868; Helen Leonard to E. M. Cravath, Milledgeville, 9 Mar. 1871; Abbie Howe to E. P. Smith, Albany, 20 Feb. 1869.

52. Ira Pettibone to George Whipple, Savannah, 1 Dec. 1865.

53. Carl R. Osthaus, *Freedmen, Philanthropy, and Fraud*, pp. 43, 60–63, 230–34.

54. John Rockwell to J. R. Lewis, Macon, 13 Mar. 1869, FOR (series 937, vol. 298, p. 15), BRFAL.

55. Osthaus, *Freedmen, Philanthropy, and Fraud*, pp. 27, 64; Walter L. Fleming, *The Freedmen's Savings Bank*, pp. 22–23, 47.

56. Fleming, *Bank*, pp. 144–50.

57. Osthaus, *Freedmen, Philanthropy, and Fraud*, pp. 93, 96, 125–26, 176. In his study of mid-nineteenth century Newburyport, Massachusetts, Stephan Thernstrom found that "it was common for unskilled workmen to have savings accounts" (*Poverty and Progress*, p. 128). One Georgia teacher told of a pupil who had saved his nickels and dimes faithfully until he had twenty-eight dollars in his account at the Savannah branch of the Bank. *AM* 16 (Oct. 1872):218.

58. Osthaus, *Freedmen, Philanthropy, and Fraud*, pp. 100, 157–78, 213; Fleming, *Bank*, pp. 115–24, 142–43. E. A. Ware reported of Cory in 1868, "Several people have expressed the opinion that he is partially insane." E. A. Ware to George Whipple, Savannah, 18 Feb. 1868.

59. Quoted in Osthaus, *Freedmen, Philanthropy, and Fraud*, p. 207; C. W. Francis to E. M. Cravath, Atlanta, 10 Feb. 1874; A. Rowe to E. M. Cravath, Sept. 1874.

60. Abbie Case to Samuel Hunt, Savannah, 22 Apr. 1866.

61. H. E. Gaylord to George Whipple, Savannah, 22 Jan. 1866.

62. Sarah Stansbury to E. P. Smith, Cuthbert, 30 Dec. 1869, 11 Mar. 1870; Ruben Richards to E. P. Smith, Cuthbert, 24 May 1870.

Chapter VII

1. Ronald G. Walters, *The Antislavery Appeal*, pp. 91–110. These pages embrace the chapter entitled "Families: 'The Centre of Earthly Bliss' and Its Discontents," in which Walters describes the social significance of the family in the context of abolitionist ideology.

Secondary literature on group-living situations among middle-class women in the nineteenth century is sparse. Thomas Dublin examines the textile-mill company boardinghouses for female operatives in Lowell, Massachusetts, in his article "Women, Work, and Protest in the Early Lowell Mills." He highlights the solidarity fostered among the mill workers, and argues that strong personal relationships enabled the young women to conduct organized protests against deteriorating working conditions. The mission home-boardinghouse situations are not analogous, of course; mission homes were smaller, and were characterized by a more carefully delineated hierarchy of roles than boardinghouses. Moreover, the northern teachers lived in relative social isolation, far away from friends and family and estranged from their southern neighbors, white and black.

2. *AM* 15 (April 1871):73–74; "Atlanta Home Expenses," Apr. 1867, Ayer Papers; *AM* 16 (Jan. 1870):7; *AM* 13 (June 1869):131; Myron W. Adams, *A History of Atlanta University*, p. 58; E. K. Jencks to E. M. Cravath, Atlanta, 5 June 1871; E. A. Ware to E. M. Cravath, Atlanta, 17 July 1872; E. A. Ware to E. M. Cravath, Atlanta, 1 July 1872.

3. Laura Parmelee to E. P. Smith, Andersonville, 22 Dec. 1869; Mary K. Colburn to

Samuel Hunt, Savannah, 25 Sept. 1866; John Rockwell to E. P. Smith, Savannah, 7 Sept. 1868; Laura Parmelee to E. M. Cravath, Andersonville, 28 Oct. 1871; Laura Parmelee to E. M. Cravath, Andersonville, 11 Nov. 1872; Laura Parmelee to E. M. Cravath, Andersonville, 27 Apr. 1872; *AM* 11 (July 1867):160–61; *AM* 14 (Feb. 1870):36. For contemporary descriptions of the town of Andersonville, see Cornelia Hancock, *South after Gettysburg,* p. 282; John Richard Dennett, *The South As It Is,* p. 267; and *FR* 3 (Aug. 1869):30.

4. Abbie Case to Samuel Hunt, Savannah, 27 July 1866; William L. Clark to E. P. Smith, Albany, 19 Nov. 1867; Caroline H. Merrick to Martha Quillin, Augusta, 14 Mar. 1868, in George W. Clower, ed., "Some Sidelights on Education in Georgia in the 1860s," pp. 252–54.

5. C. W. Sharp to E. P. Smith, Savannah, 16 Nov. 1868; Harriet Gaylord to W. E. Whiting, Savannah, 15 Dec. 1865; E. A. Cooley to Samuel Hunt, Savannah, 20 Dec. 1865.

6. E. A. Cooley to W. E. Whiting, Savannah, 30 Nov. 1865; Mary P. Stewart to E. M. Cravath, Albany, 11 Nov. 1870.

7. E. M. Cravath to John Rockwell, Nashville, 6 Feb. 1866; Michael E. Strieby to E. P. Smith, Macon, 3 Dec. 1869; E. M. Cravath to Hiram Eddy, Nashville, Tenn., 17 Feb. 1866, Rockwell Scrapbook.

8. "Shipping and Receiving Department," #23069, n.d., AMA Archives.

9. F. Ayer to W. E. Whiting, Atlanta, Dec. 1866; John Rockwell to W. E. Whiting, Macon, 25 Apr. 1867; J. K. Warner to W. E. Whiting, Augusta, 13 Dec. 1867; C. W. Francis to E. M. Cravath, Atlanta, 3 Feb. 1872; E. A. Ware to E. M. Cravath, Atlanta, 13 Oct. 1870.

10. Jennie T. Ware to G. D. Pike, Atlanta, 2 Jan. 1871; E. A. Ware to E. P. Smith, Atlanta, 29 Sept. 1870.

11. John Rockwell to W. E. Whiting, Macon, 13 Jan. 1867; John Rockwell to E. P. Smith, Macon, 23 Apr. 1869; E. P. Smith to John Rockwell, Pittsburgh, Pa., 25 July 1866, Rockwell Scrapbook.

12. Julia Shearman to E. P. Smith, Augusta, 13 Dec. 1867; Julia Shearman to E. P. Smith, Augusta, 12 Apr. 1867; Caroline Merrick to E. P. Smith, Augusta, 12 Dec. 1868; Abbie W. Johnson to E. M. Cravath, Savannah, 12 May 1871; O. W. Dimick to E. P. Smith, Savannah, 28 Sept. 1867; O. W. Dimick to E. P. Smith, Savannah, 7 Mar. 1868.

13. G. L. Eberhart to Samuel Hunt, Augusta, 20 Dec. 1865; G. L. Eberhart to Samuel Hunt, Augusta, 23 Jan. 1866; W. P. Russell to Samuel Hunt, Augusta, 8 June 1866; C. S. Martindale to George Whipple, Augusta, 21 Dec. 1865.

14. Helen B. Sharp to E. P. Smith, Savannah, 4 May 1869; Helen B. Sharp to E. P. Smith, Savannah, 17 May 1869; C. W. Sharp to E. P. Smith, Savannah, 21 Jan. 1869; C. W. Sharp to E. P. Smith, 16 Apr. 1869; C. W. Sharp to E. P. Smith, Savannah, 30 Apr. 1869.

15. E. P. Smith to E. A. Ware, New York City, 18 Nov. 1868, Ware Papers; Julia Shearman to E. P. Smith, Augusta, 7 Mar. 1867; Michael Strieby to George Whipple, Macon, 31 Mar. 1869. Julia Shearman described Freedmen's Bureau Superintendent G. L. Eberhart as "but about *half a man.*" See Julia Shearman to E. P. Smith, Augusta, 12 Apr. 1867.

16. Mrs. C. W. Francis to E. M. Cravath, Atlanta, 14 Nov. 1871; Mrs. E. A. Cooley to Samuel Hunt, Savannah, 28 Dec. 1865; Caroline H. Merrick to E. P. Smith, Augusta, 31 Dec. 1868; Cornelia A. Drake to E. P. Smith, Savannah, 19 Oct. 1868.

17. A. N. Niles to E. M. Cravath, Savannah, 17 Oct. 1871; Frank Haley to E. P.

Smith, Macon, 1 Dec. 1867; J. R. and Frank Haley to W. E. Whiting, Macon, 14 May 1868; E. P. Smith to Samuel Hunt, Atlanta, 17 Mar. 1866.

18. John A. Bassett to E. P. Smith, Augusta, 16 Dec. 1867; A. N. Niles to "Miss Mina," Savannah, 16 Dec. 1870.

19. Mrs. E. A. Cooley to Samuel Hunt, Savannah, 28 Dec. 1865. See also Small, "The Yankee Schoolmarm," p. 391.

20. For examples of the charge of "unchristian behavior" leveled at teachers by superintendents, see M. J. Armstrong to George Whipple, Savannah, 16 May 1868; O. W. Dimick to E. P. Smith, Savannah, 13 Apr. 1868; and Frederick Ayer to E. P. Smith, Atlanta, 22 July 1867.

21. G. L. Eberhart to Samuel Hunt, Augusta, 23 May 1866; G. L. Eberhart to Samuel Hunt, Augusta, 4 June 1866; J. E. Bryant to Secretary, AMA, Augusta, 12 June 1866; W. P. Russell to Samuel Hunt, Augusta, 22 May 1866; Julia Shearman to W. E. Whiting, Augusta, 6 Feb. 1867; Mary J. Welch to Samuel Hunt, 26 Feb. 1866; Davis Tillson to George Whipple, Augusta, 4 July 1866; E. B. Bingham to John R. Lewis, Augusta, Jan. 29, 1869, FOR (series 772, vol. 154, p. 16), BRFAL. See also Leon F. Litwack, *Been in the Storm So Long*, pp. 491–501.

22. Hattie C. Foote to Samuel Hunt, Augusta, 19 July 1866; G. L. Eberhart to Samuel Hunt, Augusta, 11 Sept. 1866; J. W. Lawton to Samuel Hunt, Augusta, 6 Sept. 1866; G. L. Eberhart to Samuel Hunt, Augusta, 4 June 1866; Mary E. Hart to E. P. Smith, Macon, 15 June 1870.

23. Helen M. Leonard to E. P. Smith, Macon, 23 June 1870; Hattie C. Foote to E. P. Smith, Macon, 23, 24 June 1870; Hattie C. Foote to E. P. Smith, Macon, 26 Sept. 1870; N. D. Sneed to E. P. Smith, Macon, 27 Sept. 1870; Helen M. Leonard to E. P. Smith, Macon, 8 Oct. 1870; Hattie C. Foote to E. M. Cravath, Macon, 10 Oct. 1870.

24. Julia Shearman to E. P. Smith, Augusta, 29 May, 6 June, 1 July, 27 Nov. 1867; A. N. Niles to E. P. Smith, Savannah, 19 May 1870.

25. Charles Prince to E. P. Smith, Augusta, 7 June 1867; E. E. Rogers to E. M. Cravath, Savannah, 21 Sept. 1871.

26. J. K. Warner to E. P. Smith, Augusta, 26 Nov. 1867.

27. Frederick Ayer to E. M. Cravath, Atlanta, 5 Sept. 1867, Ayer Papers; C. W. Francis to E. M. Cravath, Atlanta, 2 Mar. 1871; C. W. Francis to E. P. Smith, Atlanta, 20 Oct. 1869; C. W. Francis to E. P. Smith, Atlanta, 27 Oct. 1869. For more information on the teacher-matron feud, see correspondence originating in Atlanta from September to November 1870.

28. Anna Snowden to E. P. Smith, Atlanta, 22 Dec. 1869; E. A. Ware to W. E. Whiting, Atlanta, 4 June 1870; Amy Williams to E. M. Cravath, Atlanta, 29 July 1872.

29. George Walker to E. M. Cravath, Atlanta, 3 May, 29 Nov. 1873.

30. Annie R. Wilkins to E. P. Smith, Darien, 23 Apr. 1869.

31. A. L. Etheridge to E. P. Smith, Augusta, 28 Mar. 1867; *AM* 12 (Aug. 1868):175; *AM* 13 (July 1869):149; Quarterly Report of J. F. Chalfant, 1 Apr. to 1 July 1866, FASME Archives; J. H. Caldwell to J. F. Chalfant, LaGrange, 3 Apr. 1866, FASME Archives; Charles Stearns, *The Black Man of the South, and the Rebels*, pp. 132, 166–67.

32. Mary Withington to E. P. Smith, Augusta, 30 Apr. 1868; Helen Leonard and Evelyn Plummer to Mrs. Pond, Columbus, 19 Dec. 1867; Caroline Merrick to G. D. Pike, Augusta, 10 May 1869; A. N. Niles to E. M. Cravath, Savannah, 29 Apr. 1871; C. W. Francis to E. M. Cravath, Atlanta, 22 Nov. 1870. For an example of a particularly intense relationship between two female teachers, see the correspon-

dence from Emeline A. Hawley originating in Atlanta in November and December 1870.

33. O. W. Dimick to E. A. Ware, Oak Hill, Newton, Mass., 14 Sept. 1868, Ware Papers; E. B. Bingham to E. A. Ware, Augusta, 10 Feb. 1869, Ware Papers; "Sketch of the Life of Edmund Asa Ware," typescript, Ware Papers; E. P. Smith to E. A. Ware, New York City, 28 Oct. 1868.

Lizzie Parsons had a particularly tragic experience. Of all the teachers, she was the only one to marry a native southerner. When he died within half a year after their marriage, he bequeathed all his possessions to a child by a previous marriage, and left all his debts to his bride. Lizzie Parsons to E. M. Cravath, Bainbridge, 22 Mar. 1873; William L. Clark to E. M. Cravath, Thomasville, 2 Dec. 1873.

34. C. W. Francis to E. M. Cravath, Atlanta, 25 Feb. 1872; H. W. Cobb to Michael E. Strieby, Savannah, 27 Feb. 1869; *AM* 12 (May 1868):111–12; *AM* 12 (June 1868):134; Rufus Saxton to E. A. Ware, 28 May 1869, Ware Papers.

35. Frank Haley to E. P. Smith, Macon, 1 Dec. 1867; George A. Hood to E. P. Smith, Savannah, 26 Oct. 1869.

36. A. N. Niles to G. D. Pike, Savannah, 3 Mar. 1871; O. W. Dimick to E. P. Smith, Savannah, 10 Mar. 1868; Sarah Stansbury to E. M. Cravath, Macon, 11 Oct. 1871.

37. E. A. Ware to Ednah D. Cheney, Atlanta, 30 Dec. 1867, GSE, LS, BRFAL; Abbie Clark to E. M. Cravath, Savannah, 25 Oct. 1872.

38. Sophia Russell to E. P. Smith, Brunswick, 31 Jan. 1868; Abbie E. Howe to E. P. Smith, Albany, 12 Apr. 1869; Mary Dyer to E. P. Smith, Madison, 29 Dec. 1868; Douglas Risley to E. P. Smith, Brunswick, 28 Nov. 1867; Virgil Hillyer to E. P. Smith, Berne, 11 June 1868; Josie Barbour to E. A. Ware, Madison, 2 Dec. 1868, Ware Papers.

39. Lucretia Thayer to E. P. Smith, Darien, 5 Dec. 1868; O. H. Howard to E. P. Smith, Savannah, 9 Apr. 1869; Hattie Emerson to E. P. Smith, St. Mary's, 5 June 1868; *FR* 2 (July 1866):133.

40. Esther W. Douglass to "Dear Brother," Wild Horn, 14 Nov. 1866, Douglass Papers; "Joy in Service: My Life Story," pp. 12, 16, 19; Esther W. Douglass to "Dear Nephew," Wild Horn, 16 Jan. 1867, Douglass Papers; Sarah Stansbury to E. M. Cravath, Albany, 31 Oct. 1871.

41. Douglas Risley to E. P. Smith, Brunswick, 21 Sept. 1868; Clara Janes to E. P. Smith, Brunswick, 19 Nov. 1868; Fred Brownlee, *New Day Ascending*, p. 102 (letter from a Liberty County teacher dated 8 Jan. 1868).

42. Sophia Russell to E. P. Smith, Brunswick, 29 May 1868; Mary Dyer to E. P. Smith, Madison, 20 Apr. 1869; Caroline Damon to E. P. Smith, Griffin, 1 June 1867; Sarah Champney to E. P. Smith, Brunswick, 1 Jan. 1868; O. H. Howard to E. P. Smith, Savannah, 9 Apr. 1869; P. Maria Lee and Jennie N. Cooke to E. P. Smith, Thomasville, 1 Apr. 1869.

43. Sophia Russell to E. P. Smith, Brunswick, 1 Mar., 1 May 1868; Lizzie Parsons to E. M. Cravath, Bainbridge, 2 Nov., 2 Jan. 1871; Minnie C. Owen, St. Mary's, Dec. 1868, TMR, BRFAL.

44. S. Ranks to John R. Lewis, Waynesboro, 7 Jan. 1867, GSE, LR, BRFAL; Sidney Andrews, *The South Since the War*, p. 360.

45. Minnie E. Hanson to E. M. Cravath, Newton, 24, 27 Dec. 1870.

46. Josie Barbour to E. P. Smith, Madison, 29 Dec. 1868; Sarah Stansbury to E. M. Cravath, Cuthbert, 6 Feb. 1871; P. M. Lee to E. P. Smith, Thomasville, 25 May 1869; Lizzie Parsons to M. E. Strieby, Bainbridge, 31 Mar. 1873; Minnie Owen to E. P. Smith, Darien, 12 May 1870; Sarah Champney to E. P. Smith, Brunswick, 31 Jan. 1868.

Chapter VIII

1. Jacob D. Enos to E. M. Cravath, Valdosta, 5 June 1870; E. P. Smith to W. E. Whiting, Augusta, 10 Apr. 1868.

2. U.S. Department of the Interior, "Report of U.S. Commissioner of Education," (1880), vol. 3, pp. 61–65; Georgia State School Commissioner, First *Annual Report*; William Preston Vaughn, *Schools for All*, p. 60.

3. Sarah Stansbury to E. M. Cravath, Cuthbert, 2 Mar. 1871; A. N. Niles to E. M. Cravath, 19 May 1873, 3 June 1874; R. F. Markham to M. E. Strieby, Savannah, 2 Oct. 1875; William A. L. Campbell to M. E. Strieby, Macon, 3 Sept. 1875; M. E. Sands to E. M. Cravath, Macon, 5 June 1873. In 1874 William L. Clark wrote that the AMA teachers in Atlanta were now "in the preserve of our enemies." Clark to E. M. Cravath, Atlanta, 6 Jan. 1874.

4. Lizzie Parsons to E. M. Cravath, Macon, 5 June 1872; Mary P. Stewart to E. M. Cravath, Albany, 4 Jan. 1871.

5. C. W. Francis to M. Farwell, et al., Atlanta, Feb. 1872; Mrs. T. N. Chase to E. M. Cravath, Atlanta, 8 July 1872.

6. Unsigned letter from an Augusta teacher to T. N. Chase, 15 Feb. 1878; R. F. Markham to M. E. Strieby, Savannah, 7 Oct. 1878.

7. Article, Atlanta *Daily Times*, 21 July 1876, AMA Archives. See also James M. McPherson, *The Abolitionist Legacy*, pp. 20–21. On state aid to Atlanta University, one Georgia newspaper editor wrote in 1875, "It cannot reasonably be expected . . . that the class upon which the burden of taxation chiefly falls will consent to support an institution wherein the mischievous doctrine of social equality is practically inculcated." Newspaper clipping, Jan. 1875, AMA Archives.

8. Frank Haley to E. M. Cravath, Atlanta, 29 June 1874; R. F. Markham to M. E. Strieby, Savannah, 21 May 1876.

9. A. N. Niles to E. M. Cravath, Savannah, 2 May 1874; S. S. Ashley to M. E. Strieby, Atlanta, 31 July 1876; R. F. Markham to M. E. Strieby, Savannah, 7 Jan. 1877. The Reverend Henry M. Turner, the fiery black leader in Savannah, was another "leading spirit among the Colored People" who tried to improve black public schools at the expense of the AMA's Beach Institute. A. Rowe to George Whipple, Savannah, 31 Aug. 1874. See also Howard N. Rabinowitz, "Half a Loaf," pp. 565–94.

In both Macon and Savannah, blacks supported schools taught by an order of black Roman Catholic nuns. This suggests, again, that the race of the teacher was a decisive factor in shaping the people's preferences for their teachers. See Petition to M. E. Strieby, Macon, 1 July 1875, AMA Archives; William A. L. Campbell to M. E. Strieby, 30 June 1875.

10. A. N. Niles to E. M. Cravath, Savannah, 15 Jan. 1875; T. N. Chase to E. M. Cravath, Atlanta, 2 Feb. 1875.

11. Mrs. S. C. Bierce to M. E. Strieby, Macon, 27 Nov. 1876; William A. L. Campbell to M. E. Strieby, Macon, 8 July 1875; McPherson, *Abolitionist Legacy*, p. 175.

12. T. N. Chase to M. E. Strieby, Macon, 4 Oct. 1877; S. S. Ashley to M. E. Strieby, Atlanta, 1 Sept. 1877. See also McPherson, *Abolitionist Legacy*, p. 176; Rabinowitz, "Half a Loaf," p. 575. Georgia correspondence in the AMA Archives ends in 1878.

13. For the dispute over Williams's salary, see the correspondence from Atlanta workers in March and April 1871. Mrs. S. C. Bierce to D. E. Emerson, Macon, 16 May 1876.

14. McPherson, *Abolitionist Legacy*, pp. 64–65, 262–95; Raymond Wolters, *The New Negro on Campus*. Georgia AMA workers gave up trying to establish

Congregational churches in Georgia in the late 1870s.

15. U.S. Department of the Interior, "Report of U.S. Commissioner of Education," (1880), vol. 3, pp. 58–59. This report includes a "Summary of Education Statistics of Georgia—1871 to 1880." See also *Annual Reports* of the U.S. Commissioner of Education, 1870–1890.

16. Louis R. Harlan, *Separate and Unequal*, p. 11; U.S. Department of Commerce, Bureau of the Census, *Thirteenth Census*, vol. 1 (Population), p. 1198; Rabinowitz, "Half a Loaf," p. 589.

17. For a discussion of the "competitive" typology of race relations as it applies to southern society in the 1870s, see C. Vann Woodward, *American Counterpoint*, pp. 243–44, 253; and Vernon Burton, "Race and Reconstruction," pp. 31–56.

18. Roger L. Ransom and Richard Sutch, *One Kind of Freedom*, pp. 85, 184–85.

19. J. Morgan Kousser, *The Shaping of Southern Politics*, pp. 67, 210, 214, 218, 220.

20. M. E. Sands to E. M. Cravath, Macon, 7 Oct. 1874.

21. R. F. Markham to M. E. Strieby, Savannah, 3 Jan. 1876, 17 Jan. 1877. See also John W. Blassingame, "Before the Ghetto," pp. 479–80; John M. Matthews, "Negro Republicans in the Reconstruction of Georgia," pp. 159–60; Howard N. Rabinowitz, "From Reconstruction to Redemption in the Urban South," pp. 169–94.

22. Ransom and Sutch, *One Kind of Freedom*, pp. 177–78; William Harris, "Work and the Family in Black Atlanta, 1880," p. 321.

23. M. Blanche Curtiss to M. E. Strieby, Dalton, 31 Oct. 1877.

24. This discussion is based on the following works: Martin Abbott, *The Freedmen's Bureau in South Carolina*; Peter Kolchin, *First Freedom*; Robert G. Sherer, *Subordination or Liberation?*; Ransom and Sutch, *One Kind of Freedom*; Joe M. Richardson, *The Negro in the Reconstruction of Florida*; Alrutheus Ambush Taylor, *The Negro in the Reconstruction of Virginia*; Joe Gray Taylor, *Louisiana Reconstructed*; William P. Vaughn, *Schools for All*; Vernon Lane Wharton, *The Negro in Mississippi*; Joel Williamson, *After Slavery*; and Leon F. Litwack, *Been in the Storm So Long*.

25. S. S. Ashley to Michael E. Strieby, Atlanta, 29 Aug. 1876.

26. This paragraph employs the theoretical framework of nineteenth-century women's history devised by Nancy F. Cott (*The Bonds of Womanhood*) and Carroll Smith-Rosenberg ("The Female World of Love and Ritual"). The quotation is from Cott, *Bonds of Womanhood*, p. 100.

Bibliography

Primary Sources

MANUSCRIPTS

American Missionary Association Archives. Amistad Research Center, New Orleans, Louisiana (available on microfilm).
Frederick Ayer Papers. Negro Collection, Atlanta University Center Trevor Arnett Library, Atlanta, Georgia.
Chase Family Papers. American Antiquarian Society Library, Worcester, Massachusetts.
Esther W. Douglass Papers. Rackham Library, University of Michigan, Ann Arbor, Michigan.
Archives of the Freedmen's Aid Society of the Methodist Episcopal Church. Interdenominational Theological Center (Gammon Seminary), Atlanta, Georgia.
John A. Rockwell and Martha D. Ayres Scrapbook. Amistad Research Center, New Orleans, Louisiana.
United States Bureau of the Census. Manuscript Population Schedules for the Eighth and Ninth Census (1860 and 1870). National Archives, Washington, D.C. (available on microfilm).
Records of the United States Bureau of Refugees, Freedmen, and Abandoned Lands (Record Group 105). Reports of the Georgia Superintendent of Education, 1865–70 (available on microfilm). Records of the Field Offices of the Bureau, 1865–70. National Archives, Washington, D.C. (available on microfilm).
Edmund Asa Ware Papers. Negro Collection, Atlanta University Center Trevor Arnett Library, Atlanta, Georgia.

BOOKS

Addams, Jane. *Twenty Years at Hull-House*. New York: Macmillan Co., 1936. Orig. pub. in 1910.
Andrews, Eliza Frances. *The War-Time Journal of a Georgia Girl, 1864–65*. Edited by Spencer Bidwell King, Jr. Macon: The Ardivan Press, 1960.
Andrews, Sidney. *The South Since the War: As Shown by Fourteen Weeks of Travel and Observation in Georgia and the Carolinas*. Boston: Houghton Mifflin Co., 1971. Orig. pub. in 1868.
Brockett, Linus Pierpont. *Woman's Work in the Civil War: A Record of Heroism, Patriotism, and Patience*. Philadelphia: Zeigler, McCurdy and Co., 1867.

Caldwell, John H. *Reminiscences of the Reconstruction of Church and State in Georgia*. Wilmington, Del.: J. M. Thomas, 1895.

Child, Lydia Maria. *The Freedmen's Book*. Boston: Ticknor and Fields, 1865.

The Condition of Affairs in Georgia: Statement of Hon. Nelson Tift to the Reconstruction Committee of the House of Representatives, Washington, February 18, 1869. Freeport, N.Y.: Books for Libraries Press, 1971. Orig. pub. in 1869.

Dennett, John Richard. *The South As It Is: 1865–1866*. New York: The Viking Press, 1965.

Du Bois, W. E. Burghardt. *The Souls of Black Folk: Essays and Sketches*. Chicago: A. C. McClurg and Co., 1904.

Eaton, John. *Grant, Lincoln, and the Freedmen: Reminiscences of the Civil War*. New York: Longmans, Green, and Co., 1907.

Hancock, Cornelia. *South After Gettysburg: Letters, 1863–1868*. Edited by Henrietta Stratton Jaquette. New York: T. Y. Crowell Co., 1956.

Kemble, Frances Anne. *Journal of a Residence on a Georgian Plantation in 1838–1839*. Edited by John A. Scott. New York: Alfred A. Knopf, 1961. Orig. pub. in 1863.

Killion, Ronald, and Waller, Charles, eds. *Slavery Time When I Was Chillun Down on Marster's Plantation: Interviews with Georgia Slaves*. Savannah: Beehive Press, 1973.

Leigh, Frances B. *Ten Years on a Georgia Plantation Since the War*. New York: Negro Universities Press, 1969. Orig. pub. in 1883.

Myers, Robert Manson, ed. *The Children of Pride: A True Story of Georgia and the Civil War*. New Haven: Yale University Press, 1972.

Nordhoff, Charles. *The Cotton States in the Spring and Summer of 1875*. New York: D. Appleton and Co., 1876.

Norton, Arthur O., ed. *The First State Normal School in America: The Journals of Cyrus Peirce and Mary Swift*. Cambridge: Harvard University Press, 1926.

Rawick, George P., ed. *The American Slave: A Composite Autobiography*. 19 vols. Vols. XII–XIII (Georgia Narratives). Westport, Conn.: Greenwood Press, 1972.

Reid, J. M. *Missions and Missionary Society of the Methodist Episcopal Church*. Cincinnati: Cranston and Stowe, 1879.

Reid, Whitelaw. *After the War: A Southern Tour*. New York: Moore, Wilstach and Baldwin, 1866.

Slaughter, Linda Warfel. *The Freedmen of the South*. Cincinnati: Elm Street Printing Co., 1869.

Stearns, Charles. *The Black Man of the South, and the Rebels: Or, the Characteristics of the Former, and the Recent Outrages of the Latter*. New York: Negro Universities Press, 1969. Orig. pub. in 1872.

Swint, Henry L., ed. *Dear Ones at Home: Letters from Contraband Camps*. Nashville: Vanderbilt University Press, 1966.

Taylor, Susie King. *Reminiscences of My Life in Camp*. New York: Arno Press, 1968. Orig. pub. in 1902.

Trowbridge, J. T. *The South: A Tour of Its Battlefields and Ruined Cities*. Hartford, Conn.: L. Stebbins, 1866.

ARTICLES AND PAMPHLETS

Abbott, Lyman. "The Results of Emancipation in the United States of America." New York: American Freedman's Union Commission, ca. 1865.

Alvord, J. W. "Letters from the South Relating to the Condition of Freedmen, Addressed to Major General O. O. Howard, Commissioner, Bureau R., F., and A. L." Washington, D.C.: Howard University Press, ca. 1870.

American Missionary Association. "Woman's Work for the Lowly as Illustrated in the Work of the American Missionary Association Among the Freedmen." Boston: South Inquirer Press, 1873.

American Temperance Union. "Band of Hope Melodies: Adapted to Band of Hope, Cadet, and Other Temperance Meetings." New York: American Temperance Union, 1860.

————. "The Band of Hope Rituals, To Which is Prefaced a Form of Constitution and Rules for the Use of Bands of Hope." Rockland, Mass.: Z. Pope Vose, 1860.

Beecher, Catharine. "Statistics of Female Health." In *The Ovenbirds: American Women on Womanhood, 1820–1920*, edited by Gail Parker, pp. 165–78. New York: Anchor Books, 1972.

Calkins, N. A. "Objective Teaching: Its Value, and Extent of Its Adaptation to School Instruction." *The Addresses and Journals of Proceedings of the National Educational Association . . . 1872*. Peoria, Ill.: N. C. Nason, 1873.

Calvin, Martin V. "Recent Progress of Public Education in the South: A Paper Read Before the Georgia Teachers' Association at Savannah, May 5th, 1870." Augusta: Chronicle and Sentinel Steam Printing Establishment, 1870.

Campbell, Tunis G. "Sufferings of the Rev. T. G. Campbell and His Family in Georgia." Washington, D.C.: Enterprise Publishing Co., 1877.

Campbell, William A., ed. "A Freedmen's Bureau Diary by George Wagner." *Georgia Historical Quarterly* 48 (1964):196–214, 333–59.

Clower, George W., ed. "Some Sidelights on Education in Georgia in the 1860s." *Georgia Historical Quarterly* 37 (1953):249–55.

Georgia Equal Rights Association. "Proceedings of the Freedmen's Convention of Georgia, Assembled at Augusta, January 10th, 1866. . . . " Augusta: Loyal Georgian Press, 1866.

————. "Journal of the Proceedings of the Convention of the People of Georgia . . . 1867." Augusta: E. H. Pughe, 1868.

————. "Proceedings of the Convention of the Equal Rights and Educational Association of Georgia held in Macon, October 29, 1866." Augusta: Loyal Georgian Press, 1866.

Mayo, Amory D. "Methods of Moral Instruction in Common Schools." *The Addresses and Journals of the Proceedings of the National Educational Association . . . 1872*. Peoria, Ill.: N. C. Nason, 1873.

Pierson, H. W. "A Letter to Hon. Charles Sumner with Statements of Outrages upon Freedmen in Georgia . . . by the Ku Klux Klan." Washington, D.C.: Washington Chronicle, 1870.

Reed, John Calvin. "What I Know of the KKK." *Uncle Remus's Magazine* 1 (1908):24–26, 60–61, 92–95, 122–23, 154–55, 236–38, 282–83, 291–94.

Robertson, James I., Jr., ed. "The Diary of Dolly Lunt Burge Robertson." *Georgia Historical Quarterly* 44–46 (1960–62): (44) 186–219, 321–37, 434–55; (45) 57–72, 155–70, 257–74, 367–84; (46) 59–78.

Rust, Richard S. "Educational Work in the South by the Freedmen's Aid Society of the Methodist Episcopal Church." Cincinnati: Western Book Concern, 1882.

————. "The Freedmen's Aid Society of the Methodist Episcopal Church: Its Organization and Work." n.p., ca. 1882.

JOURNALS AND NEWSPAPERS

American Freedman. Vols. 1–2 (1866–68). Washington.
American Missionary. Vols. 5–17 (1861–73). New York.
Colored American. Vol. 1 (1865–66). Augusta, Georgia.
Freedman's Friend. Vols. 1–10 (1864–74). Philadelphia.
Freedmen's Advocate. Vols. 1–2 (1864–65). New York.
Freedmen's Bulletin. Vols. 1–2 (1864–66). Chicago.
Freedmen's Record. Vols. 1–5 (1865–70). Boston.
Freemen's Standard. Vols. 1–2 (1868–70). Savannah.
Loyal Georgian. Vols. 1–2 (1866–67). Augusta.
National Freedman. Vols. 1–2 (1865–66). New York.

GOVERNMENT DOCUMENTS AND ANNUAL REPORTS

Barnard, H. "History of Schools for the Colored Population." *Special Report of the U.S. Commissioner of Education*. Washington, D.C.: Government Printing Office, 1871.
Freedmen's Aid Society of the Methodist Episcopal Church. *Annual Reports*. 1866–73. Cincinnati: Western Book Concern.
Georgia, State of. *First Annual Report of the State School Commissioner of the State of Georgia*. Atlanta: Public Printer, 1871.
Presbyterian Church in the U.S.A. Board of Missions for Freedmen. *Annual Reports*. 1864–71. Publisher varies.
United States. Bureau of Refugees, Freedmen, and Abandoned Lands. *Semi-Annual Reports on Schools for Freedmen*. 1866–70. Washington, D.C.: Government Printing Office.
_____. Department of Commerce. Bureau of the Census. *Population*, Eighth through Thirteenth Censuses (1860–1910). Washington, D.C.: Government Printing Office.
_____. Department (later Bureau) of Education. *Annual Reports of the Commissioner of Education*. 1868–80. Washington, D.C.: Government Printing Office.
_____. "Illiteracy in the U.S. with Appendix on National Aid to Education." By Charles Warren and J. L. M. Curry. Pamphlet. Washington, D.C.: Government Printing Office, 1884.
_____. Department of the Interior. "Report of the U.S. Commissioner of Education," in the *Report of the Secretary of the Interior* (1880). House of Representatives Executive Document Number 1, 46th Congress, 3rd Session. Washington, D.C.: Government Printing Office, 1882.

Secondary Sources

BOOKS

Abbott, Martin. *The Freedmen's Bureau in South Carolina, 1865–1872*. Chapel Hill: University of North Carolina Press, 1967.
Adams, Myron W. *A History of Atlanta University, 1865–1929*. Atlanta: Atlanta University Press, 1930.

Beard, Augustus Field. *A Crusade of Brotherhood: A History of the American Missionary Association.* Boston: Pilgrim Press, 1909.

Bentley, George R. *A History of the Freedmen's Bureau.* Philadelphia: University of Pennsylvania Press, 1955.

Blassingame, John W. *The Slave Community: Plantation Life in the Ante-bellum South.* New York: Oxford University Press, 1972.

Brownlee, Fred. *New Day Ascending.* Boston: Pilgrim Press, 1946.

Bryan, T. Conn. *Confederate Georgia.* Athens: University of Georgia Press, 1953.

Bullock, Henry Allen. *History of Negro Education in the South, from 1619 to the Present.* Cambridge: Harvard University Press, 1967.

Cash, W. J. *The Mind of the South.* New York: A. A. Knopf, 1941.

Conway, Alan. *The Reconstruction of Georgia.* Minneapolis: University of Minnesota Press, 1966.

Cott, Nancy F. *The Bonds of Womanhood: "Woman's Sphere" in New England, 1780–1835.* New Haven: Yale University Press, 1977.

Coulter, Ellis Merton. *College Life in the Old South.* New York: Macmillan Co., 1928.

Curti, Merle. *The Social Ideas of American Educators.* Totowa, N.J.: Littlefield, Adams, and Co., 1968. Orig. pub. in 1935.

Dawley, Alan. *Class and Community: The Industrial Revolution in Lynn.* Cambridge: Harvard University Press, 1976.

Douglas, Ann. *The Feminization of American Culture.* New York: Alfred A. Knopf, 1977.

Elson, Ruth Miller. *Guardians of Tradition: American Schoolbooks of the Nineteenth Century.* Lincoln: University of Nebraska Press, 1964.

Flanders, Ralph Betts. *Plantation Slavery in Georgia.* Chapel Hill: University of North Carolina Press, 1933.

Fleming, Walter L. *The Freedmen's Savings Bank: A Chapter in the Economic History of the Negro Race.* Chapel Hill: University of North Carolina Press, 1927.

Flexner, Eleanor. *Century of Struggle: The Woman's Rights Movement in the United States.* New York: Atheneum, 1970.

Foner, Eric. *Free Soil, Free Labor, Free Men: The Ideology of the Republican Party Before the Civil War.* New York: Oxford University Press, 1970.

Foster, Charles I. *An Errand of Mercy: The Evangelical United Front, 1790–1837.* Chapel Hill: University of North Carolina Press, 1960.

Fredrickson, George. *The Black Image in the White Mind: The Debate on Afro-American Character and Destiny, 1817–1914.* New York: Harper and Row, 1971.

Genovese, Eugene D. *Roll, Jordan, Roll: The World the Slaves Made.* New York: Vintage Books, 1976.

Gerteis, Louis S. *From Contraband to Freedman: Federal Policy toward Southern Blacks, 1861–1865.* Westport, Conn.: Greenwood Press, 1973.

Gutman, Herbert G. *The Black Family in Slavery and Freedom, 1750–1925.* New York: Pantheon, 1976.

Hareven, Tamara K., ed. *Anonymous Americans: Explorations in Nineteenth-Century Social History.* Englewood Cliffs, N.J.: Prentice-Hall, 1971.

Harlan, Louis R. *Separate and Unequal: Public School Campaigns and Racism in the Southern Seaboard States, 1901–1915.* New York: Atheneum, 1968.

Hersh, Blanche G. *The Slavery of Sex: Feminist-Abolitionists in America.* Urbana: University of Illinois Press, 1978.

Johnson, Michael P. *Toward a Patriarchal Republic: The Secession of Georgia.* Baton Rouge: Louisiana State University Press, 1977.

Kaestle, Carl F. *Evolution of an Urban School System: New York City, 1750–1850.*

Cambridge: Harvard University Press, 1973.

Katz, Michael B. *Class, Bureaucracy, and Schools: The Illusion of Educational Change in America.* New York: Praeger Press, 1971.

_____. *The Irony of Early School Reform: Educational Innovation in Mid-Nineteenth Century Massachusetts.* Boston: Beacon Press, 1968.

Kett, Joseph F. *Rites of Passage: Adolescence in America, 1790 to the Present.* New York: Basic Books, 1977.

Kolchin, Peter. *First Freedom: The Responses of Alabama's Blacks to Emancipation and Reconstruction.* Westport, Conn.: Greenwood Press, 1972.

Kousser, J. Morgan. *The Shaping of Southern Politics: Suffrage Restriction and the Establishment of the One-Party South, 1880–1910.* New Haven: Yale University Press, 1974.

Kraditor, Aileen S. *Means and Ends in American Abolitionism: Garrison and His Critics on Strategy and Tactics, 1834–1850.* New York: Random House, 1970.

Lerner, Gerda. *The Grimké Sisters from South Carolina: Pioneers for Woman's Rights and Abolition.* New York: Schocken Books, 1971.

Levine, Lawrence W. *Black Culture and Black Consciousness.* Oxford: Oxford University Press, 1977.

Litwack, Leon F. *Been in the Storm So Long: The Aftermath of Slavery.* New York: Alfred A. Knopf, 1979.

McFeely, William S. *Yankee Stepfather: General O. O. Howard and the Freedmen.* New Haven: Yale University Press, 1968.

McLoughlin, William G. *The Meaning of Henry Ward Beecher: An Essay on the Shifting Values of Mid-Victorian America, 1840–1870.* New York: Alfred A. Knopf, 1970.

McPherson, James M. *The Abolitionist Legacy: From Reconstruction to the NAACP.* Princeton: Princeton University Press, 1975.

_____. *The Struggle for Equality: Abolitionists and the Negro in the Civil War and Reconstruction.* Princeton: Princeton University Press, 1964.

Magdol, Edward. *A Right to the Land: Essays on the Freedmen's Community.* Westport, Conn.: Greenwood Press, 1977.

Messerli, Jonathan. *Horace Mann: A Biography.* New York: Alfred A. Knopf, 1972.

Morrow, Ralph Ernest. *Northern Methodism and Reconstruction.* East Lansing: Michigan State University Press, 1956.

Nathans, Elizabeth Studley. *Losing the Peace: Georgia Republicans and Reconstruction, 1865–1871.* Baton Rouge: Louisiana State University Press, 1968.

Novak, Daniel A. *The Wheel of Servitude: Black Forced Labor After Slavery.* Lexington: University Press of Kentucky, 1978.

Orr, Dorothy. *A History of Education in Georgia.* Chapel Hill: University of North Carolina Press, 1950.

Osthaus, Carl R. *Freedmen, Philanthropy, and Fraud: A History of the Freedman's Savings Bank.* Urbana: University of Illinois Press, 1976.

Perry, Lewis. *Radical Abolitionism: Anarchy and the Government of God in Antislavery Thought.* Ithaca: Cornell University Press, 1973.

Ransom, Roger L., and Sutch, Richard. *One Kind of Freedom: The Economic Consequences of Emancipation.* Cambridge: Cambridge University Press, 1977.

Richardson, Joe M. *The Negro in the Reconstruction of Florida, 1865–1877.* Tallahassee: Florida State University Press, 1965.

Roark, James L. *Masters without Slaves: Southern Planters in the Civil War and Reconstruction.* New York: W. W. Norton and Co., 1977.

Rodgers, Daniel T. *The Work Ethic in Industrial America, 1850-1920*. Chicago: University of Chicago Press, 1978.

Rose, Willie Lee. *Rehearsal for Reconstruction: The Port Royal Experiment*. New York: Oxford University Press, 1964.

Rothman, David J. *The Discovery of the Asylum: Social Order and Disorder in the New Republic*. Boston: Little, Brown and Co., 1971.

Schultz, Stanley K. *The Culture Factory: Boston Public Schools, 1789-1860*. New York: Oxford University Press, 1973.

Sherer, Robert G. *Subordination or Liberation? The Development and Conflicting Theories of Black Education in Nineteenth-Century Alabama*. University, Ala.: University of Alabama Press, 1977.

Sklar, Kathryn Kish. *Catharine Beecher: A Study in American Domesticity*. New Haven: Yale University Press, 1973.

Smith, John Montague. *History of the Town of Sunderland, Massachusetts*. Greenfield, Mass.: E. A. Hall and Co., 1899.

Spain, Rufus B. *At Ease in Zion: Social History of Southern Baptists, 1865-1900*. Nashville: Vanderbilt University Press, 1967.

Spivey, Donald. *Schooling for the New Slavery: Black Industrial Education, 1868-1915*. Westport, Conn.: Greenwood Press, 1978.

Stowell, William Henry Harrison. *Stowell Genealogy: A Record of the Descendants of Samuel Stowell of Hingham, Massachusetts*. Rutland, Vt.: Tuttle Co., 1922.

Swint, Henry L. *The Northern Teacher in the South, 1862-1870*. Nashville: Vanderbilt University Press, 1941.

Taylor, Alrutheus Ambush. *The Negro in the Reconstruction of Virginia*. Lancaster, Pa.: Lancaster Press, 1926.

Taylor, Joe Gray. *Louisiana Reconstructed*. Baton Rouge: Louisiana State University Press, 1974.

Thernstrom, Stephan. *The Other Bostonians: Poverty and Progress in the American Metropolis, 1880-1970*. Cambridge: Harvard University Press, 1973.

_____. *Poverty and Progress: Social Mobility in a Nineteenth-Century City*. Cambridge: Harvard University Press, 1964.

Trelease, Allen W. *White Terror: The KKK Conspiracy and Southern Reconstruction*. New York: Harper and Row, 1971.

Troen, Selwyn K. *The Public and the Schools: Shaping the St. Louis System, 1838-1920*. Columbia, Mo.: University of Missouri Press, 1975.

Tyack, David B. *The One Best System: A History of American Urban Education*. Cambridge: Harvard University Press, 1974.

Vaughn, William Preston. *Schools for All: The Blacks and Public Education in the South, 1865-1877*. Lexington: University of Kentucky Press, 1974.

Walters, Ronald G. *American Reformers, 1815-1860*. New York: Hill and Wang, 1978.

_____. *The Antislavery Appeal: American Abolitionism after 1830*. Baltimore: Johns Hopkins University Press, 1976.

Wharton, Vernon Lane. *The Negro in Mississippi, 1865-1890*. Chapel Hill: University of North Carolina Press, 1947.

Williamson, Joel. *After Slavery: The Negro in South Carolina during Reconstruction, 1861-1877*. Chapel Hill: University of North Carolina Press, 1965.

Wishy, Bernard W. *The Child and the Republic: The Dawn of Modern American Child Nurture*. Philadelphia: University of Pennsylvania Press, 1968.

Wolters, Raymond. *The New Negro on Campus: Black College Rebellions of the 1920s*. Princeton: Princeton University Press, 1975.

Woodson, Carter Godwin. *The Mis-Education of the Negro.* 1933. Reprint. New York: AMS Press, 1973.
Woodward, C. Vann. *American Counterpoint: Slavery and Race in the North-South Dialogue.* Boston: Little, Brown and Co., 1971.
Works Project Administration. Georgia Writers Project, Savannah Unit. *Drums and Shadows: Survival Studies among the Georgia Coastal Negroes.* New York: Doubleday and Co., 1972.
Wyatt-Brown, Bertram. *Lewis Tappan and the Evangelical War against Slavery.* New York: Atheneum, 1971.

ARTICLES AND PAMPHLETS

Banner, Lois. "Women's History: Culture and Feminization." *Reviews in American History* 6 (1978):155–62.
Bernard, Richard M., and Vinovskis, Maris A. "The Female School Teacher in Antebellum Massachusetts." *Journal of Social History* 10 (1977):332–45.
Billman, Carol. "McGuffey's Readers and Alger's Fiction: The Gospel of Virtue According to Popular Children's Literature." *Journal of Popular Culture* 11 (1977):614–19.
Blassingame, John W. "Before the Ghetto: The Making of the Black Community in Savannah, Georgia, 1865–1880." *Journal of Social History* 6 (1973):463–88.
Burton, Vernon. "Race and Reconstruction: Edgefield County, South Carolina." *Journal of Social History* 12 (1978):31–56.
Carter, Dan T. "The Anatomy of Fear: The Christmas Day Insurrection Scare of 1865." *Journal of Southern History* 42 (1976):345–64.
Dublin, Thomas. "Women, Work, and Protest in the Early Lowell Mills: 'The Oppressing Hand of Avarice Would Enslave Us.'" *Labor History* 16 (1975):99–116.
Gordon, Ann D., and Buhle, Mari Jo. "Sex and Class in Colonial and Nineteenth-Century America." In *Liberating Women's History: Theoretical and Critical Essays*, pp. 278–300. Edited by Berenice A. Carroll. Urbana: University of Illinois Press, 1976.
Graff, Harvey J. "Patterns of Dependency and Child Development in the Mid-Nineteenth Century City: A Sample from Boston, 1860." *History of Education Quarterly* 13 (Summer 1973):129–44.
Gutman, Herbert G. "The Reality of the Rags to Riches 'Myth': The Case of Paterson, New Jersey, Locomotive, Iron, and Machinery Manufacturers, 1830–1880." In *Essays in American Working-Class and Social History*, pp. 209–33. Edited by Herbert G. Gutman. New York: Alfred A. Knopf, 1976.
Harris, William. "Work and the Family in Black Atlanta, 1880." *Journal of Social History* 9 (1976):319–30.
Howe, Daniel Walker. "American Victorianism as a Culture." *American Quarterly* 27 (1975):507–32.
Kaestle, Carl F. "Social Change, Discipline, and the Common School in Early Nineteenth-Century America." *Journal of Interdisciplinary History* 9 (1978):1–18.
Katz, Michael B. "Origins of the Institutional State." *Marxist Perspectives* 1 (1978):6–23.
Kett, Joseph F. "Growing up in Rural New England, 1800–1840." In *Anonymous Americans: Explorations in Nineteenth-Century Social History*, pp. 1–16. Edited by Tamara K. Hareven. Englewood Cliffs, N.J.: Prentice Hall, 1971.

Litwack, Leon F. "Free at Last." In *Anonymous Americans: Explorations in Nineteenth-Century Social History*, pp. 131–71. Edited by Tamara K. Hareven. Englewood Cliffs, N.J.: Prentice Hall, 1971.

Matthews, John M. "Negro Republicans in the Reconstruction of Georgia." *Georgia Historical Quarterly* 60 (1976):145–64.

Morehouse, Henry L. "Historical Sketch of the American Baptist Home Missionary Society for Fifty Years." In *Baptist Home Missions in North America . . . Proceedings and Addresses of the Jubilee Meeting*, pp. 291–619. New York: Baptist Home Mission Rooms, 1883.

Nieman, Donald G. "Andrew Johnson, the Freedmen's Bureau, and the Problem of Equal Rights, 1865–1866." *Journal of Southern History* 44 (1978):399–420.

Norton, Mary Beth. "Youthful Men and Domestic Women." *Reviews in American History* 6 (1978):171–77.

Olsen, Otto H. "Setting the Record Straight on the Reconstruction South." *Reviews in American History* 3 (1975):333–39.

Osofsky, Gilbert. "Cardboard Yankee: How Not to Study the Mind of Charles Sumner." *Reviews in American History* 1 (1973):595–605.

Parmelee, Julius H. "Freedmen's Aid Societies, 1861–1871." In *Negro Education: A Study of the Private and Higher Schools for Colored People in the United States*, pp. 268–95. Edited by Thomas Jesse Jones. 1917. Reprint. New York: Arno Press, 1969.

Rabinowitz, Howard N. "From Reconstruction to Redemption in the Urban South." *Journal of Urban History* 2 (1976):169–94.

————. "Half a Loaf: The Shift from White to Black Teachers in the Negro Schools of the Urban South, 1865–1890." *Journal of Southern History* 40 (1974):565–94.

Singleton, Gregory H. "Protestant Voluntary Organizations and the Shaping of Victorian America." *American Quarterly* 27 (1975):549–60.

Small, Sandra E. "The Yankee Schoolmarm in Freedmen's Schools: An Analysis of Attitudes." *Journal of Southern History* 45 (1979):381–402.

Smith-Rosenberg, Carroll. "The Female World of Love and Ritual: Relations between Women in Nineteenth-Century America." *Signs* 1 (1975):1–29.

Temin, Peter. "The Post-Bellum Recovery of the South and the Cost of the Civil War." *Journal of Economic History* 36 (1976):898–907.

Vaughn, William P. "Partners in Segregation: Barnas Sears and the Peabody Fund." *Civil War History* 9 (1964):260–75.

Vinovskis, Maris A., and Bernard, Richard M. "Beyond Catharine Beecher: Female Education in the Antebellum Period." *Signs* 3 (1978):856–69.

Welter, Barbara. "The Cult of True Womanhood, 1820–1860." *American Quarterly* 18 (1966):151–74.

Wood, Ann Douglas. "The 'Fashionable Diseases': Women's Complaints and their Treatment in Nineteenth-Century America." *Journal of Interdisciplinary History* 4 (1973):25–52.

Wright, Richard R. "Brief Historical Sketch of Negro Education in Georgia." Savannah: Robinson Printing House, 1894.

DISSERTATIONS AND TYPESCRIPTS

Adams, Myron. "The Founding of Atlanta University." Typescript, n.d. Edmund Asa Ware Papers, Atlanta University Center Trevor Arnett Library, Atlanta, Georgia.

Anderson, James D. "Education for Servitude: The Social Purposes of Schooling in the Black South, 1870–1930." Ph.D. dissertation, University of Illinois, 1973.

Boylan, Anne Mary. "'The Nursery of the Church': Evangelical Protestant Sunday Schools, 1820–1880." Ph.D. dissertation, University of Wisconsin-Madison, 1973.

Drake, Richard B. "The American Missionary Association and the Southern Negro, 1861–1888." Ph.D. dissertation, Emory University, 1957.

Johnson, Clifton, Herman. "The American Missionary Association, 1841–1861: A Study of Christian Abolitionism." Ph.D. dissertation, University of North Carolina, 1958.

Johnson, Henry Morrison. "The Methodist Episcopal Church and the Education of Southern Negroes, 1862–1900." Ph.D. dissertation, Yale University, 1939.

Jones, Jacqueline. "The 'Great Opportunity': Northern Teachers and the Georgia Freedmen, 1865–1873." Ph.D. dissertation, University of Wisconsin-Madison, 1976.

Mohr, Clarence L. "Before Sherman: Georgia Blacks and the Union War Effort, 1861–1864." Unpublished paper in the author's possession.

———. "Georgia Blacks During Secession and Civil War, 1859–1865." Ph.D. dissertation, University of Georgia-Athens, 1975.

Morris, Robert C. "Reading, 'Riting, and Reconstruction: Freedmen's Education in the South, 1865–1870." Ph.D. dissertation, University of Chicago, 1976.

Index

Abolitionism, 10, 14, 18–23, 26–27, 233 (n. 10). *See also* Neoabolitionism
Addams, Jane, 235 (n. 50)
Adlington, Ellen, 154
African Methodist Episcopal Church, 17, 155–56
Albany, Georgia, 62, 161, 171, 188, 193
Alvord, Reverend John W., 73, 75, 93, 162
American Baptist Home Missionary Society (ABHMS), 17, 37, 88, 90, 101, 108, 198
American Freedman, 98
American Freedmen's Union Commission (AFUC), 101, 153, 246 (n. 26); teachers sponsored by, 16–17, 35–39, 183, 209; in Savannah, 71; cooperates with Freedmen's Bureau, 88–90, 95; fund-raising activities of, 97–98; ceases operations, 107, 191, 204; and physical punishment in schools, 115, 125; and moral instruction, 122. *See also* Freedmen's aid societies
American Missionary, 9, 29, 34, 95, 98, 136; articles quoted, 27, 35, 113, 147, 154
American Missionary Association (AMA), 11–13, 14, 204; in Georgia, 16–17, 111, 120; ideology of, 18–30; teachers sponsored by, 35–39, 54, 69–71, 131, 132, 140, 142, 189, 192–98, 201, 202, 209; and Savannah Education Association, 73–76, 99; cooperates with Freedmen's Bureau, 88–96, 100–103, 107–8, 186; fund-raising activities of, 97–100; and physical punishment in schools, 115, 125; and moral instruction, 122; founds Atlanta University, 135–38; policy on charity, 144–45; attitudes toward black family

life, 149–51; establishes orphan asylum, 152; religious activities in Georgia, 155–58; sponsors temperance societies, 158–61; and Freedman's Bank, 161–64; teachers' mission homes, 167–90 passim; concentrates on higher education, 191, 198; and Georgia public school system, 191–98; in Macon, 1870s, 196–97. *See also* Freedmen's aid societies; Teachers
Americus, Georgia, 68
Amherst College, 33
Andersonville, Georgia, 63, 82, 120, 124, 130, 131, 135, 143, 149, 157, 159, 168–69
Athens, Georgia, 83, 133, 150, 198
Atlanta, Georgia, 13, 81, 89, 100, 101, 105, 117, 119–20, 124–53 passim, 160, 161, 169, 180–82, 188, 191, 194, 196, 198, 204
Atlanta University, 13, 135–38, 151, 195, 196, 247 (n. 56), 255 (n. 7)
Augusta, Georgia, 17, 28–29, 34, 46, 59, 72, 89, 93, 99, 107–25 passim, 144, 160, 161, 169, 175, 178, 180, 183, 189, 192, 195
Ayer, Frederick, 38, 181
Ayres, Martha D., 147–48

Bainbridge, Georgia, 85, 96, 130
Baptists: northern, 17, 125; southern black, 158. *See also* American Baptist Home Missionary Society
Beach Institute (Savannah), 92, 106, 197
Beecher, Catharine, 40, 235 (n. 49)
Beecher, Reverend Henry Ward, 23
Bingham, Egbert B., 34, 88, 183
Black codes, in Georgia, 57
Blassingame, John W., 71, 72
Bradley, Aaron A., 72, 75

267